NATURALISM
in
AMERICAN
FICTION

NATURALISM

in

AMERICAN

FICTION

The Classic Phase

JOHN J. CONDER

THE UNIVERSITY PRESS OF KENTUCKY

Library of Congress Cataloging in Publication Data

Conder, John J.
    Naturalism in American fiction.

    Bibliography: p.
    Includes index.
    1. American fiction—19th century—History and
criticism.   2. American fiction—20th century—History
and criticism.   3. Naturalism in literature.   I. Title.
PS374.N29C66   1984   813'.009'12   84-8661
ISBN 0-8131-1522-1; 0169-7

CONTENTS

Preface   vii

Acknowledgments   ix

1. American Literary Naturalism:
From Hobbes to Bergson   1

2. Stephen Crane and the Necessary Fiction   22
"The Open Boat" 22   "The Blue Hotel" 30
Maggie 42   *The Red Badge of Courage* 52

3. Norris and Hard Determinism: *McTeague*   69

4. Dreiser's Trilogy and the Dilemma of Determinism   86
The Financier 88   *The Titan* 95   *The Stoic* 108

5. Dos Passos and Society's Self: *Manhattan Transfer*   118

6. Steinbeck and Nature's Self: *The Grapes of Wrath*   142

7. Faulkner and Naturalism's Selves:
The Sound and the Fury   160

Notes   197

Bibliographical Essays   209

Index   225

To my mother and father
and (again) to Barbara

PREFACE

Mine is a thesis book. Literary naturalism as a concept and American literary naturalism as a movement may once have been hidebound by theoretical considerations, but I believe that discussions of both in the past twenty years have been so absorbed in denying theory, or else have so drifted away from theoretical considerations, that the term *literary naturalism* has been rendered essentially meaningless in American literature. My first chapter addresses this situation and attempts to establish a working view of American literary naturalism in its classic phase, a phase that hindsight grants us to see as beginning roughly in the 1890s and ending a little before America entered the Second World War. In this phase determinism plays a unifying role, and I try to trace its course throughout succeeding chapters. My own hunch is that determinism still plays a central role in the contemporary period—at least if the concept of determinism is rightly understood. Nonetheless I confine my claims to the period on which we can have some perspective.

Although mine is a thesis book, I do not believe my approach is so idiosyncratic that it points only to features of the fiction and the movement never before noticed, or that every one of its observations is unique. Anyone aware of the mass of material relevant to my subject knows that would hardly be possible. At the same time, I have tried to develop an original argument. In the process, I encountered a problem. I wanted to recognize other points of view, parallel or opposed, but I also wanted to retain the flow of my own argument in my text and to make the most pertinent acknowledgments in my notes, without including in either my text or my notes distracting arguments with opposed points of view or distracting explanations of important differences between my line of thought and lines of thought parallel to it.

To handle the problem, I introduced a separate bibliographical essay pertaining to each chapter and to the notes for that chapter. The method had several advantages for me. In an essay I could acknowledge parallel points of view and quickly note important differences. I could briefly indicate different views by advising the reader that my work can be read against the backdrop of someone else's. I make this recommendation to emphasize contrasts and to eliminate the need to get into sustained argument with a critic either in my text or in my notes. Such argument was necessary in my opening chapter, but I saw the further necessity of keeping the procedure to a minimum thereafter. Finally, in a time of textual controversy, a bibliographical essay could also serve the purpose revealed in the one I wrote on *The Red Badge of Courage*.

For the most part, I treat references in those bibliographical essays as essential acknowledgments of the work and do not feel compelled to note a parallel or contrast in the notes if it appears in an essay. Where I do depart from this practice, I do so to consider a controversial matter that lies outside the center or centers of interest of any single bibliographical essay or to fill some obvious need like citing a quotation from a work appearing in the essay. Even with such departures, however, my supporting materials—both bibliographical essays and notes—are not as inclusive as they might have been had I not been limited by considerations of length. In some cases I have cited a single work as representative of a particular point of view without being able to pay it the courtesy of showing how it differs from other works with similar points of view, and without being able to pay these other works even the courtesy of a mention.

ACKNOWLEDGMENTS

From the time when I first undertook this study, years ago, my wife, Professor Barbara McCamus Conder, has been my principal reader, critic, and supporter. Her scholarly mind aided me in clarifying my thoughts; her generosity of spirit impelled her to contribute her own. Even while working on her own study of Hardy, she found time to help me. Thank you, Barbara.

Now for others whom I acknowledge with pleasure. G. Thomas Tanselle, a former Wisconsin colleague, read and criticized the manuscript. A valued reader, he was also a valued advisor who contributed to supporting my morale, especially with his sense of humor. T. Daniel Young was another valued reader and advisor; his sympathy for this project made him a very special Vanderbilt colleague. I understand why he commands the admiration of so many of his students. Walter Sullivan called the manuscript to the attention of the University Press of Kentucky. I am grateful for the help of the Vanderbilt University Research Council and for the support of Deans Wendell Holladay, Jacques Voegeli, John Venable, James Wesson, and Ruth Zibart, and that of chairmen Rupert Palmer and James Kilroy. In one way or another these colleagues made it possible for Vanderbilt University to give me a leave and a reduced load of teaching and other responsibilities so that I could work on the book.

ONE

American Literary Naturalism: From Hobbes to Bergson

It is now clear that no critical consensus exists to explain the commonly used term *literary naturalism* as distinct from *literary realism* in American fiction, and some background is necessary in order to understand the complexities of the problem raised by the term and the approach taken here to help resolve that problem. It is generally agreed that, in late nineteenth-century America, a body of fiction arose that is rather different from the fiction represented by the term *American literary realism.*[1] It is also certain that earlier literary critics saw in the works of several of these fin-de-siècle writers—Crane, Norris, and Dreiser are the major ones—a pessimistic determinism that they called *naturalism.*[2] The term *naturalism,* with this meaning, was also applied to describe the works of later writers—Dos Passos, Farrell, Steinbeck, Hemingway, and even Faulkner—although this list is hardly inclusive.[3]

This meaning for American literary naturalism is still accepted by some, although recent critics who use it in this sense do so in order to deny the "naturalism" of writers classified as such. Crane is a major example of a writer whose naturalism is now denied, but he is not the only one. Using the old definition of the term, one critic has denied the very existence of such a literary movement in America.[4]

But even before this critic reached his conclusion, two others insisted that this literary phenomenon did exist but had to be understood in less rigid terms. Charles Child Walcutt found that the movement possessed a central philosophical coherence, for he saw all the writers as expressing a philosophy of determinism.[5] Nonetheless he denied that they were all thoroughgoing pessimists, for he found many of them optimistic about the possibilities for improving the human lot, despite the premises on which their art was based. He saw nothing contradictory about an optimistic intention propelling the creation of a pessimistic, deterministic novel. If will is absent in the novel, it is "transferred to the reader and to society at large,"[6] and so the novel's destructive determinism acts as a stimulus to improve the human condition.

Walcutt therefore had no problem reconciling conflicting attitudes issuing from conflicting doctrines so long as the conflicts existed between the world of the reader and the world of the novel, for each world has its own logic. But he could not accept such conflicts when they surfaced *within* the world of the novel because they marred the logic of that world. Thus he was led to conclude that, with the exception of Crane's fiction, most of the work by other naturalistic writers suffered because of a failure to reconcile a belief in progress through human initiative with a philosophy of determinism.[7] The private optimism of these writers seemed to creep into their works to conflict with the pessimism of the works' determinism. Compounding the conflict between attitudes was a conflict between doctrines, for Walcutt saw surfacing within single works the doctrine of freedom of the will as well as that of determinism.[8]

For Walcutt, then, these conflicts were flaws *within* the novels; but Donald Pizer called them sources of strength. He also went on to deny that the movement had any philosophical coherence.[9] He translated Walcutt's flaws into a tension within a work between "the individually significant and the deterministic" that existed not to promote a philosophy of determinism but to affirm the importance of the values threatened or destroyed by the deterministic forces.[10]

In order to see that Pizer's response to Walcutt is inadequate, it is important to emphasize the ultimate source of Walcutt's sense of flaws in a work. It lies in the contradiction between the doctrine of determinism and the doctrine of the freedom of the will.[11] Walcutt felt that a deterministic novel could not logically contain a belief in purposive progress or growth, which depends on man's freedom of the will, just as it could not logically judge human agents morally if they lack such freedom. Associated with this primary doctrinal opposition, of course, is a secondary opposition in attitudes between pessimism (associated with determinism) and optimism (associated with freedom of the will). A deterministic novel showing that man does what he can, not what he ought, is pessimistic. If it introduces overt or covert expressions of convictions that are by-products of a belief in freedom of the will, it introduces an attitude that conflicts with its pessimism. If, for example, the novel includes the view that purposive growth or progress is possible, it introduces an optimistic view that conflicts with the pessimistic view inherent in its determinism. In such a novel even the appearance of another by-product of a belief in free will—moral judgment of individuals—harbors a degree of optimism conflicting with its pessimism because such judgment rests on the assmption that the most "evil" of men can nonetheless behave other than as they do.

Pizer's "translation" of Walcutt's two contradictions into a single tension is therefore not an adequate translation at all because it ignores the basic contradiction between freedom and determinism and focuses instead on the subordinate conflict between the *attitudes* associated with each of these doctrines. In finding affirmations of "the individually significant" Pizer strengthened the sense of the optimism of a work—its view that one value or another makes life worth the living—even as he diminished its pessimism by seeing the disruptive deterministic forces functioning to serve the positive purpose of underscoring the importance of the values threatened by them. In working with these opposed attitudes in this way, however, Pizer left unresolved the conflict central to Walcutt's critique. Pizer's strengthening the novel's affirmative view of life hardly strengthened the novel's sense of freedom. The logical opposite of determinism is freedom. If determinism is used to arrive at an affirmation of the importance of "the individually significant," the individually significant does not thereby become an affirmation for the existence of freedom. Even the most die-hard determinist can vouch for the individually significant, for value, as Dreiser does for Cowperwood's aesthetic tastes despite the fact that they are functions of chemisms beyond his control. An author can even affirm the worth of values within a morally ambiguous world without affirming the existence of that freedom without which moral choice is meaningless. Indeed, such an author may in fact be rigorously deterministic if his moral ambiguity exists because characters appear to have a freedom that they do not possess in reality. Since "the individually significant" can appear even in such a novel, it is possible that these works are more steadfastly deterministic than Pizer suggests.[12] One is therefore left wondering to what extent Walcutt's sense of the primary contradiction in individual works is valid, and whether determinism does not in fact give philosophical coherence to the movement after all.

This book is written to urge that there does exist an important body of fiction, once called naturalistic, that does indeed possess philosophic coherence, and that such coherence depends on the evolution of a concept questioning man's freedom. Even if the questioning leads to both determinism and freedom, no individual work studied here suffers from a logical contradiction as a result. On the contrary, when these seemingly irreconcilable opposites appear in a work, its inner coherence is as strong as that of a work that is monolithic in its denial or assertion of man's freedom.

But critical readings of Crane show the need to raise and answer another question before proceeding with this undertaking: Can the philosophic coherence argued for in later pages sensibly be called naturalistic? Three representative critics of Crane show the terms of the problem. Two of them agree that naturalists, because they see man as a part of the continuum of nature, are philosophical monists. These two critics therefore agree that this perspective views man as like the animals in the sense that he lacks freedom of the will, and that such monism logically proscribes a concern for morality and value, a concern that is the domain of dualists. On this basis one of these critics calls Crane a naturalist and praises his work for the consistency of its monism. The other, finding in Crane's work an emphasis on morality and value, denies that Crane is a naturalist, because this emphasis makes him a dualist. The third critic agrees that Crane indeed is a dualist but insists that he is a naturalist nonetheless.[13]

Clearly, we must ask not only what Crane is, but what naturalism is. Because there is no consensus on the issue, furthermore, we must permit the introduction of criteria from sources outside the literature once associated with naturalism in order to justify applying the term *naturalistic* to works considered here. This procedure does not deny our primary loyalty to the works themselves. It only constitutes a recognition that we must not be arbitrary in calling "naturalistic" whatever kind of unity we find among a body of works; that simply because works have been associated with "naturalism" in the past, what we find in them in the present does not thereby become legitimate evidence of "naturalism." Indeed, the readings of Crane included in this book required an understanding of a particular philosophic tradition in order to show the plausibility of calling him a naturalist. The inquiry that led to this finding also forced a reassessment of the standard critical view of what it means to be a part of nature.

The way in which most literary critics answer this question still remains at odds with the view expressed several decades ago by one of literary naturalism's spokesmen, James Farrell. Their dogmatic assertion that the answer is to be found in a *deterministic* monism stands in sharp contrast to Farrell's flexibility. Farrell admits he is a naturalist, and his adherence to the philosophy of John Dewey suggests that he thinks of man as a part of the continuum of the natural world; but he clearly rejects the first answer given by critics to the question of what it means to be a part of nature. "I have been called a naturalist and I have never denied it,"[14] he states in an essay, "On Naturalism, So Called," but he also declares: "I am not a monistic determinist."[15] However, his definition of naturalism permits a rejection of the second conclusion of literary critics, that a writer who empasizes morality and value is necessarily a dualist who cannot think man is a part of nature: "My own conception of naturalism is not that which is usually attributed to me. By naturalism I mean that whatever happens in this world must ultimately be explainable in terms of events in this world."[16]

Farrell's view of naturalism is thus monistic, but the scientific mentality with which he associates this view in the same essay makes it clear that the monism represented by his comment is a methodological and not necessarily an ontological one.[17] That is, his view of explaining human events demands the same perspective as the explaining of nonhuman ones. This posture is central to naturalism and need not entail an ontological monism, the view that there is one thing in the universe (only matter, for example, or only mind) or, in another version, the view that, though "there are many things . . . there is only one *kind* of thing."[18]

However, methodological monism can lead to an ontological monism of a special sort, one that says that man is a part of nature though significantly different from other things in nature. The link between the two is succinctly expressed in Sterling Power Lamprecht's own definition of naturalism. In an essay included in his *Metaphysics of Naturalism,* he writes: "Suffice it to say that in this essay 'naturalism' means a philosophical position, empirical in method, that regards everything that exists or occurs to be conditioned in its existence or occurrence by causal factors [compare Farrell] within one all-encompassing system of nature, however 'spiritual' or purposeful or rational some of these things and events may in their functions and values prove to be."[19]

Although Lamprecht's philosophical views are in part a reaction against the philosophical tradition that is central to American literary naturalism, specifically to the concept that questions man's freedom, his conception of a "sound" philosophical naturalism is relevant here because it provides some help in the critical controversy. His particular ontological monism, based on an empiricism so similar to Farrell's, allows him to reject that materialistic monism so frequently identified with literary naturalism, as well as those dualistic visions sometimes used to deny the naturalism of a writer. Though he sees man as part of nature, Lamprecht, like Farrell, eschews a monistic materialism because of its reductiveness, its failure to distinguish between the causal factors of things and "the values to which the same things lend themselves."[20] He rejects the view that man's ideals "are but compensatory imaginings by which we describe hidden bodily functions and drives,"[21] because nature, for Lamprecht, is more expansive than this view allows, providing for both man's values and freedom: "However naturalism be defined, it ought certainly to involve the position that man and his ways (including his moral aspirations and his rationally formulated ideals) are as 'natural' as lightning and its ways, or as sunshine and its ways."[22]

Even though unique in nature, therefore, man is still part of nature, and for Lamprecht this fact does not work against a monistic vision of the world of human beings and nonhuman things. Indeed, he insists that a "sound"[23] naturalism must oppose all dualisms: "To suppose that mind, because it is distinguishable from matter and distinctive in its essential nature, did not have an origin in natural events antecedent to it, is to become at once mythological, to appeal to what has no possible empirical support."[24]

As seen by Lamprecht, therefore, naturalism need not be pessimistic, or materialistic, or deterministic. He therefore diverges from traditional views of naturalism among literary critics not simply by permitting naturalism to embrace widely cherished human values, for these can be embraced and celebrated by the determinist. He diverges from them by the character of his ontological monism, which permits him to see man as a part of nature even while possessing freedom. His ontology does not commit him "to any particular theory of the degree of systematic connection among things and events"[25] such as a deterministic view would, and he specifically eschews determinism. Influenced by John Dewey, who would concur in Lamprecht's view that man possesses freedom, Farrell no doubt would follow suit, agreeing that in strictly philosophical terms, man can be viewed as free, not determined.[26] But it is interesting to observe the qualifications on man's freedom that Farrell notes in his essay "On Naturalism, So Called."

One of those qualifications subtly undermines the popular notion that freedom of the will is just *there*, existing in all normal adults from the fall of Adam on—in fact, before. Farrell believes free will to be not "an inherent attribute of man" but "an achievement of men, gained individually and collectively, through knowledge and the acquisition of control, both over nature and over self."[27] And related to this reservation is a far more important one that explicitly introduces the subject of determinism. Although he denies being a determinist, Farrell does not dislike determinism as a doctrine. He dislikes, rather, critics who have an ideological loathing of the concept and who turn on literary naturalism because they think it harbors that view of the way the human world is arranged. He himself admires the precocity of a literature that anticipated the concerns later engaging sociologists and psychologists, and is vexed, if not downright angered, that it should be rejected on ideological grounds. "When a critic of naturalism logically demonstrates the existence of free will," he writes, "he is merely proving what he wants to prove," and those "who base their criticisms on free will do so on grounds of temperament."[28]

Judged by their tone, critical responses today take on a similar temperamental zeal seemingly born of ideological conviction, though now they are devoted less to denouncing determinism and more to "saving" authors like Crane from association with such a point of view.[29] Farrell was less sensitive about the subject. Despite his statement that men can achieve free will, his own belief in the will's freedom is highly qualified: "It is important here to observe that usually those who pose this question pose it in terms of a flat either/or. Is man free or is he not free? Does man have free will, or is he completely determined? To me, this is an unanswerable question."[30] In his essay, at least, he thus leaves as problematic what for an orthodox literary realist is an unquestionable truth.

Farrell's remarks suggest a crucial difference in focus between the vision of a modern literary naturalist and that of a philosophic naturalist who is Farrell's contemporary. Lamprecht's views repudiate "the metaphysics on which the philosophy of much of the last three hundred years— 'modern philosophy'—has been based," a philosophy based "upon the metaphysics which was the working out of ontological assumptions implicit in 17th century science."[31] Hence, despite qualifications he sees on man's freedom, Lamprecht focuses on the fact that man is indeed free. But as Farrell makes clear in his essay, he and other literary naturalists are concerned with restrictions on man's freedom that arise within the framework of the more traditional view of modern philosophy, and within that tradition the existence of man's freedom, far from being viewed as quite as "natural" as lightning, was precisely the point in question. And the unresolved critical controversy over Crane's work raises the issue of whether Crane is part of this naturalistic tradition, or of any naturalistic tradition at all. The terms of the controversy, furthermore, suggest that central to understanding his meaning as well as his place (if any) in literary naturalism is the status of freedom in his work, just as much the same thing can be said about the importance of the role of freedom in the works of other writers once associated with naturalism.

Critics who find a firm moral axis in Crane clearly give freedom an unambiguous presence in his works, just as those who see only determinism deny its presence altogether. In between these camps emerge views of a Crane who is ambiguous. These same views of his ambiguity either blindly affirm the existence of freedom in his pages or leave its status to fend for itself by not pursuing the matter in any depth. At any rate, the ambiguous Stephen Crane, like his famous squirrel, is "no philosopher of his race" and so lacks a coherent vision.[32] Now, such differing views of Crane may emerge because of simple misinterpretations of what exists on the written page—one view is right, that is, and the others are wrong—but it is also possible that the critical problem exists because Crane possesses a vision with a special kind of philosophic consistency that, if misunderstood, invites substituting a part for the whole or seeing no whole at all.

Remarks by Farrell lead to this conclusion. When he states that naturalism *explains* "whatever happens in this world . . . in terms of events in this world,"[33] he associates this perspective with "a different mental climate," calling it the result of "the scientific superseding of the Aristotelian world" and a function of "a conception of the world in terms of relationships rather than of essence." Those relationships emphasize the "powerlessness" of "modern tragic characters" and trace their helplessness to "social forces, social factors, social pressures and tendencies [which] play a role similar to that played by the gods, by Fate and Nemesis, in ancient Greece."[34]

One need only add, then, that the scientific mentality that emphasizes causality easily leads in the direction of determinism, a point not difficult to accept if one keeps in mind a proper definition of the concept:*

> Determinism is the general philosophical thesis which states that for everything that ever happens there are conditions such that, given them, nothing else could happen.[35]

---

*Part of the caveat that Bernard Berofsky applies to philosophical discussions of human freedom certainly applies as well to discussions of the problem by literary critics: "In discussions of human freedom it is not uncommon to omit a definition or clarification of the thesis of determinism, although reference to it may be made. This is quite serious if one considers . . . the fact that this thesis often plays a fundamental role in conceptions of human freedom." Bernard Berofsky, ed., "General Introduction: Determinism," *Free Will and Determinism* (New York: Harper & Row, 1966), p. 1

Viewing human affairs from a methodologically monistic point of view hence can lead to an emphasis not on action or character but on conditions fostering both, and such a view can produce critical confusion about an author's philosophic vision, as some critics point to the power of conditions and others the power of human will, while still others find no clear authorial vision of who or what is in control. That very emphasis on conditions which is the source of critical confusion, however, can in turn breed that tolerance of determinism which appears in Farrell's remarks on both free will and determinism.

But it can lead to more. The person who feels the compelling power of causal factors in human as well as nonhuman affairs might very well hone his vision to see man as *both* determined and free, irreconcilable though the oppositions between determinism and freedom of the will may seem. Such double vision has been around for quite some time. Although no literary critic has associated literary naturalism with it, a specific, coherent philosophical vision embracing these oppositions is part of the philosophical tradition of the Western world, arising in the late seventeenth century as a response to scientific advances. Its component elements are easily stated, though when completely assimilated into the form of a literary text they generate fascinating complexities, not to mention endless disagreements among critics. For these very reasons, however, this vision is worth recalling. It can grant Stephen Crane that complex, coherent vision now denied him. It can also expose a coherent philosophical development at the center of American literary naturalism, no matter what else naturalism may entail in American literature.

Thomas Hobbes is the figure who shaped the mental climate to which Farrell refers and which, two centuries later, surfaced in the naturalistic novel. He was concerned to view man in natural rather than in theological or supernatural terms, and thus to view human affairs as part of the causal processes of nature. Hobbes was a materialist, though what is of interest here is not his materialism but the outline of his views of voluntary acts of the will, as well as his related views of liberty in relation to self. His many spiritual heirs are more sophisticated than to locate all causes of human action in physiological changes in the brain, for they concentrate on psychological and environmental as well as biological sources of behavior. But although they have abandoned his materialism, their views of cause-effect relationships relative to choice and self follow a Hobbesian pattern.[36]

Hobbes asserted that all events in nature, including voluntary human acts of the will, are caused, for "nothing taketh beginning from itself."[37] He located the causes of voluntary acts in changes in brain matter. Before these changes are completed to produce the act of the will—while they are still in process, that is—they manifest themselves in the competing appetites or motives of aversion and desire. Deliberation is a state in which contrary appetites vie within the individual, and voluntary action is thus caused by the resolution of these competing motives. An act of the will is caused by the "last appetite," which is the final preference that moves the will to act. Hence all voluntary action is reducible to such causes; that is, action is necessitated.[38]

Necessitated though acts of the will are, Hobbes nonetheless granted freedom to man. Defining liberty as the "absence of all the impediments to action that are not contained in the nature and intrinsical quality of the agent,"[39] he said that man was free when impediments or external restraints were not imposed on his will. He is free in the same way that water is free when it flows unimpeded downhill. Water is not thereby free to flow uphill, but this fact does not deny its freedom, since it is its "nature and intrinsical quality" to flow downhill. In like manner an individual is "free" to act and to choose whenever impediments "not contained in the nature and intrinsical quality" of himself are absent.[40]

The very brevity and simplicity of this outline of Hobbes's "solution" to the problem of freedom and causation should bring out its most troublesome feature: the compelling relation between cause and effect that Hobbes found adequate to account for freedom and its corollary, moral vision. For he did assert that men must be held responsible for their actions, and this, despite the fact that he believed that the cause ("the last appetite") compelled the occurrence of its effect (the act of the will). Of course partisans of free will find it most unreasonable to hold men morally responsible for action if their acts of the will are caused in this sense. If a man acts because his "last appetite" compels the action, and if he has no control over the conditions that give rise to that appetite, in what sense can he be free? Believers in free will assert that "a free agent is one who, when all things necessary to produce a given action are present, can nevertheless refrain from that action."[41] But Hobbes found this illogical, for it was equivalent to saying "that conditions might be sufficient to produce a given effect without that effect's occurring, which is a contradiction."[42]

Nor does the Hobbesian view of liberty in relation to self help matters, since Hobbes's view of this subject unravels in the direction of determinism as well. If liberty is indeed the "absence of all the impediments to action . . . not contained in the nature and intrinsical quality of the agent," how can one judge morally an agent whose "nature and intrinsical quality" have been purely shaped since birth by an environment over which he has no control? As in the case of voluntary actions, this view of liberty reduces itself to pure determinism because the self (its thought processes, emotions, and choices) is a pure product of its environment.

Hobbes—and those like him who insisted on having it both ways, on seeing man as free and yet also subject to the causal world in every regard—both alarmed and attracted the scorn of one philosopher. In "The Dilemma of Determinism," William James warned against "free-will determinists." To contrast them to the honest variety of "hard" determinists who openly denied man's freedom of the will, James scornfully dubbed them "soft determinists" because they deceptively acknowledge man's free will but, by emphasizing causal factors in its exercise, take away with the other hand what they give with the first.[43] James had philosophers in mind when he baptized this kind of determinism, but his classification has a literary application as well; for the dilemma that a scientific mentality has created for views of freedom and causation since the seventeenth century ultimately affected the world of letters.

To put the matter most comprehensively, that mentality forced men to ask what it *means* to be free, and in the nineteenth century answers to this question permeate the novel because the mental climate, formed by the new truths of science reflected in the burgeoning social sciences of Comte, Spencer, and their popularizers, made the time ripe for the question to surface and for answers to be offered.[44] Such a question sometimes emerges directly within works considered in this study, but more often lies outside them. More important, the central thrust of thought in these works lies in their witnessing life in Hobbesian terms, viewing either choice or self in Hobbesian fashion in order to answer the question. An age stressing the influence of force on man was hardly one to grant man Kant's categorical freedom in moral choices in order to escape determinism, nor was it one to state, with Hume, that causes "do not compel the occurrence of their effects." So the center of interest shifts, from action and character to conditions producing both.[45] That shift is characteristic of many novels labeled naturalistic and is the source of their determinisms, soft and hard. An emphasis on causal factors weakens individual autonomy in direct proportion to the distance of these causes from the control of the actor. The reader is thus left with the impression that conditions control; that, given a rerun of the action under the *same* conditions, nothing else *could* happen.

The significance of this emphasis on conditions has frequently been missed or misinterpreted. Edwin Cady becomes a case in point when he refutes Charles Child Walcutt's view that Crane is a determinist:

> Walcutt holds that Crane must be "naturalistic" because "nowhere does a character operate as a genuinely free ethical agent in defiance of the author's intentions." By "free ethical agent," as the chapter develops, he appears to mean one who makes moral choices free of all contingency. Theologians have doubted that God possesses such freedom (He is conditioned by Himself). Certainly no one ever supposed that any human being had such freedom—and, if one did suppose so, it would obviously be impossible to write a novel about the libertine.[46]

One cannot, of course, write a novel about anyone without relating contingency to choice, but Cady implies that this truth necessarily denies the possibility of seeing contingency as an important factor in a work's determinism. This is not so. Most of the novelists considered here either reduce choice to condition—give, that is, the condition or contingency full authority over the choice; or else they create a perfect equation between the authority of both so that it is impossible to say that choice rules condition, that man has freedom. It is one of these relations between condition and choice (or condition and self) that emerges in American naturalistic fiction as a distinguishing factor signifying the presence of determinism.

But there was more than one way to cope with the Hobbesian dilemma, and Henri Bergson's confrontation with it illuminates a view of man that gradually emerges in American naturalistic writing; that man has two selves, one determined, one free; and that the freedom of the second self is beyond the confines of that determinism into which the Hobbesian view unravels. Acknowledging that man was a part of nature, Bergson began his career by arguing that the Hobbesian view of man, which leads to determinism, is inadequate because it fails to grasp that man's uniqueness in nature depends on his possession of an inner being whose special character cannot be understood by the methods of the natural sciences. In *Time and Free Will*, his first major work, he alleges that deterministic views of man arise because "the English school" of philosophers, among others whom he mentions, apply to man's psychic life a mechanical or spatial view of time, a time measurable by spatial objects like clocks, a time that is scientific and mathematical, a time that, indeed, dominates the life of social man.[47]

In Bergson's view, mechanists (physical determinists) measure time by changes of events in space, events that they perceive as succeeding each other in causal fashion. And mechanists use the same spatialized concept of time to explain changes in the psychic life of human beings. They witness a present psychic state and call it the effect of a condition external to it, its cause. So, too, they view a prior psychic state. They thus separate the states, making it appear that they succeed each other at intervals measurable by the clock, as though these psychic states took place in space much as their presumed external causes did. Since mechanists logically believe that causal relations are binding, the self—its feelings, its thoughts, and its choices—is thereby as readily reducible to a social environment over which it has no control as Hobbes's self is. [48]

From this same mechanistic point of view, Bergson argues, proceeds psychological determinism, psychological state A becoming the compelling cause of state B because each is viewed as separate from the other, one succeeding the other, as though in space. But Bergson escaped the Hobbesian dilemma of freedom and causation and its resolution into determinism by postulating the existence of another kind of time besides spatial, clock time in which all events are determined. To this kind of time he opposes "pure time," a personal sense of change or "duration" in which man's psychic states flow *inseparably* one into another so that the past state is always within another but altered by that fact. Only man can live in "pure time," and there one escapes the tyranny of cause-effect relations that spatial time inevitably creates. In "pure time" the mechanistic view of psychic states cannot hold because no external force alone can be said to be the sufficient cause of any single psychic state. Even assuming that the psychic state could be frozen for an instant without changing (a fact Bergson denies), its cause would also be all the previous psychic states experienced by the individual, since all merge. Nor can the psychological view of psychic states hold true in "pure time," for the same reason. No single psychic state can be held as sufficient cause for producing a succeeding one, because *all* previous psychic states blend together indistinguishably with a present one. Cause and effect thus become one and the same thing because they are inseparable. [49]

The self that lives in "pure time" is therefore free. Because it is forever "becoming," the fluidity of its psychic states transcends deterministic relations between itself and the external world, or between one psychic state and another. But though in duration man possesses a free self, what will here be called a durational self, Bergson nonetheless concedes that man cannot avoid spatializing time. As a social creature, he lives most of his life in a social environment that is controlled by the clock, which measures mechanical or spatial time. As a consequence he develops a social self (Bergson refers to it as his "shadow") that usually conceals the self living in pure time. The shadow self that man develops hence is a product of society and that spatialized time which governs it. That self's acts, too, are fully determined by society. Hence, though Bergson believes that man possesses freedom, he feels that free acts are rare because man is rarely in contact with the self capable of performing them. By distinguishing between two selves, therefore, he grants the validity of the Hobbesian view of freedom relative to choice and self, a view that reduces itself to determinism; but he applies this view to only one portion of the person, the "shadow" self.[50]

The approach presented here is that the Hobbesian view of causality, manifested both in his view of choice and in his view of liberty in relation to self, represents the tradition within which American literary naturalism grows, and that it issues in a Bergsonian view of two selves, one determined, the other free. The tensions of the Hobbesian vision, nowhere resolved, are most perfectly embodied in the work of Stephen Crane, and this fact is responsible for the diametrically opposed views of Crane as determinist and as moralist, and for the view that his determinism leads to an affirmation for value, with the view of freedom simply left in limbo. Crane is a "soft determinist." Without himself resolving the issue posed by causation and choice—the issue, that is, of determinism and freedom—he constructs his work in such a way that the reader is forced to unravel freedom into its opposite, and this unraveling is forced on the reflective reader as surely as if he were to pursue the implications of Hobbes's view of self or choice.

If Crane uses the form of the Hobbesian paradox (man is free but his acts of the will are caused) to create a perfect tension between freedom and determinism, other naturalistic writers introduce the polar opposites of this vision with varying degrees of resolution of its oppositions in a single work, a factor explaining why no naturalistic writer in America, Dreiser included, remained a thoroughgoing determinist throughout his career. Norris, for example, wrote a completely deterministic work in *McTeague* but later expanded his vision to embrace both freedom and determinism in *The Octopus*. Dreiser's life and work best exemplify the struggles between these irreconcilable opposites inherent in the position of the free-will determinist. As a reformer he wished for the betterment of mankind but, as he put it in *Notes on Life,* "Without Free Will—how?"[51] His trilogy reflects the changed resolution of these oppositions in his thought—the first two volumes written from a rigidly deterministic point of view, the last escaping its confines.

This book therefore agrees that determinism plays a central role in American literary naturalism, but it argues that it is a determinism emanating from a specific vision that generates the complexities of this literary tradition. One of its major objects, hence, is to explain the misunderstood ways in which determinism appears when the work's center of interest is causation in relation to the crucial issues of choice and self. But this book's other object is to trace an evolution in American literary naturalism, a progressive development that shows, among other things, a paradoxical shift in conceptions of nature and the self. In other words, this book tries to demonstrate that American literary naturalism possesses philosophical coherence, and this goal also was a consideration in deciding on the authors and works included or excluded. Short of Faulkner, and apart from Farrell, the other authors are the chief representatives of American literary naturalism in its classic period of development. Farrell is excluded because the point made about the second self in *Manhattan Transfer* is easily transferrable to *Studs Lonigan,* and Dos Passos seems a more important author, incisive though Farrell's critical insights into literature may be. The book does not go into the contemporary period. No doubt most of the work of Thomas Pynchon, for example, does continue the tradition, but it seems better to take advantage of the critical perspective it is possible to have on writers whose full canon has been established, and who have been and are the center of debate on what "naturalism" is, than it does to move forward into the contemporary period and lose that advantage. Naturalism, like any vital literary movement, will continue to develop, but understanding of subsequent developments is best based on sounder understanding of the earlier fiction. The study stops with Faulkner because he seems to be the chief inheritor of naturalism as described in this book.

The exclusion of two specific works by authors included in the book probably needs a word of explanation. *The Octopus* is excluded because the opposition between the mechanical and the instinctual so important to that work also occurs in *The Grapes of Wrath* (included), which has the further advantage of showing the emergence of a dual self in man. *USA* is excluded because Dos Passos's conception of a dual self appears more clearly in *Manhattan Transfer*. Furthermore, the conception of self developed in *Manhattan Transfer* is the assumed ground of character portrayal in *USA*, so character portrayal in the trilogy is best understood in the light of the earlier work. Other exclusions and inclusions are more easily accounted for by a commentary on the book's overall design in order to show the reader that the chapters that follow possess a logical sequence.

It is reasonable to accept the common critical practice of applying the term "naturalistic" to any work of fiction predicated on an ontological monism of the kind that avers that man is a part of nature, even if the work is not philosophically deterministic. Works of this kind are largely excluded here because of this book's focus on the classic phase of American literary naturalism, in which determinism plays a definitive role. However, there are three deviations from this pattern, and since the first deviation introduces the next chapter, its appearance can usefully be explained now.

This book begins with a discussion of Crane's "The Open Boat," a story that exhibits a vision akin to Lamprecht's because it views man as a part of nature, but a story that is not deterministic. It does so, however, because that story's naturalistic vision is implicit in Crane's other major work, though with one sharp difference: in that other work it is the basis for Crane's developing a Hobbesian vision with perfect tensions between freedom and determinism. In *Maggie* he works with a Hobbesian view of liberty in relation to self (liberty as the absence of obstacles to action not inherent in the intrinsic character of the agent) by equating the self with the environment of which it is product. In "The Blue Hotel" and *The Red Badge of Courage* he employs a Hobbesian view of choice, in which "freely-willed" choices and actions are equated with the conditions inspiring them.

Crane leaves it to his Easterner in "The Blue Hotel" to raise the issue of freedom and determinism, a tactic no doubt designed to sustain the tensions between polar opposites without drawing the narrative voice into a position in which it might be forced to resolve them. But in *McTeague* Norris, unlike Crane, raises the issue in his own—or at least his narrator's—voice specifically to question traditional moral concepts, and thus to question the concepts of freedom and responsibility that moral vision entails. And unlike Crane he resolves the tension of the Hobbesian view of choice into pure determinism, hence denying that the Hobbesian vision justly permits moral evaluations of action.

Dreiser sustains this denial in the first two volumes of his trilogy by declaring throughout his narrative that apparent choices are determined, not free. But the real interest of that work is its exploration of the implications of determinism, which finally drove the author onto the horns of that dilemma which William James so clearly identified in "The Dilemma of Determinism": despair or aestheticism. In the trilogy Dreiser focuses the source of the fundamental problem, the self fated to remain a creature of its chemisms, and the solution, an escape from that self.

This escape is an example of a notable development in American literary naturalism, for it postulates the existence within the individual of two selves, one determined, the other free because irreducible. Such a view of the self had already been advanced by Dos Passos in *Manhattan Transfer*. *Manhattan Transfer*, it is true, basically renders a milieu. It portrays, that is, the conditions in which its characters must act. But unlike Norris, Dreiser, and the Crane of *The Red Badge of Courage,* Dos Passos does not make "freely" willed acts and the conditions surrounding them the focus of his work. He follows the related but somewhat different aspect of the Hobbesian vision, reducing to determinism the Hobbesian view of liberty of self rather than that of choice. From his central angle of vision he sees that social conditions create a social self indistinguishable from its environment and alienated from a more fundamental self, the source of man's freedom, a second self denied development and expression in society.

Of what this second self consists, what the contents of its consciousness are, Dos Passos gives no clear indication, though both Steinbeck and Faulkner do. He does, however, endow it with a dim awareness, by way of conclusion, that man and nature are one, not two, and that this recognition is the starting point for releasing it from its social bondage and permitting it freedom. In their own ways, of course, Crane, Norris, and Dreiser share the view that man and nature are one, not two, [52] but their visions emphasize a view of nature as animated by destructive impulses. Since societies are a part of the continuum of nature, they in their relation to the individual necessarily exhibit the same destructive tendencies evident in all of nature. Dos Passos's benign view of nonhuman nature alters this angle of vision by viewing the destructiveness of human societies as part of the distinctiveness setting apart human societies from other things in nature. Man's connections to nonhuman nature, therefore, seem the possible source of man's salvation.

And they become so for Steinbeck, although his work shows significant differences in center of interest. He follows Dos Passos in working with the Hobbesian view of liberty of self rather than choice (his characters, seen as separate identities, make numerous moral choices), but his determinism focuses not on individuals but on the group treated as a single entity or individual, if you will. It also has two selves. One, its social self, is purely a product of society. The other, an animal self, is only initially a creature of determinism; for it gains its freedom, paradoxically, by virtue of the recognition by a few of its members that they do possess an animal nature relating them to all of nature and more immediately to the other animal natures of which they are by force of circumstance a part. This recognition gives nature that explicit redemptive value only dimly shadowed in *Manhattan Transfer*, and it even gives determinism a special kind of value. The group transcends biological determinism to fulfill a predicated historical one, but the determinism of its initial condition is the essential precondition for its freedom.

The book concludes with discussions of *The Sound and the Fury* and *Absalom, Absalom!*—the other exceptions to the book's main focus on determinism in American literary naturalism—in order to show that Faulkner's work is very much an outgrowth of the philosophic climate that nourishes the classic phase of American literary naturalism and is in some ways its climax. For Bergson not only illuminates a major development in American literary naturalism; because he is a direct influence on Faulkner, Faulkner's work is a part of that development. In *The Sound and the Fury*, Faulkner uses Bergsonian concepts to delineate a naturalistic vision of man in its broader sense—the sense in which the phrase applies to "The Open Boat"—that man, though unique in nature, is a part of it. Benjy is on Faulkner's dividing line between man and the animals. He is a parody of that durational self so fully developed in Dilsey, yet not so far "advanced" as Jason, who is a parody of the social self that Bergson imaged as a shadow. It is this self that Quentin tries to escape by tricking his shadow in order to remain in contact with a durational self threatened by clock time and to retain the freedom that acts performed by that self alone enjoy.

Hence, by way of Bergson, Faulkner comes into possession of all the component elements of a naturalistic vision that logically ally him to the naturalists discussed earlier. Like Dos Passos and the later Dreiser, he sees dual selves and renders social selves that are indistinguishable from society. Unlike theirs, however, his central theme is not determinism—though it is inevitably there, in Quentin's desperate attempt to escape "the sequence of natural events and their causes which shadows every man's brow even benjy's." For Faulkner's central subject is the second self, the durational self, man's true identity and the source of his freedom, and he brings it into sharpest focus by contrasting it to the shadow self. Faulkner uses the contrast, however, not to make the point that the shadow self is a product of social determinism, its acts of the will beyond moral judgment. Rather, he uses it to show the primacy of the durational self as a measure of man's spiritual condition. Thereby he portrays the pathos of Quentin Compson, whose fear is that he will lose the durational self. Thereafter he portrayed the pitiable condition of Rosa Coldfield, whose rage is that Sutpen stifled that self; the spiritual emptiness of Thomas Sutpen, whose flaw is that he abandoned it; and the freedom of Henry Sutpen, whose tragedy is that he obeyed it. The conflicts between that self and the world became the source of Faulkner's tragic vision. In *The Sound and the Fury* he forged those elements of naturalistic tragedy which Quentin Compson and his roommate use to create the tragic love story called *Absalom, Absalom!*

TWO

Stephen Crane and the Necessary Fiction

"The Open Boat"

"The Open Boat" is the center of the Crane canon and the appropriate work with which to begin a discussion of Crane's naturalism. In its brilliant starkness, the central image portrays a naturalistic vision of man. Men adrift in a boat, a human creation, confront the sea, the world of nature. Unwillingly they receive an education whose terms are understood mainly by the correspondent. The lessons he learns are central to Crane's naturalistic vision, and they emerge with remarkable clarity.

Although the correspondent would like to think of nature as having purpose, he is soon divested of that comforting illusion, for his repeated invocations to "the seven mad gods who rule the sea"* only lead him to a knowledge of her indifference. At first he "wishes to throw bricks at the temple" of nature to protest this injustice, but he can only settle for hating "deeply the fact that there are no bricks

---

*Stephen Crane, "The Open Boat," in *Tales of Adventure,* edited by Fredson Bowers with an introduction by J. C. Levenson. The University of Virginia Edition of the Works of Stephen Crane, edited by Fredson Bowers (Charlottesville: Univ. Press of Virginia, 1970) 5: 77, 81, 84. Page references to this edition will appear in parentheses in my text. References to other works by Crane will be from the University of Virginia Edition hereafter cited, where appropriate and with volume number and publication date, as Va.

and no temples." He discovers nature is not symbolic, that man cannot think in teleological terms, even though the egocentricity of an endangered man makes him "desire to confront a personification" of some force in nature and, "with hands supplicant," to beg, " 'Yes, but I love myself' " (85). No such personified force exists in Crane's nonanthropomorphic world. Still, the correspondent learns that if man's egocentricity can lead (and has led) to his creating gods to relieve the anxieties of his loneliness in the universe, it also can lead (and has led) to a more concrete reality, the creation of societies and ethical systems for the purpose of survival. The men in the boat, once safely ensconced in a steamer now wrecked, are in the original position of primitive man confronting a threatening nature. The common threat of nature gives rise to a miniature society, "the subtle brotherhood of men" (73) who cooperate out of a desire to survive, though self-preservation is not the only value offered by society. The correspondent does not wish to view the shark alone. Society also provides solace and morale to frightened men.

Moral and ethical systems have the same source as societies, indeed are indispensable to any society, for without them a society could not be self-regulative and would dissolve. Hence the story contains marked reference to ethics: "The ethics of their condition was decidedly against any open suggestion of hopelessness" (71). In short, to maintain morale becomes an ethical duty in the interest of self-preservation, and the repetition of the phrase " 'Will you spell me?' " (82, 86, 87) suggests that Crane is interested in depicting the sense of mutual obligation that arises in the face of a common danger, the source of that ethical system. The acceptance of such obligation, indeed, is explicitly stated: "The obligation of the man at the oars was to keep the boat headed so that the tilt of the rollers would not capsize her" (82).

The correspondent learns these lessons in origins not abstractly but from a lived experience that conveys to him the emotional value of the comradeship that society and ethics promote. The power of the experience dispells his former cynicism about men ashore and, in this special situation, makes "a distinction between right and wrong [seem] absurdly clear to him" (88). Of course the unambiguous moral stance at which he arrives is not a challenge to the story's naturalism, to its monistic view that man and nature are one. The brotherhood and cooperation that instantly spring into being are man's *instinctive* responses to a threatening natural world. Man's difference in nature may derive from his moral sense, but that sense is rooted in instinct, a faculty that man shares with other creatures. Man is different, but different from other things in nature.

If the men in the boat pitted against the sea permit the correspondent clarity of moral vision, a contrast between the primitive society in the boat and the advanced one on the shore prevents any hasty conclusion that the moral clarity that prevails in the first extends to the second, for a central aspect of the story is the distinction between the unusual conditions that prevail in the boat and those which commonly prevail ashore. Ultimately, those distinctions lead to a distinction between moral sensibilities as well.

Initially, the correspondent measures the difference in his own suffering flesh when he calls rowing "a diabolical punishment" rather than a social amusement (74). The advanced society of the shore, with its windmill, its "house of refuge"(76), its lighthouse, and its winter vacations, has developed beyond the point where physical exertion—in this case, rowing—is a necessity for survival; men ashore engage in such activities for mere sport, a fact that makes the correspondent lament that men cannot train for shipwrecks (74). So the physical distance between the protosociety of the boat and the society of the shore suggests a temporal one, depicting how much man's creation, society, has progressed beyond its original reason for existence, self-protection, and developed a life of its own that affects man's behavior so as to defy its primary reason for being. It is the diversions and pleasures offered by the shore society, after all, that lead the members of the winter resort hotel party thoughtlessly to assume that the men in the boat are enjoying their own pleasures.

This lesson in distance that the correspondent is so painfully learning implies another lesson both for him and the reader. If nature is indifferent and societies and their associated moral systems spring from man's instinct for survival, then societies are fictions in the sense that works of art are fictions—that is, creations of man designed to interpret the outside world in human terms, to give human meaning to a world without meaning and impose human order on a world whose natural order can be beneficent to man only if its destructive aspects are controlled. From the correspondent's perspective the shore is "set before him like a bit of scenery on a stage, and he looked at it and understood with his eyes each detail of it" (90). The equation between art (the stage scenery) and society suggests that society is an art form, a human organization of reality like art, and this equation is reinforced shortly thereafter, further promoting the view that society is a fiction: "The shore, with its white slope of sand and its green bluff, topped with little silent cottages, was spread like a picture before him. It was very near to him then, but he was impressed as one who in a gallery looks at a scene from Brittany or Holland" (91).

But Crane does something more than develop an equation between art and society. He endows his correspondent with aesthetic distance to make it clear that the latter is viewing art properly. Those who possess this faculty view the work of art in terms of its internal relations and refrain from establishing relations external to it; that is, they see the work as it is in itself without imposing practical values on it or establishing a personal relation with it that projects some part of the self or its experience onto it. And those who achieve aesthetic distance thus also achieve an understanding of the true meaning of the work, the word "distance" implying an intimate rather than a peripheral involvement.[1]

This is a faculty that Crane takes pains to show his correspondent in possession of. Readers who note his identification with the soldier of Algiers should also note that the identification is impersonal. A sense of shared situations, in short, prompts the development of aesthetic distance, with a consequent loss of self, rather than an identification that is simply external because it projects one man's personal responses onto those of another. Hence the correspondent dreams "of the slow and slower movements of the lips of the soldier"; and, losing all sense of personal self, becoming the soldier, he "was moved by a profound and perfectly impersonal comprehension. He was sorry for the soldier of the Legion who lay dying in Algiers" (86).

Although he naturally feels a personal relationship to the shore once in the water (he does not want to drown), the pictorial references to it suggest that for two brief instances he views it as he viewed the soldier—that is, with aesthetic distance—and hence can perceive the true meaning and value of each art work: the shore signifying refuge, home, life; the soldier representing abandonment, homelessness, death. This is a dramatic reversal of his former view, an external one, in which "he had never regarded it [the soldier's dying] as important." Indeed, "it was less to him than the breaking of a pencil's point" (85). On the shore, in society, he measured the value of everything in personal terms, and no experience prompted the development of aesthetic distance.

The problem with the people on the shore in this story is that they do *not* possess aesthetic distance. They view others in terms of external relations, projecting their own personal lighthearted mood onto the men in the boat, whom they view as engaging in sport like themselves. And this fact brings into bold relief the difference between the man who can view society as a fiction and with aesthetic distance and the man living within the fiction of his own creation. Immersed in the complications of an advanced society, social man forgets the original reasons for its existence and responds to other needs generated by that society—the "need," for example, for diversion and pleasure. As creations of men, advanced societies are still fictions—that is, interpretations of nature—but such interpretations can lead to a loss of communication among men (as in the case between the boat's occupants and the shore's visitors) because they no longer have their source in primal instincts for survival. Rather, their source is in needs that engender an external view of other men rather than an internal (aesthetic) view.

If there seems to be an implied moral commentary in Crane's handling of his picture motif, it should be clear by now that neither this commentary nor the correspondent's clear moral vision constitutes a flat judgment of man's moral failings. For the exercise of aesthetic distance in viewing paintings does indeed require a proper physical distance from the work, distance that is denied social man caught in the complicated social fabric (in this case, living within the world viewed as art by the correspondent). That lack of distance is certainly a circumstance mitigating the responsibility of the men on the shore who do not perceive the dangerous situation of the boat's occupants. Although the correspondent undoubtedly wishes urgently that someone could see him and his partners from the windtower, the tower is, after all, a windmill, not "a life-saving station." Crane takes care to point out somewhat earlier "that there was not a life-saving station within twenty miles in either direction, but the men did not know this fact and in consequence they made

dark and opprobrious remarks concerning the eyesight of the nation's life-savers" (76). In short, what may seem indefensible to the
men in the boat does not appear so to the reader, for there is no reason
to believe that the operators of this windmill have had knowledge of
repeated shipwrecks in their vicinity and ought therefore to use the
structure as a post to spot survivors. The complexity of shore life
suggests that the simple contrast betwen the human moral realm of
the boat and the amoral world of nature (the sea) underscores a larger,
more complicated contrast between the situations of the men in the
boat and those on the shore.

The contrast is introduced by the windtower, a human creation
harnessing the wind. This structure represents two things to the
correspondent: "nature in the wind, and nature in the vision of
men"(88). "Nature in the wind" is an odd phrase, for wind is a part of
nonhuman nature; but the phrase aptly describes nature as seen by
the snow man in Wallace Stevens's poem. Paraphrased, "The Snow
Man" means that "one must have a mind of winter" (that is, be a
snow man) in order to comprehend nature as it is in itself without
imposing on it human perceptions and emotions. "Nature in the
wind" is thus whatever nonhuman nature is in itself. In the vision of
men, "she" (nature) is, among other things, "flatly indifferent," at
least from the perspective of the correspondent. No snow man, he
inevitably personifies when he describes nature. But his reference to
"men" in the phrase "nature in the vision of men" seems to involve
more than himself and suggests that he also includes nature as seen by
the eyes of those who created the windtower. It is unlikely that they
share the correspondent's feeling that nature is "flatly indifferent" to
man, for it has taken a shipwreck for the correspondent to reach this
conclusion. But no matter what their views of nature's essential
character, they know that they can harness the wind's energies and
make it serve man's purposes: to generate electricity, to drain water,
and the like. To use nature in this way is to "interpret" nature—to
impose on it a significance which it does not in itself possess.

In the vision of men, then, the windtower represents (indifferent)
nature forced to serve the human world of purpose, and this point
establishes an important, clear difference between the situation of
the men on the shore and that of the men in the boat. Although the
world of the shore developed from a simple society symbolized by

the men in the boat, it has achieved a degree of freedom from the primitive struggle for existence that permits it to make relatively sophisticated interpretations of nature, of which the windtower is one example. Such a degree of freedom is denied the men in the boat. Their perspective on their immediate lives is sharply limited by their physical struggle to remain afloat. The first line of the story stresses the limitation of that perspective: "None of them knew the color of the sky" (68). But when they reach the safety of the shore, their perspective is no longer so limited: "When it came night, the white waves paced to and fro in the moonlight, and the wind brought the sound of the great sea's voice to the men on shore, and they felt that they could then be interpreters" (92).

After their venture they are released from the struggle for existence to reenter a world of interpreters. They can continue to interpret according to their own respective professions and thus contribute to society's fictional structure. Because of his changed situation, the correspondent can now interpret nature in a far more sophisticated way than when in the boat. The specific background of this story—Crane lived through such an adventure as a correspondent and wrote a journalistic account of the shipwreck that forced him into an open boat—permits a critic to merge character and author by saying that the story is the form the correspondent-author's interpretation takes. And the story's meaning involves a moral view of life achieved by him. But though the correspondent may have achieved a measure of clarity of moral vision as one consequence of his being thoroughly subjected to natural forces, few on the shore have been in a position to arrive at his perspective. The fundamental contrast between the situations of the two societies suggests that one has lost access to truths momentarily permitted the other. It takes a brush with death for the correspondent to arrive at his vision.

The lack of clarity of moral vision ashore derives from social complexity. The simplicity of an opposition between man and nature in "The Open Boat" becomes, in Crane's other work, the complexity of the opposition between man and society. The boat becomes an individual, floating in a sea that is society, and the complexities of this changed opposition lead to determinism. Subsequent analyses will show that there are many reasons for this difference in philosophical vision, but two can be offered here as germane to "The Open Boat." The first is that when the sea becomes society, the sharp contrast between the individual and the sea (as nonhuman nature) is lost, for the character can be viewed both as a representative of society and as an individual apart from it. A blurring of the distinction between the individual in his role as individual and in his role as social man—as oiler, correspondent, and the like—already exists in "The Open Boat," but the critical situation permits instinct to form that brotherhood which leads in the direction of clear moral vision. On the shore— that is, in the societies portrayed in Crane's other works—this blurred distinction undoes moral vision and questions the concept of freedom. When the individual is reduced to the status of social man, a product of society's values, his choices appear as deter- mined as the self that makes them.

A related, and broader, reason for the determinism of the other works lies in the central implication of Crane's view of society as a fiction, a creation of man's, as is a work of art. The implication is that society is not founded on an absolute, and therefore man lives in that world of right and wrong to which the correspondent refers, rather than in a world of good and evil. And distinctions between right and wrong are less easy to perceive than those between good and evil. This is so because good and evil are founded in an absolute outside of man, access to which religions have traditionally provided. In a world of right and wrong so- ciety's values replace those of God, and the merits of social values are frequently questionable. And without an absolute, individuals have no way of distancing themselves from such values by mea- suring them according to God's. Hence they more easily become their unconscious product rather than their autonomous wielders.

Right and wrong, furthermore, are ultimately founded in man's instinctively felt need to survive. In a simple social situation like that of the boat, instinct to survive easily creates a sense of the right and leads to brotherhood because all the men can readily enough perceive the common threat posed by the sea. Such a shared perception makes absurdly clear the moral demands of brotherhood, cooperation, and obligation. But the social situa-

tion of the shore is far more complicated. There the individual still
has an instinct to survive, and his place in society limits his
perspective just as surely as the sea limits the perspective of the
boat's occupants. But in society individuals do not necessarily
have shared, if limited, perceptions of that pressing common
danger which evokes brotherhood on the boat. Nor do they have
a substitute, a shared objective absolute to which all can give
allegiance and thus temper their instincts and improve their moral
visions. In society brotherhood and cooperation break down as
men fight men rather than the sea, and the breakdown occurs
precisely because men are at the mercy of their instincts and their
conflicting, limited perceptions. The one is a function of biological and psychological conditions over which they have no control; the other, their perceptions, a function of social conditions
that they are equally powerless to control. When perception is the
condition for right action, and when it is reducible to circumstance beyond individual control, then a clear moral vision permitting judgment of characters gives way to a deterministic one.

"The Blue Hotel"

A deterministic element in "The Open Boat" exists to show that
man's roots are in the natural world, and this view is intrinsic to
the naturalistic vision. Man cooperates and develops a sense of
mutual obligation—these are his instinctive responses to his condition, the common threat to survival, what Crane calls "the
plight of the ants" (88). Thus his moral codes derive from a nature
that embraces men as well as ants, both of which cooperate and
form societies. Of course Crane uses the reference to the ants
ironically—the men are as insignificant as ants *sub specie aeternitatis*—but the ironic mode is not simplistic, and the reference
contains both values.

  Man, of course, is "different": he can interpret, impose meanings on the world, and this ability separates him from the ants,
although his difference is still rooted in nature. Yet this latter
aspect of the story, its biological determinism, does not raise
determinism as a serious philosophical issue. For though men
possess instincts, like other creatures in the natural world, this fact

does not mean that they do not also possess freedom over and above those determinisms which wed them to nature. It is in "The Blue Hotel" that the issue is raised in serious fashion by the concluding interchange between the Easterner and the cowboy.

This interchange is marked by the spirit of "might-have-been." The Swede might be alive, according to the cowboy, had the bartender "been any good" and "cracked that there Dutchman on the head with a bottle" (169), or had the Swede not been "an awful fool," even "crazy" (170).* The Easterner initially responds "tartly" that "a thousand things might have happened" (169), as if to suggest that it is pointless to think in might-have-been terms, but it soon becomes clear that he shares the same spirit, for he cries out, "The Swede might not have been killed if everything had been square"(170). He rejects the cowboy's view, which holds the Swede largely responsible for his own death, and instead involves five men (other than the Swede) in a "collaboration" issuing in a "sin," the killing (170). "Collaboration" and "sin" are words that introduce a moral factor into the spirit of might-have-been, a factor which holds men responsible for their actions and thus presupposes their freedom.

But there is an interesting ambiguity in the sad phrase memorialized by Whittier, for "might-have-been" can mean "could have been under the same conditions" or "would have been if conditions had been altered." Applied to the Easterner's behavior, the phrase can thus mean that, in the lived moment of the action, the Easterner *could* have corroborated the Swede's charges under prevailing conditions; or it can mean that he *would* have corroborated those charges *if*—if, for example, he could have foreseen the Swede's death. Furthermore, although the Easterner applies this ambiguous phrase only to the Swede's death ("The Swede might not have been killed if everything had been square"), simple logic demands that it be applied to the conditional clause as well. If it is true that the Swede might not have been killed if everything had been square, then the reader must conclude that the Easterner feels that everything *might have been* square. And since he implicates in this collaboration not just himself and Johnnie (who knew

*Stephen Crane, "The Blue Hotel," in *Tales of Adventure*, Va. (1970) 5.

of the cheating) but Scully and the cowboy (who did not), a reader must assume that the Easterner believes that all the actions performed by these men in the story *might have been* different.

This ambiguous phrase thus embraces all the events through section viii of the story, but which of its meanings applies? Insofar as the Easterner is moral in his point of view, one must assume that he adopts a could-have-been interpretation, for the concept of moral responsibility is drained of value if men under the same conditions cannot act other than as they do. Curiously enough, however, Crane does not put words into the Easterner's mouth that could clarify this matter. Instead, he seems deliberately to obfuscate. "Sin" and "collaboration" suggest a could-have-been interpretation, but to say that "every sin is the *result* of a collaboration" (170, italics added) suggests a *would*-have-been reading. "Result" is a mathematical term denoting a closed system in which human intention is not a factor. Try as one will, two plus three will not equal six. Since this "collaboration" could not have been purposeful (the Easterner did not withhold confirmation of the Swede's charges to assure the Swede's death), the would-have-been interpretation of the Easterner's remarks is strengthened. Because one can argue that the Easterner *would* have acted differently *if* he could have foreseen the future, one is left with a plausible "would-have-been" interpretation of his remarks, an interpretation that is perfectly consistent with determinism, the thesis that states that "for everything that ever happens there are conditions such that, given them, nothing else could happen."[2] From this angle of vision the "sin" is indeed the "apex of a human movement" (170) which represents the condition for its occurrence, though no single person premeditated its commission.

If the Easterner's concluding remarks do not clarify the meaning of "might-have-been," neither does the story's structure; for it also fails to give unambiguous sanction to either a moral or a deterministic meaning for events. Section viii, for example, seems to indict the community for hypocrisy in tolerating a gambler because he is "so judicious in his choice of victims" (166) and because, apart from his gambling, he is in all other matters "so generous, so just, so moral, that, in a contest, he could have put to flight the consciences of nine-tenths of the citizens of Romper"

(167). One can argue that this indictment strengthens the story's moral vision by extending the scope of the Easterner's. Clearly, if the Swede was in the gambler's company because of the moral failing of five men, the gambler was in his company because of a community's moral failure.

The "moral" vision of section viii, however, is counterbalanced by foreshadowings within the tale at odds with a moral interpretation because they strengthen a deterministic reading. The Swede early in the story predicts his own death; and indeed, he meets it. He is killed by a gambler who, like Johnnie, the first gambler he encounters, preys on reckless farmers: a nice bit of literary symmetry suggesting that the agent of the Swede's death is not far removed from the social context in which he feared meeting it. Out of a sense of frustration, Scully and the cowboy fervently wish the Swede's death, and their wish is fulfilled through no conscious effort on their part. And the cash machine message on which the Swede's eyes stare— " 'This registers the amount of your purchase' " (169)—can certainly be read as a confirmation of deterministic forces, rather than human free will, guiding events. If it recalls the ancient adage "As a man soweth, so shall he reap," the moral value of that adage is drained by the closed system of mathematics the message represents. The Swede does not intend his actions to produce his death, but they do.

Of course, one might argue that these deterministic elements are only ironic, but if one deprives them of deterministic intent on that basis, one can use the same argument to deprive section viii of moral intent. It is only ironic that men who think themselves moral should tolerate, even approve of, this gambler who preys on old farmers; for nowhere does the narrator suggest that such "moral" citizens could behave other than as they do, a view that is the necessary adjunct of the moral one. Their behavior thus becomes but another instance of the cosmic irony of the human situation.

In these ways one can see that Crane has created, in his story at large, the same kind of tension between the moral and the deterministic that surfaces in the Easterner's "fog of mysterious theory." In order to resolve that tension in favor of a moral reading, therefore, one must find somewhere within the story the indispensable premise on which a moralist reading rests. One must be able to see that men could have acted other than as they did under the same conditions; one must be able to aver that Crane wishes "might-have-been" to mean "could-have-been."

Testing the validity of this premise requires that the reader review events from two perspectives, that of ignorance and that of knowledge; that is, from a perspective that views events as they are lived without the Easterner's knowledge that Johnnie is cheating and without an advance knowledge that the Swede will be killed, and from a perspective that views the lived events with such knowledge. There is a difference between one's perception of events as they are lived and as they are viewed in retrospect. The Easterner may, in hindsight, impose elements upon the past that were not there in the lived moment. So, too, might a reader. Indeed, the major point that emerges from an examination of these two perspectives is that Crane seems deliberately to undercut a clear moral axis for the first seven sections by concealing the reasons for characters' actions at crucial moments. If one doesn't know why characters behave as they do, it is clearly hard to say whether they could have behaved otherwise, and by so much is a moral interpretation weakened.

In the lived moment and from the point of view of ignorance, the action poses one moral issue, and its center is the Easterner's response to the Swede's initial appeal for help. When the Swede's "appealing glance" is met only with the Easterner's "I don't understand you," the reader, who learns shortly that the Easterner in fact does understand the source of the Swede's anxieties, might very well be tempted to view this failure of brotherhood in moral terms. The reader also might be tempted to moral judgment of the Easterner from the perspective of knowledge, which raises the only other moral issue involving the Easterner, his failure to corroborate what he knows to be the truth of the Swede's charge of cheating. But from either perspective, that of ignorance or that of knowledge, several factors inhibit moral judgment of the Easterner. The major one is that the reader has no access to the Easterner's thought processes. Although in the first case he engages in "prolonged and cautious reflection" (146) before he responds to the Swede, the reader does not know the content of his thought that leads him to respond as he does. Is he thinking, "I should help this Swede, but I can't be bothered to become involved," a thought which would invite moral condemnation? Or does his thought undermine the possibility of moral judgment, as the following might: "I believe I know what's wrong with this fellow, but I am not certain; and I am afraid if I try to help, I shall only make matters worse"?

In the second case also, Crane deprives the reader of access to the Easterner's thought, and with the same effect. No matter what else the reader learns about the Easterner—that he does not find a game of cards worth a fight, for example, or that he feels sufficiently moved for the underdog in a fight that he cheers for Johnnie, the card cheat—he never learns the cause of the Easterner's "sin" of omission. And in both cases, Scully's own experience with the Swede further weakens a moral charge against the Easterner, whether leveled by the reader or by the Easterner himself. Scully's attempt to calm the Swede compensates for the Easterner's initial failure, and it backfires disastrously. So even "moral" behavior can lead to disaster. The upshot of Scully's good intentions thus rivets the reader's attention on the ironic operations of cause and effect rather than on the moral delinquencies of men. As for the Easterner's other "failure," one can conclude that any argument premised on the view that the Easterner has a moral duty to corroborate the Swede's charge can be countered by an argument that corroboration would be an inflammatory act in a rapidly deteriorating situation. An Easterner who has witnessed a change for the worse in the Swede's behavior (effected by Scully's good intentions) could very well believe that silence is the best moral response under the circumstances.

Denied access to the Easterner's thoughts, the reader can find no clear moral axis in events that might yield one. And without such access, how can a reader accept the moral legitimacy of the Easterner's self-recriminations at the story's end? If he has forgotten the common psychological phenomenon of individuals experiencing irrational guilt after an unhappy event, he can recall that after Scully's benevolent intentions fail, "the others understood from his manner that he was admitting his responsibility for the Swede's new viewpoint"(155). If Scully can experience irrational guilt for the Swede's aggressive behavior, might not the Easterner be so responding to a consequence far more serious? This question can be answered with another: Would the Easterner have felt guilty had the Swede not died, the murderer not been imprisoned? Perhaps he should feel guilty, but nothing in the story allows the reader to corroborate his feeling in fact. All that the reader can say with certainty is that in both "moral" events, the Easterner's apparent failure is in character—character here defined not necessarily as "indifferent" but as "reflective." The Easterner refuses to act without weighing the consequences of such action. To an outsider he may seem indifferent to the point of moral negligence, but that is only speculation.

There is no reason to believe, however, that Johnnie was not cheating. Certainly the contrast between his ne'er-do-well self and the respectable brother whose picture Scully shows the Swede with pride would make little literary sense were he not a cheat, and the symmetry created by one card cheat's carrying out the doom sensed by the Swede in the presence of an earlier one would be lost. Nonetheless it is risky to pin one's hopes for a clear moral axis on the fact that Johnnie cheated. For just as Crane denies the reader access to the Easterner's thoughts at crucial points, he does the same with Johnnie at one crucial moment of the lived action. The reader does not know why Johnnie cheats in a card game not played for money—a fact stressed by the cowboy in conclusion. Is he just keeping in shape for future card rivals? Is he trying, in a petty way, to get back at the Swede for the Swede's patently offensive behavior? A reader cannot know. He only knows that it is in character for Johnnie to do so.

From both perspectives, then, the only characters on whom one might pin a moral reading thwart efforts to do so because they conceal their thoughts, and so their motives. Or rather, of course, Crane conceals them, thereby clearly and significantly reversing the relationship between character and behavior that prevails in prose fiction with a moral axis. In such novels the primary function of behavior is to reveal character; that is, to display growth, development, or other change, or their lack. In "The Blue Hotel," Crane turns the horse and cart around, making character type explain behavior. It clearly is "in character" for a reflective Easterner to ruminate and it is "in character" for a ne'er-do-well to cheat. But their moral status is not clear.

Indeed, this very lack of clarity makes moral readings of the tale illogical. That moral failure to be brotherly which more than one critic finds is the central meaning of the story does at first seem plausible as its major point, all the more so because the Easterner's theory seems to embrace it and because it has a certain reasonableness alluded to earlier: had the Easterner, or others, handled the Swede differently, the Swede might not have been where he was to provoke a gambler who responded as he did. But a moment's reflection shows that the story points to the problems—better, the impossibility—of translating this thought into a moral indictment. Scully's brotherly gestures worsen matters, so moral behavior is no panacea. Furthermore, to sustain a moral reading, one must force the Swede to share guilt for his death. Good reason there may be for his behavior (he is a victim of paranoia bred by his reading of dime novels), but there is also good reason for Scully's later fury; namely, the behavior of the Swede. Because Scully does not know the merit of the Swede's charge against his son, his frustration must be put in the same "moral" category as the Swede's paranoia. If Scully must be blamed, therefore, so must the Swede. For that matter, so must everybody else not named by the Easterner, for to sustain a moralist reading, finally, one must honor the "moral" vision of section viii and brand the community that harbored the gambler. And so one arrives at the moral of a moralist reading: If everyone behaved like angels, there would be no killings and no prisons. It is difficult to believe that a writer widely hailed as a "psychological realist" would have taken the trouble to convey such a truism.

Why, then, if there is no clear moral axis in the first seven sections, does Crane introduce moral perspectives in the last two? The apparently moral perspectives of the narrator in section viii and of the Easterner in ix seem more like deliberately planned additions to the story to impale the reader on the horns of what can be called the Hobbesian dilemma:[3] man is free and can be judged morally, but his acts of the will are caused, a fact that undercuts the premise on which moral judgment is based—that under the same conditions individuals could behave other than as they do.

It is Crane's emphasis on types, on what he early in the story refers to as "creeds, classes,[and] egotisms" (142), that initially challenges that premise. The story shows that an individual's character type is one of the conditions governing behavior, a fact that makes nonsense of the idea that under the same conditions a character could act other than as he does. Perhaps so, but then he would be a different character! And as the story develops, one sees the challenge to this premise strengthened, for another dimension of character that acts as cause emerges: its elemental nature. The story presents character as type defined by class or creed and character as animallike in its egotism. Indeed, in this story, these two aspects of character become inseparable, and this twin emphasis resolutely turns the Hobbesian definition of liberty ("the absence of all the impediments to action that are not contained in the nature and intrinsical quality of the agent")[4] into a deterministic vision.

In order to see that both aspects of character operate as conditions that govern behavior, the reader must be aware of how thoroughly Crane blurs the distinction between the human and the nonhuman worlds. He does this primarily by presenting the story as though it were a scientific experiment, the subject of which is human responses. The unusual color of the hotel, blue, suggests its role as a laboratory where the experimental scientist blends the "creeds, classes, egotisms, that streamed through Romper on the rails day after day." Those, like the Easterner, who came from "the brown-reds and the subdivisions of the dark greens of the East" had "no color in common" with the "opulence and splendor" of the hotel—or so the reader is told (142). But Crane's naturalistic vision manipulates color to show that even a sophisticated Easterner is, finally, a part of nature and can be viewed as such in a laboratory.

The first hint of this comes from the particular colors that this color-conscious author chooses to emphasize in his story. The East is equated with brown-red and dark green; the West, with blue. Red, green, and blue-violet are primary colors—not the pigment primaries of the painter, to be sure, but the light primaries of the physicist, more appropriate to the perspective of the narrator as that of a detached scientist. To understand the narrator's "scientific findings," however, the reader must ignore

Crane's choice of *brown*-red and his omission of violet as the tone of his blue. Eastern subdivisions, after all, are not fire-engine red, and it would be awkward to call the story "The Blue-Violet Hotel." Granting Crane this privilege, the reader can see that Crane deliberately reduces regions and the particular "creeds, classes, egotisms" that they breed to color; he blends together in the hotel not the subtractive primaries of the painter, which combine to produce black, but the additive primaries of the physicist—red, green, and blue—whose blending produces white.[5] So the characters do, after all, share a "color in common." White, furthermore, is the color (really noncolor) of the snowstorm, and so blending these character-colors together equates all of them with the world of physical nature—even the Easterner, despite his civilized veneer. Crane, indeed, emphasizes the sophisticated Easterner's association with physical nature. His name is Blanc, French for white. And Mont Blanc, the highest peak in the Alps, is eternally covered with glaciers and snow, a fact that inspired Coleridge and Shelley and very likely Crane as well.

But the story is named "The *Blue* Hotel," and Crane gives equal emphasis to that color to make the point that man is a part of nature. The hotel's color seems to set it apart not just from the world of the East but, by its sharp contrast to the white of the snowstorm, from the world of physical nature as well. But the blue is also associated with physical nature, for it covers the snow with its "unearthly satin" (158); thus, the human creation—the hotel—and nature share a common color, suggesting that the division between the two worlds of man and nature is tenuous at best. Furthermore, people grow blue when they are cold and, though the hotel is supposed to protect them from this condition, it is in this very blue hotel that temperaments so commingle as to force them into the world of nature that will make them blue.

Crane's use of color, then, partly translates into a philosophical meaning akin to Ishmael's final speculations in the chapter "The Whiteness of the Whale" in *Moby-Dick* (chapter 42). Colors may distinguish one type of man from another type, and they indeed seem to separate man from the world of nature, which is snow-white-colorless. But in fact the human world represented by color is part of the continuum of nature because the whiteness of nature contains all colors—if the mixing of the colors produces white, the colors are *in* the white. Or, as Ishmael puts it, whiteness is not just "the visible absence of color" but is "at the same time the concrete of all colors." Hence, nature and man are one, not two, in "The Blue Hotel."

If the usual distinctions between the human and nonhuman worlds ultimately collapse, then one can legitimately examine human responses as a biologist examines the responses of birds or bullocks. And Crane's narrator does exactly that. His investigation shows that character operates as condition in *both* its social and its animal dimensions. In other words, the narrator's angle of vision is Hobbesian, and that angle of vision issues in a Hobbesian view of freedom because it views man's civilized self, with its "freedom," in the same way that it views man's animal nature. Initially the emphasis falls on character type—that is, social type—as one important condition that causes certain emotional responses and leads to certain characteristic actions.

He introduces the Swede's first paranoid response, one that has its conditions: his foreignness, the locale, and his familiarity with the clichés of dime novels. And that paranoid response acts as the condition sparking the initial responses of others, differing types responding in different ways to one condition. Thus, the action that unfolds in the opening sections seems perfectly reasonable— "reasonable" in the sense of explicable and plausible rather than rational. Each character seems to have good reason to behave as he does, given his respective type. But by the end of section vii the reader can perceive that beneath the different types a common "savagery" emerges, though the expression of that violent emotional response again varies with the character type. That is, some people are more civilized than others and require greater external provocation before becoming like their fellow animals—before becoming, that is, creatures of instinct and emotion rather than creatures of a social class. Section vii ends with the cowboy and Scully vying in expressions of frustration as they repeat how they would like to kill the Swede, though Scully's stronger ethical sense prevents the cowboy from taking him on. The Easterner does not participate in section vii's verbal orgy, but he is hardly exempt from the emotional responses there expressed. For that section's marked emphasis on savage responses prepares for the final and most important response in the story, the Easterner's in section ix. It is there that his place in nature, and so in Crane's laboratory experiment, becomes apparent.

The Easterner's "fog of mysterious theory" seems to proceed naturally from the reasoned and reflective character type assigned him earlier, a type in marked contrast to others in the work. But the cowboy's protestations against the Easterner's assertion, "The Swede might not have been killed if everything had been square" (170), "reduced him [the Easterner] to rage." He is no more exempt from frustration than the cowboy, as the following words indicate: " 'You're a fool!' cried the Easterner *viciously*" (emphasis provided, 170). He is enraged by the cowboy's obtuseness, and his rage proceeds from a sense of guilt generated by a knowledge of the conclusion of his encounter with the Swede. This "fog of mysterious theory," then, hardly possesses a rational base, and in his desire to relieve himself of the anguish of guilt, the Easterner dilutes it by imposing it on four others as well. It would be logical, of course, to blame the Swede, too; indeed, the whole community, which supported the "unfortunate gambler" whose action of killing the Swede is "the apex of a human movement" (170). But such logic would only be for one not caught in the throes of guilt. Where everyone is guilty, no one is, and the Easterner's guilt feelings are too intense to allow for their complete dissipation. But their very intensity also demands that they be shared. Hence, though he observes that "usually there are from a dozen to forty women really involved in every murder" (a comment that suggests that guilt can be widely distributed to the point where the concept becomes meaningless), he acknowledges his own felt guilt by implicating himself and just four others in the killing.

Seen in the lived moment of action, hence, the story contains a psychological determinism dependent on character type. Psychic states determine not just the obvious emotional responses of a simple cowboy who shrieks "Kill him" during the fight but also the apparently reasoned concluding observations of the sophisticated Easterner. But viewing events in retrospect, the reader is forced to the determinism that is part of the Easterner's

theory, that historical determinism which describes every sin as
the "apex of a human movement," a determinism that is the
natural complement of the psychological; for indeed any present
moment is "the apex of a human movement" in a past in which
men's behavior is a function of conditions then prevailing.

These two ways of witnessing the action show that the Easterner both is and is not Crane's spokesman. The moral aspect of
his theory is false because it involves only five men as collab-
orators in a "sin." But because his theory embraces both the moral
and the deterministic, thereby reducing "sin" to a "result," "the
apex of a human movement," his theory in broad outline does
indeed represent the story's preferred philosophical vision. For the
Easterner forces the reader to think in two sets of opposed terms,
and so does Crane, who structures his story to embody a classic
modern vision expressed by the Easterner, the Hobbesian paradox that undoes liberty with causation. That human movement
whose apex is the Swede's death may be the result of characters
performing "freely-willed" actions, but each action is reducible to
conditions over which the character has no control. This paradox
is the source of richness in "The Blue Hotel" and moves it
resolutely in the direction of determinism. More important, the
clear surfacing of the Hobbesian paradox in this, one of Crane's
late works, suggests that his earlier works contain a dual vision
that is responsible for such thoroughly incompatible interpretations of them.

Maggie

Crane's Hobbesian view of the liberty of the self is most perfectly
reflected in two extended statements he made that are important
to an understanding of *Maggie*. Hobbes defined that liberty as the
"absence of all the impediments to action that are not contained in
the nature and intrinsical quality of the agent,"[6] but, as explained
in the first chapter, the implications of that definition inevitably
lead to determinism. The same can be said of Crane's two views of
Maggie. When actually implemented within the form of prose
fiction, they make liberty a facade, a mere appearance behind
which lies the reality of determinism inherent in Hobbes's own
definition of liberty.

The first quotation, inscribed by Crane in copies of his novel, emphasizes the force of environment in the life of Maggie and, by implication, in the lives of others:

> It is inevitable that you will be greatly shocked by this book but continue please with all possible courage to the end. For it tries to show that environment is a tremendous thing in the world and frequently shapes lives regardless. If one proves that theory one makes room in Heaven for all sorts of souls (notably an occasional street girl) who are not confidently expected to be there by many excellent people.[7]

This is the heart of the inscription, although it runs on for another sentence. It is important because it relieves Maggie of responsibility for her career as prostitute and her subsequent suicide. But it is not unambiguously deterministic. Nowhere does it state that Maggie does not possess the faculty called free will, nor does it say that her self is a product of its environment. It merely emphasizes environment as a cause explaining the shape of her life; and a reader familiar with the story can interpret it to mean that environment shapes her life in the sense that those who reject her give her no other alternative to prostitution when they force her into the streets. This view is supported by the form of her appeal to Pete after he rejects her: " 'But where kin I go?' "* Since she has no other option, such a view seems to relieve her of moral condemnation but to permit moral judgments of the people who constitute her environment, those who deny her another option. And Crane seems to be engaged in such judgment in comments on Bowery life he makes in a letter that concludes with direct reference to *Maggie*:

> I do not think that much can be done with the Bowery as long as the [*word blurred*] are in their present state of conceit. A person who thinks himself superior to the rest of us because he has no job and no pride and no clean clothes is as badly conceited as Lillian Russell. In a story of mine called "An Experiment in Misery" I tried to make plain that the

*Stephen Crane, *Maggie*, in *Bowery Tales*, edited by Fredson Bowers with introductions by James B. Colvert. Va. (1969) 1:67.

root of Bowery life is a sort of cowardice. Perhaps I mean a lack of ambition or to willingly be knocked flat and accept the licking. The missions for children are another thing and if you will have Mr. Rockefeller give me a hundred street cars and some money I will load all the babes off to some pink world where cows can lick their noses and they will never see their families any more.[8]

The letter's references to "conceit" and "cowardice" call Bowery inhabitants to account in moral terms; but just as the inscription referred to above is not unambiguously deterministic, neither is this letter unambiguously moral. Crane's desire to cart Bowery children away from their parents suggests his view that their environment will inevitably induce in the children that very "conceit" and "cowardice" by which he morally indicts their parents, themselves presumably products of their environment. The fact that each letter can be read to deny the main thrust of its argument suggests Crane's moral ambiguity. And separate authorial comments implying opposed interpretations of the same story further suggest that the story unites both poles of his interpretation into a single vision.

The view urged here is that Crane's fiction goes beneath what his letter calls "the root of Bowery life," a "cowardice" and willingness to "be knocked flat and accept the licking." It digs up the roots of the cowardice and the willingness in order to expose the environment in which they grow. In this way it shows, in the words of the inscription, "that environment is a tremendous force in the world and frequently shapes lives," and by so showing, it undermines moral judgment of the lives that grow in that environment. Certainly Crane's perspective on Jimmie's "conceit" in *Maggie* is environmental. Ironic though it be that this lowly figure thinks himself superior to Christians and aristocrats, his "conceit" has its roots in childhood conditions to which Crane devotes the first four sections of his story. A reader's moral judgment of that "conceit" which distinguishes his character, therefore, is undermined by his knowledge of the conditions, beyond his control, that produced it. And this view of his conceit applies also to his "cowardice" in rejecting his sister. Crane's portrayal of Jimmie is but one illustration of the story's Hobbesian vision. In any present moment of action, Jimmie seems free, in the sense that no obstacle to action not inherent in his character is present. He thus seems to be a target for moral judgment. But by repeated reminders that his intrinsic character is formed by his environment, Crane reduces his "voluntary" actions to a self that is product of, rather than autonomous agent in, its world.

Part of that environment is the Christian mission that Jimmie attends, and Crane makes slighting remarks about such missions in his letter, though there he does not mention one obvious reason provided by the story for criticizing them—they offer to satisfy the physical need for food as a bribe for the acceptance of their religious views. The unfortunates in *Maggie* who must attend these missions sense the grossness of this situation but cannot comprehend a larger grossness: the missions are the source of that double standard pervading Maggie's environment and leading to her destruction. In criticizing this aspect, among others, of her environment, Crane introduces a moral factor into his work. Because he blames not specific individuals but institutions and the larger moral environment they foster, however, he promotes determinism even as he criticizes the environment that determines. He suggests that people are so much a part of their environment that only the environment, not the individual, can be judged morally. His determinism does not destroy a moral vision of a corrupt environment, nor does the moral vision of that environment destroy its determining effect on individuals. What is destroyed by his Hobbesian vision is a clear moral focus that permits readers to state that *Maggie* is a story about conscious hypocrisy and that three hypocrites in particular—Maggie's mother, brother, and seducer—ought roundly to be condemned.[9]

As already stated, *Maggie* is the story of a double standard, which is the heart of the social environment determining Maggie's life and the life of others. To see how that standard functions to undermine moral judgment of individuals in Maggie's world, one must note that world's major distinct characteristic. Associated with the obvious struggle for physical survival is a subtler but more devastating battle. In Crane's world, people not only have a biological instinct to survive (as in "The Open Boat"); they also have a psychological instinct for self-esteem. This latter instinct is a natural corollary of the biological instinct for survival, the social dimension of the physical. In society people can only gain a sense of self-esteem by achieving a social position, for this gives them "honor" and "respectability," both of which satisfy the primary psychological need. In the novel's very first sentence, a reader finds Jimmie standing "upon a heap of gravel for the honor of Rum Alley"; Pete responds to the ruined Maggie "with the anger of a man whose respectability is being threatened"; "Jimmie publicly damned his sister that he might appear on a higher social plane," and Mrs. Johnson also employs the double standard to improve her position with the law: "She used the story of her daughter's downfall with telling effect." She does much the same thing with her neighbors, in this way gaining status, that "moral standin' " to which the "gnarled old woman" refers (7, 66, 56, 56, 64).[10]

The double standard is thus impressed into the service of establishing a pecking order that exists to give individuals that "honor" and "respectability" required by their psychological need for esteem in society. In the Bowery its usage takes distinctive forms, becoming a part of the pattern of its violence and leading to Maggie's death. But the Bowery is unique only in the distinct forms that the pecking order there assumes. It differs from the rest of society in terms of the violence, drunkenness, and poverty that characterize its world, not in terms of the dynamics animating it and uniting it to the larger social world. Hence the minister who "saved his respectability" by sidestepping Maggie as she approached him for help is engaged in pecking quite as much as Jimmie is. His "silk hat and . . . chaste black coat" distinguish him from Jimmie, but this "picture of benevolence and kind-heartedness" (67) otherwise looks remarkably like the Jimmie who earlier rejected his sister while "radiant virtue sat upon his brow and his repelling hands expressed horror of contamination" (64). Both use sexual mores in the service of their self-image and in this way preserve or improve their position in the pecking order.

The central element of this story's pecking order, therefore, is a moral attitude divorced from that religion of forgiveness which generated it and translated into a social world animated by Darwinian principles.[11] In society, it is called the double standard. The fact that it commands allegiance from all strata of society is of some importance because it enlarges the scope of that environment which is really the central character in *Maggie*. Since the double standard knows no class boundaries, *Maggie* is a story both of the Bowery and of Christian America. In *Maggie*, the larger culture, symbolized by the double standard, mixes with the specific conditions of Bowery life to determine the way in which individuals fulfill their primary psychological need: self-esteem. This mixture therefore produces a Bowery type and yields a tension in the novel between the character as individual and as social man. Maggie relates to individuals whom she conceives in personal terms as a brother, a mother, and a lover. But they are something more than these things. They also represent Maggie's environment. In general, they represent the Bowery; but ultimately, in their allegiance to the double standard, they also represent the social classes considered superior to the Bowery.

Maggie stands in relation to society as the men in the open boat stand in relation to the sea. Society and its inhabitants are every bit as threatening to her as the sea and the shark are to those men—and about as responsible, as moral agents. For as types, the characters comprising her environment are not agents acting in society but creations of it, both products and purveyors of the values of the larger society. Through the use of such types the novel conveys its determinism, Jimmie being the central vehicle here, and it is with the forces that molded Jimmie that the first four chapters of the story deal.

Just how important those chapters are can immediately be seen if one begins by considering the way in which Jimmie's moral sense is affected by his need for esteem, his need for a sense of psychological importance. After Jimmie first learns that Pete has ruined Maggie, he enters the rooms he calls home.

> Jimmie walked to the window and began to look through the blurred glass. It occurred to him to vaguely wonder, for an instant, if some of the women of his acquaintance had brothers. Suddenly, however, he began to swear.

"But he was me frien'! I brought ' im here! Dat's d' hell of
it!" (43)

Thereafter he announces Maggie's ruination to his mother, who
reacts as though she had been disgraced by her daughter. He
distinguishes between the fallen Sadie and Maggie ("Sadie was
nice an' all dat—but—see—it ain't dessame as if—well, Maggie
was diff'ent"), and these words follow: "He was trying to formulate a theory that he had always unconsciously held, that all
sisters, excepting his own, could advisedly be ruined"(44).

All of these passages are important.[12] Were Jimmie to have an
authentic sense of obligation, it would be to Maggie, not to
himself; yet it seems clear that the stain on Maggie here touches
himself alone. He feels betrayed by a friend (he has betrayed no
friends). His distinguishing between Maggie and Sadie makes
Maggie different because *he* is her brother; he is concerned not
because she has been hurt but because he has. He tries to formulate
a theory to protect his own reputation, and in the next chapter he
fights Pete to avenge not Maggie's honor but his own. Thus Crane
shows that he has not progressed beyond the opening lines of the
novel, where the little boy Jimmie fought "for the honor of Rum
Alley" (7).

This interpretation of Jimmie's perception of ethics and moral-
ity is confirmed in another introspective moment. After Mrs.
Johnson wails that Maggie "ill-treated her own mudder" (56),
Crane takes pains to stress Jimmie's equally solipsistic response:

> Jimmie thought he had a great idea of women's frailty,
> but he could not understand why any of his kin should be
> victims.
> "Damn her," he fervidly said.
> Again he wondered vaguely if some of the women of his
> acquaintance had brothers. Nevertheless, his mind did not
> for an instant confuse himself with those brothers nor his
> sister with theirs. (56)

Jimmie wonders whether the women he has seduced have
brothers, and one might argue that he is, however vaguely, concerned for these women. But in the context of the passage, it is as

plausible to argue that he wonders "vaguely" whether he has harmed their *brothers* through these seductions. At any rate, the concluding line of the passage is crucial. His sense of honor is a function of an egotism that renders him incapable of operating within a moral framework involving forgiveness. One can, of course, judge egotism morally, but Crane's portrayal of Jimmie thwarts the attempt to do so. (More about that in a moment, for it is a central issue.) One more moral moment of insight remains, and it comes closer to one's usual sense of that phrase: "Of course Jimmie publicly damned his sister that he might appear on a higher social plane. But, arguing with himself, stumbling about in ways that he knew not, he, once, almost came to a conclusion that his sister would have been more firmly good had she better known why. However, he felt that he could not hold such a view. He threw it hastily aside" (56).

Jimmie comes close to a humane attitude toward his sister, but his need for honor prohibits his acceptance of it. Such a humane attitude, the adoption of which constitutes his moral duty here, would recognize extenuating circumstances—Maggie's loveless family environment, of which Jimmie is a part—and lighten blame, paving the way for forgiveness. But Jimmie's failure to adopt such an attitude itself has extenuating circumstances, and a reader's temptation to charge him with hypocrisy and consequent moral turpitude is undercut by a knowledge of the world that made him the egotist he is.

The opening lines of the story display Jimmie translating his natural need for esteem into a violent assertion of "position" that will bring "honor" to Rum Alley. Thereafter Crane shows that the particular form taken by Jimmie's quest for esteem is determined by his family background. As a child subjected by his parents to the same treatment his mother applies periodically to her furniture, he inevitably becomes the "young man of leather" described in the opening of chapter 4, after three chapters of family background explaining why "the inexperienced fibres of the boy's eyes were hardened at an early age" (20).

Specifically, Jimmie becomes a man of leather in the sense that his family background has deprived him of the opportunity to develop any ideals. Certainly his mother's behavior is not a sound beginning for an idealized view of women, nor is his father's for a healthy view of family. But the absence of ideals leads not only to Jimmie's contempt for women and family; it leads to a profound contempt for the world generally. "He never conceived a respect for the world, because he had begun with no idols that it had smashed"(20). Deprived of something outside the self to worship, forced to wrest from the world the esteem his psyche demands, Jimmie inevitably becomes asocial man and a supreme egotist. He becomes self-centered to the point where the world exists only as a function of his own ego, so that "he and his order were kings" (21) and his "down-trodden position" had "a private but distinct element of grandeur" (22).

There is irony here, of course, and it appears because the reader recognizes the disparity between Jimmie's view of himself and his actual position.[13] But the ironic thrust, within the context of the first four chapters, also conveys the truth of psychological necessity, a fact that undermines any temptation to judge this young man morally. Indeed, one can argue that the ironic mode is perfect for the expression of Crane's Hobbesian vision, for together they tempt and then prevent. The ironic disparity between the character's view of self and reality and the reader's fuller view tempts to moral judgment, but a host of other factors inhibit its expression. Indeed, the novel's greatest irony makes the whole structure serve this end. It is ironic that the price of psychological survival should be Maggie's death, and this fact unites the parts of an apparently disunited novel into a single Hobbesian outlook.[14] *Maggie* contains many chapters in which its central character does not appear; yet those in which she figures and those in which she does not compose a single whole. Chapters 1 through 4 lay the groundwork for Jimmie's response to his sister in chapters 10, 11, and 13. When Maggie appeals to her brother for help as her mother forces her out of the house (she uses a single word, "Jimmie"), he responds with social man's "horror of contamination" (64). There seems to be a moral axis here, but it is undercut by the first four chapters. Crane tempts, but he prevents.

For understandable reasons in this compact novel, Pete's background is not given the same detailed treatment as Jimmie's, but Crane provides clues to indicate that he is as much a product of society as Jimmie. He is associated with Jimmie's fighting in the novel's opening. Older than Jimmie, he has a "chronic sneer"(9), the same as that "sneer" in Jimmie which "became chronic" as Jimmie developed (20). This clue, and their shared attitudes toward women, suggest that they are products of the same forces, and require the reader to view Pete in the same way he does Jimmie. As for Mrs. Johnson, the only other major figure in the novel besides Jimmie and Maggie, a reader can assume she is a product of her environment even though her background is not described. An author need not multiply case histories to make a point. If her son is a product, she must be too. Certainly she shares his need for self-esteem and fulfills it in the ironic way he does—at the expense of Maggie.

And what of this girl who "blossomed in a mud puddle"? Though "none of the dirt of Rum Alley seemed to be in her veins" (24), appearances can be deceiving, for she is a victim of her environment not only as a scapegoat for the ego of others but in much the same way as the others are. She too needs self-esteem, and with her blossoming into maturity that need takes a sexual form. And Pete offers, besides the love to bolster self-esteem, the fulfillment of a need that will sustain it—namely, order, a need all the stronger in Maggie because it is initially induced by her environment. Pete brings that point home to the reader when he tells the story of his boss's commendation for subduing an unruly patron of the bar at which he works: "Pete, yehs done jes' right! Yeh've gota keep order an' it's all right." As Maggie listens, "The broken furniture, grimy walls, and general disorder and dirt of her home of a sudden appeared before her and began to take a potential aspect." She fears the aristocratic Pete "might soil" (26) and that he might reject her, anxieties that reflect a fear of losing someone who offers an escape from disorder. Little wonder that she idolizes Pete. Love always distorts vision, but add to that effect the wish fulfillment, fantasies, and blindness born of an intolerable environment, and one understands Maggie quite as much as one understands her victimizers, whose roots are in the same mud puddle.

In one other way Crane calls the Hobbesian paradox to the reader's attention, for the form of the novel is a genre providing a literary content perfect for raising the issue of freedom and determinism. Eric Solomon shows that *Maggie* is a parody of the conventions of melodrama.[15] One need not rely on his specific arguments to see that the very concept of this kind of parody gives *Maggie* a special philosophic richness. The fact that Crane's characters are treated, not in depth, but as stereotypes—a drunken mother, a hypocritical brother, a virtuous girl, a scheming cad— recalls the form of melodrama. And, despite the irony of it all, the fact that the mother, the brother, and finally the community join in censuring Maggie's sin recalls the strong moral axis of melodrama and the expected audience response, the repudiation of evil. But if the form is melodramatic, its content is not. It does not portray men as "unmistakably bad" the way the melodramas within the story do. Its moral axis is blurred by the stress on extenuating circumstances alleviating guilt. This tension between the associations the reader makes with the form and the actual content of *Maggie* gives it its power and contributes to its Hobbesian vision.

Because that tension breaks in the direction of determinism, in *Maggie* Crane implies that the existence of that freedom, without which moral judgments cannot be applied, is a fiction because it does not in fact exist in reality. But Crane does not simply leave the matter there. He develops this view further. After *Maggie*, he employs his Hobbesian vision to show that society requires the concept of freedom, fictional though it is, as an analysis of *The Red Badge of Courage* will demonstrate.

The Red Badge of Courage

The Red Badge of Courage dramatizes the meaning of two words, "cowardice" and "courage," by portraying specific actions to which they are supposed to apply. The novel also studies the psychological effects of two emotions on an individual's behavior: fear and guilt. The interplay between the actions inspired by these emotions and the value judgments that society places on those actions gives energy to the novel. Its sharply limited focus on a single individual's feelings, thoughts, and perceptions makes it Crane's masterpiece of psychological realism, an achievement

that is a logical development from *Maggie.* The earlier work treats
the interplay between the psychological need for esteem and the
social conditions through which that need is fulfilled. Those
conditions are primary, the analysis of psychological need secondary, limited to a few staccato references to the need to maintain a
respectable pose and presented, in the person of Jimmie, with
only the barest suggestions of psychic struggle. *The Red Badge of
Courage* reverses this emphasis, playing down social conditions as
causal factors of action and stressing the psychic conflict to which
such conditions can give rise.

The immediate source of this conflict which dominates the
central part of the action is the clash between man's fear of
extinction and his psychological capacity for experiencing guilt.
The one, his animal instinct for survival, binds him to nature;[16]
the other, his capacity to internalize social codes and hence to
experience guilt, defines his distinctiveness in nature. This psychological faculty, of course, does not separate him from nature
either in *The Red Badge of Courage* or elsewhere in Crane's work.
Rather, if in "The Open Boat" Crane could see that moral systems
and cooperativeness arise from the instinct to survive, in *The Red
Badge* he could see that under certain conditions biological instinct
can threaten such systems. A major point of the story is that guilt
is the mechanism on which society relies to sustain itself. Hence,
when Henry discovers at the conclusion of chapter 6 that his
regiment had indeed not run, he experiences at the beginning of
the seventh chapter the next emotion (fear was the first) determining his actions and thoughts: "The youth cringed as if discovered
at a crime" (45). *

In this novel the condition inspiring the physical fear that
determines behavior is clear enough; but Crane is also specific, if
less obvious, in pinpointing the origins of that guilt which is the
other important determinant in his young soldier's life. Henry
Fleming's thoughts about his departure for war early in the novel
are central. They constitute a flashback occurring after Henry's
earlier dreams of glory have been deflated so that he regards

*Stephen Crane, *The Red Badge of Courage,* edited by Fredson Bowers with an
introduction by J. C. Levenson. Va. (1975) 2. See bibliographical essay for choice of
edition.

himself as but a member of the "blue demonstration" (8). In the
flashback the reader discovers that Henry's initial, obsessive fear
of running—a fear born in part of Henry's ethical sense that he
will succumb to physical fear—and his later guilt have their source
in moral strictures passed on to him by his mother in her role as
conduit for society's values. No doubt Henry also initially fears
running because that act would extinguish any flickering hopes he
still has of becoming a hero; but to become a hero requires
honoring the ethical restraint against running under fire, and the
very intensity of Henry's guilt after running shows how much he
shares social ethical standards, which thus are a ground of his
initial fear as well. The transmission of such standards is the center
of the flashback, focused in the mother's words, "Don't think of
anything 'cept what's right" (7), and this moral focus is reinforced
by Crane's reference to her "ethical motive" (6). The complex of
attitudes that shape Henry's environment become instrumental
factors determining his subsequent behavior, and the flashback is
a central element of the novel's deterministic vision because it is
the final ground, the ultimate condition for one of two chains of
causation stressed in the novel. Just as Henry's running is reducible to his panic, then to the perception that others are running
under attack, then to his own self-doubts earlier within the story,
so too his subsequent guilt is reducible to his knowledge that the
regiment held fast and that he ran, then to his knowledge of "the
right," then to his mother's words, "Don't think of anything 'cept
what's right."

Every novel, of course, contains conditions explaining the
motives prompting characters' actions and affecting their
thoughts, yet that fact need not make them deterministic. Nor
does this novel's flashback initially seem so. But the reader who
finishes this novel knows that Crane uses his narrator's detach-
ment to study Henry's feelings, thoughts, perceptions, and actions as though he were a product of the biological and social
world rather than a self-governing agent. Crane, in other words,
emphasizes the *supremacy* of condition. Since a considerable portion of the narrative *before* Henry flees from battle is devoted to
Henry's fear that he will do so, the reader naturally asks for the
source of that ethical sense which badgers the youth for five

chapters by telling him in effect that it is wrong to desert battle. And the reader finds the cause in the flashback, where Crane provides the condition for the youth's initial conflict, just as he provides the full conditions of all other relevant aspects of Henry's career in these pages. Henry's moral sense thus becomes part of the causal world of these pages. Like other effects that become causes of subsequent effects, Henry's moral sense is both effect (of training) and cause (of early fear and subsequent guilt). The flashback thus contributes to the novel's naturalism by placing even morality within a behavioral rather than an ethical framework.

This flashback is also important in two other ways worth mentioning. Through its references to idealized newspaper accounts of battle, village gossip, and related details, Crane stresses the conditions for Henry's enlistment quite as much as he does those for Henry's running from battle. Since conditions compel or inhibit action in battle, the reflective reader is forced to ask whether battlefield conditions do not bring out in bold relief the actual position of man in ordinary life, though his true situation is concealed by the placidity of ordinary existence. Just by raising the question, the flashback points to the novel's tripartite structure, a movement toward and away from a center of indisputable determinism in the major section of the novel. And the fact that conditions in all parts of the novel are part of a related network of causation suggests that this structure is really a movement from soft determinism (conditions dictate action, though not obviously so) into hard determinism (conditions obviously dictate action), with a return to soft determinism in conclusion.

The other importance of the flashback lies in its emphasis on stories of bravery and heroism presupposing a grandeur in battle that is at odds with Henry Fleming's initial army experience as a member of a "blue demonstration." The flashback thus stresses the illusionary nature of public views of war and hence sets the stage for a major thrust of the novel's argument: the illusionary nature of the concepts embodied in words like "courage" and "cowardice," both of whose meanings presuppose a measure of freedom that in fact man, whose actions are dictated by conditions, does not possess in the lived moment of action. But though the assumption on which the words rest does not withstand the test of rational analysis, the novel does not reject their usefulness. To the contrary, they are viewed as fostering necessary illusions. Without them, Henry Fleming could never achieve "manhood."

The first six chapters of the novel display a movement to hard determinism, with fear the dominant emotion affecting thought. Sometimes fear distorts fact, as when Henry feels "he had never wished to come to the war"; nor had he "enlisted of his free will" (from a conventional point of view, he had). At other times fear expresses itself through fact, as when Henry sees that "there were iron laws of tradition and law on four sides" of his "moving box" (23), and that these laws threaten those who desert the box. Always, fear makes its presence known by manipulating the content of his thought. But despite his fear, Henry fights successfully in his first skirmish because prevailing conditions permit him to control his biological fear so that he does not act on it to escape: "If he had thought the regiment about to be annihilated perhaps he could have amputated himself from it. But its noise gave him assurance" (34–35). At this point to escape the group would threaten his security more than to remain with it. But conditions favoring desirable military behavior do not prevail in the next skirmish. The youth who sees one man run and another "smitten abject" (41) loses all sense of "the subtle battle-brotherhood" sustaining him earlier and himself runs, his fear turned to panic by a loss of that feeling of group solidarity that earlier made him "not a man but a member" (34). But just as it is impossible to admire Henry's earlier fighting as courageous, it is impossible to condemn his fleeing as cowardly, for he is only an unfortunate creature of circumstance. If narrator and reader know that Henry exaggerates the ability of those "redoubtable dragons" (41), the enemy, the exaggeration is no less real to the youth exaggerating. One cannot judge Henry's flight morally, in short, because the detailed circumstances surrounding his act indicate that he is compelled to run. He has no control over the conditions that induce his ungovernable panic.

While neither reader nor narrator can condemn Henry for running, society certainly would. Society is not concerned with the conditions prompting the act but with the act's implications; with its threat to the army as an implementer of social goals. As a product of society, Henry thus experiences guilt when he discovers that his unit in fact has held fast, a feeling that the reader understands is normal enough, even if in philosophical terms it possesses no moral legitimacy. And he further understands that, philosophical inconsistency notwithstanding, society is correct in branding his action in moral terms as criminal. Unless it did it could not depend upon man's sense of guilt to uphold moral systems, and such systems thus could not be effective deterrents to undesirable social behavior. Whereas first Henry was determined by an ethical fear of biological fear, then by biological fear alone, now he will be determined by culture and conscience: by a psyche experiencing guilt for violating a cultural demand.

Henry's experiencing guilt fulfills one condition for his social redemption, but such redemption cannot take place immediately. His guilty feeling is so intense that it drives him to rationalize the act producing it in order to deny the social legitimacy of his conscience's message: his behavior has been "cowardly." Hence he adopts the familiar arguments in self-defense presented in chapter 7, all of which fail as it becomes clear even to him that an anonymous dead soldier does not support the "evidence" provided by a squirrel, nor does the later sight of Jim Conklin's death. Nature is not really "a woman with a deep aversion to tragedy" (46). But if nature now seems indifferent, Henry is reminded that society is not, and so guilt impels him to "sin" rather than to return to society when the tattered man's innocent questions strike the raw nerve left exposed by the failure of Henry's rationalizations: "The simple questions of the tattered man had been knife-thrusts to him. They asserted a society that probes pitilessly at secrets until all is apparent" (62). His rationalizing having failed by chapter 11, Henry abandons it and wishes instead for circumstances—his own army's defeat or his own death—to deliver him from conscience.

Because of his dread of exposure, itself intensified by guilt, Henry's must be a private wrestling with guilt until chance intervenes to free him from his paralysis and permit his return to his regiment, there to expiate his sin in military fashion. Chance accommodates in Crane's usual ironic form, a panic-stricken soldier fleeing from battle giving Henry his needed red badge (chapter 12). He can now return and say, "I got shot, too!" (chapter 13: 76). He notes the change in Wilson, the formerly loud but now battle-chastened soldier (chapter 14), but he does not get the message of that change. He is preoccupied with his relief at escaping disgrace, at returning with the semblance of honor, and the packet of letters from Wilson acts as further protection from exposure from that quarter. Soon he feels, indeed, "immensely superior" to Wilson, for he "had performed his mistakes in the dark, so he was still a man" (chapter 15:86). If his "generous" (87) return of Wilson's packet without comment fills him with what seems a gallingly unmerited pride, one can nonetheless see the mechanisms of his responses. Released from the bonds of the superego, the ego expresses its great relief through adopting illusions of the self at variance with reality. For that matter, Crane's attention to conditions suggests that even distortions can have their salutary effect.[17] One partially true perception of Henry's past experience emerges in his range of vision: "He had been taught that many obligations of a life were easily avoided. *The lessons of yesterday had been that retribution was a laggard and blind.* With these facts before him he did not deem it necessary that he should become feverish over the possibilities of the ensuing twenty-four hours. He could leave much to chance" (Emphasis added, 86).

The lesson Henry learns is a distorted one, for fickle chance does not always assure that retribution is "a laggard and blind." But it was so for him, and the distorted conclusion at which he arrives has the beneficial effect of releasing him from fear of fear; releasing him, that is, from a fear of succumbing to that biological fear the succumbing to which provokes social censure. And this release gives an unexpected value to his illusions that "he had fled with discretion and dignity" (87) and that because "he had performed his mistakes in the dark . . . he was still a man" (86). Together with his belief that retribution is "a laggard and blind," his false sense of self becomes the condition for nurturing a self-confidence which, from a military point of view, is highly desirable: "A faith in himself had secretly blossomed. There was a little flower of confidence growing within him. He was now a man of experience. He had been out among the dragons, he said, and he assured himself that they were not so hideous as he had imagined them" (86).

With these changes in him, Henry Fleming can now at least engage in battle, as he does from the following chapter (16) through the penultimate one of the novel. Conditions that previously inhibited his engagement in purposeful military activity have been altered to permit him to take military action. His release from the fear of fear and from his false pride are the conditions for a self-confidence that allows Henry to follow his guides without quailing. But though he can now at least fight, his self-confidence alone does not guarantee that he will fight with the enthusiasm demanded of a good soldier.

To be a good soldier, Henry must hate the enemy; and in fact he subsequently fights with a passionate hatred of his foe. But just as the condition for this hatred cannot be found in self-confidence alone (for it need not breed hatred), neither can it be located in his preenlistment days. Henry did not join the army to free the slaves or to preserve the union. He joined for personal glory, and the discovery of its inaccessibility makes him a poor rather than a good risk for the army. As mere part of a "blue demonstration," he does not have the incentive to fight on the ground for which he originally enlisted; nor does he have ideological cause outside the self to substitute for personal glory. Always with an eye to condition, however, Crane supplies the missing link to account for this last ingredient vital to the good soldier. In Henry's case, it is to be found in his experiences between the times of his flight from and reinstatement into his unit. At the beginning of chapter 17, therefore—that is, directly before Henry first fights successfully—Crane endows Henry with hatred by making a vital connection between a past and present hate, once again establishing cause-effect relationships that determine—in this case, determine the making of the good soldier, Henry Fleming:

He had received his fill of all exertions and he wished to rest.

But those other men seemed never to grow weary; they

were fighting with their old speed. He had a wild hate for the relentless foe. *Yesterday, when he had imagined the universe to be against him, he had hated it, little gods and big gods; to-day he hated the army of the foe with the same great hatred.* He was not going to be badgered of his life like a kitten chased by boys, he said. It was not well to drive men into final corners; at those moments, they could all develope teeth and claws. (Emphasis added, 94)

The mechanism of his transference is easy enough to see. Yesterday's universe offered Henry no escape from guilt. That universe would not support his rationalizations. Its failure to do so tortured his conscience to the point where he turns with hate against it in self-defense. Crane several times refers to that hatred in the youth's bout with guilt. After Henry discovers that most of his regiment held fast, he blames his own running on "hateful circumstances"; and "a dull, animal-like rebellion against his fellows, war in the abstract, and fate, grew within him" (46). After he witnesses Jim Conklin's death, he "turned, with sudden, livid rage, toward the battle-field. He shook his fist. He seemed about to deliver a philippic" (58). Conklin risked his life; Henry did not. The universe thus makes him vulnerable to that society represented by "the simple questions of the tattered man," and so he responds in rage. When it destroys a subsequent hope that an entire regiment is retreating, thus emphasizing his own failure, he responds in similar anguished manner: "He searched about in his mind for an adequate malediction for the indefinite cause, the thing upon which men turn the words of final blame. It—whatever it was—was responsible for him, he said. There lay the fault" (64).

The connection between his guilt and his hatred for the foe should now be clear. He had been badgered by guilt and the fear of its exposure, which would visit shame upon him. Now, he is badgered by the enemy. Yesterday, the universe drove him into a corner. Today, the enemy does the same thing. His guilt concealed, his hatred still remains, this time directed toward a socially approved target which, through superior fighting, might still bring shame on him. Hence he fights with hate. And he fights

blindly. He fights long after his comrades have ceased. His fighting is a "dream" in which "he lost sense of everything but his
hate," for he "was not conscious that he was erect upon his feet"
(95). Further, he fights without a sense of cause, a point made
three times in the novel (105, 105, 107). This emphasis upon the
blindness of fighting born not of ideological conviction but of
simple hatred is marked in several places in this part of the novel,
and it is accompanied by another emphasis, upon love—for the
flag—as a complementary impulse guiding the youth in battle.
This love is born during the second skirmish, when he sees the
flag held by the dying flag bearer: "Within him, as he hurled
himself forward, was born a love, a despairing fondness for this
flag which was near him. It was a creation of beauty and invul-
nerability. It was a goddess, radiant, that bended its form with an
imperious gesture to him. It was a woman, red and white, hating
and loving, that called him with the voice of his hopes. Because no
harm could come to it, he endowed it with power" (108).

Henry Fleming becomes a creature of the state. His primary
emotions, love and hate, have been polarized for society's purposes: love (for our flag), hatred (for theirs). Later he displays
great zeal in capturing the enemy's flag, together with four of the
enemy soldiers. "Shame was upon" one of the captured youth,
"and with it profound regret that he was perhaps no more to be
counted in the ranks of his fellows" (131). As love and hate are
polarized, so too are pride and shame: pride when "our" flag
prevails, shame when "theirs" does. These emotions comprise the
"courageous man," Henry Fleming.

The man whose affective life is determined by and serves only
the interests of the state is, of course, a robot, a product of
cultural-psychological determinism; society's man, not his own.
The word *man* thus is deprived of its vital meaning; an individual
capable of courageous action. In this novel, a word like *courage*
cannot be associated with autonomous action, and hence it loses
its moral connotations in the same way that "cowardice" does. As
creatures of society, furthermore, it is not surprising that these
men vacillate in their feelings of self-esteem, for the social view of
their performance is frequently at odds with their own personal

sense of achievement. In their judgment, they fight successfully in one skirmish—so well, in fact, that they feel they can gaze "about them with looks of uplifted pride" (115). "And they were men," the chapter (20) concludes. But in the next, their efforts are criticized, and the former pride of "men" becomes shame as "they bore upon their bended shoulders the coffin of their honor" (117).

In this late skirmish Henry learns what he has had ample opportunity to observe throughout the novel—that his own perceptions are frequently at variance with reality. Resent though he does the criticism of his efforts, that resentment is tempered by the "bitter justice" (117) that his own perceptions reveal after the skirmish. They had not fought so long nor covered so great a territory as they had thought. Because the public perception was correct and his own wrong, pride becomes shame. But Henry must also learn that the public view is not endowed with a privileged omniscience;[18] it is not an infallible source of a realistic view of life, nor are his own private views always wholly without merit. From the beginning of the novel he gives the public view a special authority, and so long as Henry Fleming lives solely in the public eye, he must remain the robot of society to which a chain of conditions has reduced him.

Reductive circumstance, however, is not without its possibilities. Even those conditions which create the robot contain the seeds permitting that robot to grow into its opposite, the true man—or at least the illusion of one. The same skirmish that earns for Fleming the lieutenant's praise as "wild-cat" draws the general's comment that the unit performed like "mule-drivers" (97, 101). Although this perception does not draw the lesson of the fickleness of the public view, it does lead to an equally important lesson: "And the most startling thing was to learn suddenly that he was very insignificant" (101). The general's comment represents the crucial condition beginning Henry Fleming's education into "authentic" manhood. And it is at this point that the novel begins its return to the world of soft determinism appearing in the flashback, but now seen from a different perspective.

First, the concluding chapters trace the conditions that allow Henry to free himself from the boy's romantic illusions about war, created in the world of the flashback, and also from the fear and guilt whose seeds lie in that world. But far from bringing Henry into a world of freedom where he will operate as a free agent, the last chapter shows him developing new illusions. In this case, however, they are illusions that the battlefield itself revealed are necessary fictions: the fiction that man is free and therefore morally responsible for his actions; and the fiction that the world was made for man. Though the army does not require the illusion of heroism, from which Henry divorces himself, it does need the fictions of cowardly and courageous actions. But Henry needs these too, for his own self-respect. Hence the necessity of the illusion on which those illusions depend: man is free. Henry embraces the army's fiction and asserts his own freedom when he "knows" in conclusion that he can follow his guides wherever they lead without quailing. And this belief in his freedom allows the development of another illusion, one that all individuals need because they have all been through the ugliness of battles, though not necessarily military ones: the illusion that the world is made for man. But even the development of these illusions has its conditions, and these are the focus of the third part of the novel.

To repeat, the general's comment is the crucial condition beginning Henry's education into manhood. Chapter 12 represents the turning point of Henry Fleming's isolation, for there he receives the wound permitting his reinstatement with his regiment. In chapter 13 he is greeted by a "loud" soldier (75) changed from an audacious and inexperienced "child" of "tinsel courage" (14:82) into a chastened and humble man. Crane then shows Henry has not yet changed—he still would like to have reason to be the braggart the loud soldier once was (15:87-88)—and at the same time establishes for the reader the terms that Henry will meet to become a man in the third part of the novel.[19]

Conditions are not ripe for him to do so, but when the general calls Henry's unit a pack of "mule-drivers" and Henry realizes his insignificance (101), one learns that the time is nearing. To effect his change into manhood, after all, Henry must be in a position to renounce the pronounced value that he places on public commendation by recognizing that the public valuation of effort can never embrace the full facts behind even a limited achievement in battle. He comes to this recognition when a colonel sustains the general's

view of his unit as "mule-drivers" by reproaching their performance, and it buds into his "tranquil philosophy":

> The youth developed a tranquil philosophy for these
> moments of irritation. "Oh, well," he rejoined, "he proba-
> bly didn't see nothing of it at all and got mad as blazes and
> concluded we were a lot of sheep, just because we didn't do
> what he wanted done. It's a pity old Grandpa Henderson got
> killed yesterday—he would have known that we did our
> best and fought good. It's just our awful luck, that's what"
> (119).

This tranquil philosophy is an important development. It permits Henry to see that generals and colonels judge him and his
fellows from the perspective of larger goals, not from the perspective of those who endure the heat of battle. As such it shows him,
by virtue of the tranquility of the philosophy, on the road toward
acceptance of his own insignificance and modification of the
importance of public approval. But if, because the time is ripe for
him to do so, he has learned certain lessons—his insignificance,
the inbuilt distortions of the public eye—he is still too caught up in
battlefield conditions to put them together into a mature view of
life. He must be able to accept both his insignificance and the
public distortions of his (and his fellows') efforts and (this is
important) still maintain a sense of personal worth. Without time
to reflect on what he has learned, without time to coalesce his
lessons into this vision of manhood, he still lives in the public eye
and values its judgments because they permit him to escape his
knowledge of his personal insignificance. The very chapter (21)
that shows his emerging "tranquil philosophy" ends by showing
his forgetting the lessons leading to its creation, as he and a fellow
soldier respond excessively to public praise for holding their flag
aloft in battle. The time for true learning, for learning the larger
lesson of his insignificance and of the distortions inherent in
public vision, arrives later, with surcease from battle and consequent escape "from scenes where many of his usual machines of
reflection had been idle" (133).

This escape takes place in the last chapter, and the escape is the
"new condition" that permits him "to look upon" his past acts "in

spectator fashion and to criticize them with some correctness" (133). The words are ambiguous, because they can mean that, as spectator, Henry views himself from the public's angle of vision—the public is a spectator of Henry's acts both in reality and in his imagination; or they can mean that, as spectator, Henry views himself from the narrator's angle of vision—the narrator is, after all, a spectator of Henry from beginning to end. In fact, both senses of the word *spectator* apply to Henry as he views himself in the novel's conclusion, although they do not apply simultaneously; for he moves from one spectator's position to another.

He begins his reflections by reviewing his acts solely from the perspective of the public eye, taking great joy in past deeds, performed publicly, that earned commendation and suffering great remorse for running from battle, and even greater anguish for his "sin," his abandonment of the tattered man. These last deeds were not witnessed, but Henry judges them as though they had been; and in adopting a public perspective on them, he is as merciless in his judgment as the public eye would be—perhaps more so. But when he musters "force to put the sin at a distance," he immediately thereafter gains a new perspective ("his eyes seemed to open to some new ways"); and despite the qualification implied by the verb "seemed," this is clearly a new perspective, for it permits him to renounce "the brass and bombast of his earlier gospels and see them truly" (135). He has, in other words, developed a perspective different from that of the public eye; and Henry thereafter achieves the narrator's spectator-view of Henry. In renouncing his "earlier gospels" and seeing "them truly," Henry renounces the distortions of the public eye from which those gospels proceed and that the narrator has exposed to the reader from the novel's very beginning.

Interestingly enough, Henry's putting his sin at a distance immediately precedes his emancipation from a need for public glory: "Yet gradually he mustered force to put the sin at a distance. And at last his eyes seemed to open to some new ways. He found that he could look back upon the brass and bombast of his earlier gospels and see them truly. He was gleeful when he discovered that he now despised them" (135). By emphasizing an order of succession in the mental events taking place in Henry's

mind—first Henry's putting his sin at a distance, then his renun-
ciation of his "earlier gospels"—Crane shows that Henry's emancipation from the need for the favor of the public eye has a
condition. And by stressing one particular condition for Henry's
emancipation, Crane imparts to his cause-effect relationship the
sharp logic of a keen psychological sense. Without a private
conviction of inner worth, Henry must forever depend on public
approval for a sense of personal worth. His distancing himself
from his sin shows he has achieved a private sense of inner worth
despite his knowledge of the scorn that a public view of his sin
invites, and despite the fact that he shares this view of his sin so
much that he experiences intense shame for its commission. And
this sense of inner worth, which emancipates him from the harsh
stare in the public eye by removing him to some distance from
that eye, is the condition for his fuller emancipation from his
desire for the public eye's admiring looks, which commend him as
a "hero" and "knight." His sense of inner worth now can sustain a
private feeling of manhood not dependent on public commendation.

But what permits Henry to muster the force to put his sin at a
distance? Or since the answer to this question is clear—he has
achieved a sense of inner worth—it is more precise to ask for the
origin of this sense. In this novel emphasizing causality, it can only
come from the conditions yielding his tranquil philosophy. The
lessons in which it temporarily issued taught him that the public,
represented by the harsh view of a colonel, doesn't "see nothing of
it at all" but gets "mad as blazes" if someone doesn't do what it
"wanted done." These lessons also taught him that if the public
could witness actions from the point of view of the performing
actor, it would know "that we did our best and fought good."
And because at the novel's end Henry finds the tranquillity that is
the "new condition" permitting him to be a "spectator" of himself
from the narrator's point of view, he can perceive that he did his
best, too, inadequate though some of his actions might be to the
public eye. Henry sees more of the conditions surrounding his
sin's commission than the public can, and therefore he can forgive
himself, at least to the extent of putting his sin at a distance. By
virtue of this fact, he can accept the implications of self-
forgiveness, the existence of a self worth forgiving.

In rejecting the bombast of his earlier ways, Henry Fleming absorbs an earlier lesson behind his tranquil philosophy, the awareness of his insignificance. For his rejection of such bombast means he accepts his insignificance, despite the social admiration some of his deeds command. And in putting his sin at a distance, he accepts his inner worth despite the social scorn that other deeds can draw. Finally, in feeling "a *quiet* man-hood, *non-assertive* but of sturdy and strong blood" (135, emphasis added), he undergoes the same transformation that the initially "loud" soldier experienced after battle. At last, Henry "was a man."

By endowing Henry's "spectator" view of himself with "some" of the "correctness" of the narrator's view, Crane shows that Henry achieves the novel's norm for manhood. And by noting that Henry's eyes only "*seemed* to open to new ways" (emphasis added), Crane sustains his Hobbesian vision to the end.[20] Although at the moment Henry indisputably puts his sin at a distance and renounces his adolescent gospels, Crane's world does not permit the certainty that Henry's eyes will remain permanently open to these new ways, just as it denies the certainty that Henry will not run again. In Crane's world, conditions dictate the outcome of the future, just as they create the realities of the present moment.

But Henry Fleming at least has been restored to a belief in the existence of that freedom whose existence battlefield conditions earlier compelled him to deny. That freedom is an illusion, though a necessary one, as Henry's career testifies. In the novel's conclusion (135), his ignorance of the illusory nature of his belief bears many blessings. Only a belief in his freedom could give him the "assurance" that "he would no more quail before his guides wherever they should point." And such assurance permits Henry to confirm in a positive way that sense of personal worth implied by his putting his sin at a distance. It permits him to arrive at a position that gives a sense of personal worth to men who learn their personal insignificance in the distorted vision of society. This position is the illusion that they have the freedom to work purposefully, albeit modestly, in their station in life. And this felt belief permits the creation of another necessary illusion, one whose "truth" Henry Fleming can embrace all the more because of his release from the condition of "an animal blistered and sweating in the heat and pain of war." Such release breeds the feeling of the lover thirsting for "images of tranquil skies, fresh meadows, cool brooks; an existence of soft and eternal peace." Of course these images constitute the illusion of the lover;[21] for though the sun seems to indicate that this illusion is a realistic view of the world by shining through the leaden rain clouds, the truth is that nature is indifferent. But in such a world man needs the illusion "that the world was a world for him" despite its "oaths and walking-sticks." Without the illusion of the lover Henry Fleming, who is an everyman, cannot psychologically survive the battles of life, just as without the illusions of "courage," "coward-ice," and "freedom," he could not become a "man."

Though this story's happy ending seems to imply that the sun will prevail over the rain in Crane's world generally, that is not the case. Two years later, he wrote "The Blue Hotel."

THREE

Norris and Hard Determinism: *McTeague*

In *McTeague*, Norris raises the question of freedom of the will explicitly. Of McTeague's struggle with his animal or sexual self he asks, "Was he to blame?" (27)* Of Trina's attraction to McTeague, he spells out the question for even the most obtuse reader to comprehend: "Did she choose him . . . of her own free will?" (77). These questions raise a major issue for the reader, and though they here refer to sexual attraction, it is clear that they are meant to apply to cultural matters as well. For Norris stresses the influence of specific cultural backgrounds on his two central characters. When Norris observes McTeague's response to Trina's presumably good fortune, her winning five thousand dollars ("He . . . was trying to realize what its effect would be upon his life . . . and Trina's" [111-12]), he thus links a cultural issue to a sexual one: the effect of money on the lives of a married couple, each partner having a specific cultural background. Hence, in answering the question "Are they to blame?" one must take into account cultural and sexual influences together.

Just as the answer to this question is not limited to Trina's and McTeague's sexual life, so too it is not limited to their behavior alone.

*Quotations from *McTeague* are from *The Complete Edition of Frank Norris* (Garden City, N. Y.: Doubleday, Doran & Co., 1928), vol. 8. Page references in the text also apply to the reissue of *McTeague* in *Complete Works of Frank Norris*, vol. 8 (Port Washington, N. Y.: Kennikat Press, 1967).

This is a story of ethnics who are portrayed as the popular archetypes of the groups they are supposed to represent. In this way Norris stresses the influence of culture on the behavior of the characters in the subplots. Because of the many parallels in action and behavior between the central characters and those in the subplots, the question applying to Trina and McTeague necessarily embraces all these figures. Therefore it becomes, Is anyone to blame? And the answer to this question is offered more explicitly than it is in the work of Crane: No. No one is to blame. Of Trina and McTeague, Norris writes, "Chance had brought them face to face, and mysterious instincts as ungovernable as the winds of heaven were at work knitting their lives together" (78). Of course the instincts referred to here are sexual, not cultural, but in *McTeague* the two are inseparable and make its determinism all-pervasive. For that reason *McTeague* embodies hard determinism, not the soft determinism of Crane, and the novel emphasizes sexual and cultural determinism as the central conditions inspiring the motives on which its characters act.

This hard determinism represents the view underlying another variety of the naturalistic novel, a view that inevitably questions the applicability of traditional moral concepts to character. Norris frequently alludes to these concepts in the early part of his novel. Surely he relies upon the reader's knowledge of the fall of man when he writes of McTeague: "A woman had entered his small world and instantly there was discord. The disturbing element had appeared. Wherever the woman had put her foot a score of distressing complications had sprung up, like the sudden growth of strange and puzzling flowers" (46). Trina becomes "the woman," the primal force who destroys the Adamic McTeague,[1] and the coming together of these two is questioned in marked religious terms: "Was it a blessing? Was it a curse? It was all one; she was his, indissolubly, for evil or for good" (78). The most important religious reference, to original sin, appears in the famous passage following a description of McTeague's kissing the unconscious Trina: "Below the fine fabric of all that was good in him ran the foul stream of hereditary evil, like a sewer. The vices and sins of his father and of his father's father, to the third and fourth and five hundredth generation, tainted him. The evil of an entire race flowed in his veins. Why should it be? He did not desire it. Was he to blame?" (27).

Norris seemingly grants status to these concepts, all of which imply man's freedom, responsibility, and guilt; but he questions them, and the novel's determinism repudiates their adequacy for evaluating the world of *McTeague*.

What is described here, of course, is not the larger philosophical vision of Norris's later work, which embraces both a cosmic determinism and freedom of the will,[2] but rather the vision of *McTeague*. Norris here has written a rigorously deterministic work whose structure shows the challenge to the artist of conveying a deterministic point of view without wearying the reader with repeated authorial intrusions to explain the governing forces behind the novel's multiple events. That same structure shows that he rose to the challenge.

The novel's first line of conflict derives from the major characters' struggle to observe social taboos (their moral standards) in the face of sexual temptation. The conflict in McTeague is described at some length in the early scene depicting Trina in the dentist's chair (chapter 2). Trina's similar conflict emerges in the description of the lovers sitting in an equally unromantic spot, the roadbed of a railroad track, where they pause after their picnic in Scheutzen Park. McTeague succumbs to his temptation by kissing the unconscious Trina "grossly, full on the mouth" (27); and, despite some initial resistance, Trina essentially succumbs to McTeague's later kiss near the track because it awakens "the Woman, and, whether she would or no, she was his now irrevocably" (77-78). Sexual determinism triumphs, and the conflict between desire and taboo is resolved in the socially approved institution of marriage.

This theme of sexual determinism appears blatantly in the narrator's explicit statements, and it is heightened by the parallel and contrast between Trina's and McTeague's relationship and that of Old Grannis and Miss Baker. The romance between the latter two remains unfulfilled for a very long time. Though circumstance gives them physical proximity in adjoining rooms, they remain apart because, in their sixties, they do not have the urgent sexual drive that so quickly unites Trina and McTeague. Without this contrast the old people would seem more foolish than they already are. But in matters of sex, they are probably not markedly different from McTeague and Trina. The young people have the driving force of youthful sexual passion to overcome their pronounced social inhibitions against overt sexual response. Without that passion, they would probably be as shy as the old couple, even though their shyness might take different form. Certainly nothing in their background suggests they would violate proprieties—save under extreme circumstances, but that is to get ahead of the story. A sexual determinism common to all men and women unites Trina and McTeague, whereas its less forceful operation in the old couple keeps them apart for some time.

The theme of sexual determinism has been much remarked upon,[3] but a second theme needs further exploring. Social determinism plays a large role in the lives of all the characters. This theme is by no means wholly separate from the first, but for purposes of analysis it can be treated as such. It appears in two ways: through emphasis on both the ethnic heritage of characters and the particular local environment in which they live. All of the characters belong to the milieu of Polk Street, a lower-middle-class environment that denies them a stable social identity. Norris makes a strong point of this environmental factor by subtitling his novel "A Story of San Francisco," by detailing a cycle of the life of Polk Street from morning through night in the first chapter, and by explicitly commenting on the uncertain social position of all these characters: "No people have a keener eye for the amenities than those whose social position is not assured" (80).

Their sense of their own social instability is the condition inspiring the motives explaining much of the behavior of these characters. Maria's illusion of her gold plate and family past takes its particular form from her own Latin background and temperament and functions to compensate for her uncertain social status. She does without the "young men" attracted to "the girls who tended the soda-water fountain," of whom "she was sick with envy" because "they were in the world, they were elegant, they were debonair, they had their 'young men' " (30). Norris uses this comment to explain why she pesters the inhabitants of the boarding house for junk to sell to Zerkow and why she steals gold from McTeague: she sells both to buy bright clothes so that she can compete with these girls. That her illusion serves the purpose of achieving social stability is marked by the fact that it disappears after her marriage to Zerkow and the birth of her short-lived child. She no longer needs the illusion once she achieves what she considers to be the stability of marriage, husband, and child. Of course her marriage and consequent loss of the need for illusion is one of the many ironies in the story, for it leads to her destruction, just as Trina's good fortune leads to her own.

Other characters share Maria's sense of insecurity. Since Norris uses stereotypes to convey his cultural determinism, he doubtless means Zerkow's greed to have its origin in his Jewish heritage. But Zerkow's social insecurity plays a role here, transforming what might have been a mildly exaggerated interest in possessions into a mania. Norris does not say this in so many words, but the clear parallelism between him and Trina suggests that the dynamics governing her behavior govern his as well. Only she exhibits the fullness of his passion for the ownership of gold, and she forces McTeague to move with her into Zerkow's flat after Maria's murder, both facts unmistakable evidence of parallelisms in a novel structured on this principle. Trina's sense of thrift comes from her German-Swiss background, but her thrift becomes pathological miserliness only after her social security is threatened by McTeague's loss of his license. Her response to the threat is to hold on to the symbol of security—her five thousand dollars in gold—by moving to the lowest level of the Polk Street world before leaving it altogether.

Like Trina's, it seems logical to conclude, Zerkow's avarice is born of insecurity. He is a Polish Jew who wandered westward from Poland to California. As a Polish Jew, he is already a social outcast. He has been thrust to the bottom of a portion of the social structure that even at its top is, in this novel, socially inferior to the mainstream of American middle-class life. Not the Man with the Hoe, laboring patiently to survive, he has become "the Man with the Rake" (38) collecting debris from "every class of society" (37).

Marcus shares the insecurity of Trina, Maria, and Zerkow. When he advises McTeague to prepare for an evening at the theatre, Norris remarks that "Marcus was not sure of himself as regarded certian proprieties" (80), and this social uncertainty results in a continual need to prove himself. Hence, his intellectually pretentious attacks on capitalists were "a pose which he often assumed, certain of impressing the dentist" (11). Because his "knowledge of the diseases of domestic animals had been picked up in a haphazard way, much after

the manner of McTeague's education," Marcus is "a bungler" as a
dog surgeon (10), and his own felt insufficiencies dictate proving
himself by a demonstration of superiority, in this case to the lowly
McTeague. His truculent behavior, his story of how he handled "an
awkward bicyclist" who nearly collided with him (" 'Say that again,'
says I to um. . . . I'd a knifed him in another minute" [9]) is another
illustration of this same characteristic. Marcus's jealousy of
McTeague's marriage has its source as much in his insecurity as it
does in the ethnic background he shares with Trina, his first cousin:
they are cut from the same German-Swiss cloth.

In his portrayal of Old Grannis and Miss Baker, Norris makes the
theme of cultural determinism most apparent and carries it to its
logical conclusion. As a stereotyped "little old maid" (13) Miss Baker
would, of course, observe propriety. Her name stands in marked
contrast to the ethnic ring of the names of the novel's other women;
an Anglo-Saxon woman of her time would doubtless distinguish
herself from those others by her sense of form. No matter how lowly
her actual social position, she would still consider herself part of
"polite society." Old Grannis's sense of form is also a function of his
cultural background. The English are reputed to have the highest
level of manners in the world, and Old Grannis is the walking
stereotype of his place of national origin. The social insecurity of
these two exaggerates their natural propensities derived from their
individual cultural past, for Norris surely includes them in a comment inspired by his portrayal of Marcus:

> Marcus was not sure of himself as regarded certain proprieties,
> nor, for that matter, were any of the people of the little world of
> Polk Street. The shop girls, the plumbers' apprentices, the
> small trades-people, and their like, whose social position was
> not clearly defined, could never be sure how far they could go
> and yet preserve their "respectability." When they wished to be
> "proper," they invariably overdid the thing. It was not as if they
> belonged to the "tough" element, who had no appearances to
> keep up. Polk Street rubbed elbows with the "avenue" one
> block above. . . . At an unguarded moment they might be
> taken for "toughs," so they generally erred in the other direc-
> tion, and were absurdly formal. [80]

Miss Baker and Old Grannis are courtesy itself; the wall that separates them is the wall of social form which their insecurity prohibits their breaking down. The novel does not say why they never married when they were younger, when their sexual drives were stronger and thus more likely to shatter such walls. The matter is of no great moment, for it does not in the least alter the novel's determinism. Still, Norris invites speculation along these lines when he muses whether this was the first romance in their lives, or whether other romances in their younger lives preceded this one. He concludes that "it was impossible to say" (14). The author knows best, of course, but one cannot help observing that a veterinarian in Victorian England would surely not have had the opportunity McTeague had with a Trina in his chair. Nor would an American dressmaker of the same period run into many men. Even their professions support the novel's cultural determinism by explaining their single state.

All of these people represent the unstable Polk Street environment in which McTeague lives, and he is more socially uncertain than they. The agonies he endures in order to take Trina and her family to the theatre attest to this conclusion. So, too, does his protest to the box-office agent, "You can't make small of me," a protest which he later echoes to Marcus (83, 126). But McTeague also differs significantly from these other figures.

In creating McTeague, Norris portrays the discernibly human, those essential elements which separate man from the animals. The numerous animal images describing him (his "jaw salient, like that of the carnivora," but so "docile" that "altogether he suggested the draught horse" [3]) suggest that he is on the borderline between the human and the animal kingdoms, and the novel's naturalistic vision reinforces this view. The vicious fighting between Trina and McTeague, Marcus and McTeague, and Zerkow and Maria is paralleled to the behavior of Alexander and the nameless Scotch collie, dogs that bark viciously at each other through a fence. Norris thus sees man as part of nature, obviously different though man may be from dogs. Some men, of course, are closer than others to the dividing line between the human world and the nonhuman, and McTeague is squarely on that line.

Zerkow receives comparable portrayal as an animal, his eyes "keen as those of a lynx," his hands possessing "claw-like, prehensile fingers" (37). But the particular animal imagery describing Zerkow serves to show that he is more socially advanced than McTeague and, hence, further from the animal world. Avarice, of course, is a social disease, and McTeague, almost alone among the central figures of the novel, is not avaricious. McTeague's "old-time miner's idea of wealth easily gained and quickly spent" contrasts sharply to Zerkow's possessiveness, just as it contrasts to Trina's own form of possessiveness. She wished to invest her income, whereas McTeague cannot comprehend the logic of interest, which "seemed wofully small" in contrast to the principal from which it was derived (114).

McTeague escapes avarice because he is socially retarded in contrast not just to Zerkow and Trina but to all the other principals of the novel. Marcus speaks "half-truths" (11), but he is at least capable of intellectual pretentiousness, as McTeague is not; and Marcus's own avarice, expressed in his jealousy of McTeague's marriage, sets him apart from the dentist. Maria's guilt in swindling and stealing from others demonstrates her social advancement over the more innocent McTeague. Clearly Old Grannis's and Miss Baker's sense of form set them squarely within the social world, not near the borderline separating it from the animals. In contrast to all these figures, McTeague is indeed "hopelessly stupid" (2) and on that borderline.

For this reason McTeague is only an observer of the social life around him at the novel's opening. "The street never failed to interest him" (4), the reader is told, but it interests him from his position as spectator from his window. That street provides him with certain basic needs and pleasures, heavy food and steam beer, for example, but as the person closest to the animal kingdom, he feels no need for further social involvement beyond that. Marcus sustains an unstable friendship with him more to satisfy his own ego than to fulfill any social need of McTeague's.

But if McTeague is closer than others to the animals, he does possess characteristics that set him apart from them. His social status in the opening pages represents a considerable advance over his boyhood in Placer County as the son of a father who became an "irresponsible animal" (2) under the influence of liquor. His capacity for social development, though limited, is thus one hallmark of his humanity, his uniqueness in nature. The pattern of the novel begins with his already accomplished social rise, then displays a further rise in his marriage to Trina, and concludes by tracing his descent to his original position in his mining days.

Other aspects of McTeague's humanity abound, but one need not be exhaustive in listing them because Norris has provided the reader with three symbols suggesting McTeague's tentative position between the human and animal worlds. One is the "huge gilded tooth" that "it was his ambition, his dream, to have" and that Trina gives him. His fascination with it connects him to the carnivores; but it also attaches him to the human world. He wants it "gorgeous and attractive" (4), so clearly he has an aesthetic sense, though limited. And because to him it further symbolizes social dignity and status giving him self-esteem, to the reader it symbolizes his human social sense as well.[4]

The canary and the concertina similarly reflect both aspects of McTeague's nature. His fundamental allegiance to the bird rather than to any single human being (he keeps it to the very end, even carrying it with him into the desert) places his affective life more in the animal than the human kingdom, but the fact that he keeps and cares for it as a pet indicates his humanity. McTeague's concertina, recalling that "music has charms to soothe a savage breast," symbolizes his membership in the animal kingdom. But that *he* plays it, soothes his own savage breast, so to speak, testifies to his humanity, his capacity in some measure to control his animal instincts, just as it points to associated elements of the human: an aesthetic sense, for example, and a personal nostalgia, for the airs that he plays, "always carried him back . . . ten years before" to his boyhood in Placer County (2).

If McTeague is inferior to the other characters, then, he is nonetheless recognizably human. And his very inferiority makes him the most sympathetic character in the novel, for it renders him guileless and helpless before others. He stands in relation to the reader roughly as he does at one point to Trina: "It was like a little child playing with some gigantic, good-natured Saint Bernard" (117). There is something Adam-like about this "young giant" (3) and Norris's references to "the foul stream of hereditary evil" in him, to "the vices and sins of his father and his father's father" and to "the evil of an entire race . . . in his veins" relate him to the reader's own humanity by suggesting that McTeague is reenacting the classic pattern of the Fall.

But if *McTeague* contains allusions to the Fall, its content is deterministic and challenges the moral axis associated with the story of the fall of man. McTeague becomes largely a victim of cultural dynamics determining the behavior of others, and he is drawn into this cultural web through that great leveler, sexual attraction. Sexual determinism unites even Trina, his social superior, to his inferior self. The themes of sexual and cultural determinism thus converge in the persons of Trina and McTeague. Their convergence first appears by way of conflict. McTeague is sufficiently aware of social ethics to condemn his natural desires and fight his sexual self. The moral conflict in Trina between social taboos and sexual desire is heightened by her own cultural past. Her German-Swiss background stresses thrift, and thrift has its source in a larger disciplined view of life. This emphasis on discipline is exhibited by the picture of her father, "a little man of a military aspect" (56), leading his family on a picnic, a rifle over his shoulder as though he were the commander of the light brigade: " 'Vorwarts!' " (58). Sexual impulses threaten such discipline because they dictate abandonment; and when the conflict in Trina revives after her marriage, it takes a specially virulent form because of her particular cultural background. For the moment, however, it is resolved for both principals in the socially approved institution of marriage.

Norris then spells out the fuller development of that resolution in preparation for exhibiting its unraveling into further conflict, which will be resolved again in more sinister form. Even from the beginning, the marriage is not a perfect blending of the sexual and the social. Norris follows the line of development suggested in an earlier comment: "With each concession gained the man's desire cools; with every surrender made the woman's adoration increases" (73). Each reader must decide for himself the legitimacy of such psychological insight. Legitimate or not, Norris patterns the McTeagues' marital life accordingly. McTeague's sexual interests diminish and are replaced by social ones. "That tempest of passion, that overpowering desire that had suddenly taken possession of him that day when he had given her ether . . . rarely stirred him now" (163). Instead, "he began to observe the broader, larger interests of life, interests that affected him not as an individual, but as a member of a class, a profession, or a political party" (164). Trina remains properly social, but she follows an opposite sexual path. Her ardor is heightened rather than diminished by marriage: "She loved McTeague now with a blind, unreasoning love that admitted of no doubt or hesitancy. . . . McTeague might cease to love her, might leave her, might even die; it would be all the same, *she was his*" (157-58).

Such bliss is unsettled by Marcus's sending the letter that deprives McTeague of his practice, an act ultimately born of an enduring jealousy that McTeague married a woman with money (p. 189)—a jealousy derived from the same cultural strain which inspires Trina's thrift and later miserliness. The consequence of this event, Trina's sense of a threat to her security, reawakens her conflict between discipline and sexuality. She becomes financially disciplined to the point of literal, cruel miserliness as she forces McTeague to lower their standard of living. After some unsuccessful resistance, he responds by having a trait of his own cultural past reawakened: he drinks heavily, just as his father did. The popular archetype of the Irishman hinted at earlier in his love for steam beer becomes, under pressure, exaggerated into the heavy drinker who behaves much like the "irresponsible animal" his father was, though not quite that yet. He bites Trina's fingers, treats her sadistically to revenge himself for her miserliness. But if Trina's sense of discipline is now also exaggerated, thus triggering her husband's behavior, she does not abandon her sexual desire. Rather than being repelled by her husband's sadistic behavior, she resolves the conflict between sex and discipline by taking masochistic pleasure in it, a fact that Norris makes perfectly clear. "Trina's emotions had narrowed with the narrowing of her daily life," he writes. "They reduced themselves at last to but two, her passion for her money and her perverted love for her husband when he was brutal" (263-64).

Even this resolution, however, is but a final step toward her ultimate degradation before her murder. After McTeague steals money that she was hoarding, at a fearful cost in deprivation of him and of herself, she removes herself from Polk Street and resolves her conflict in still different form. Her husband gone, she redirects her sexual desire away from his sadistic treatment of her to the gold dollars themselves. In passages from two succeeding paragraphs, Norris makes clear he understood the meaning of *transference*, even if he had not encountered the technical term: " 'And yet, Trina would say, I did love Mac, loved him dearly, only a little while ago. Even when he hurt me, it only made me love him more. How is it I've changed so sudden? How *could* I forget him so soon? It must be because he stole my money. That is it. I couldn't forgive anyone that' " (306). But though she must have her money, she will not abandon her sexual life easily: "One evening she had even spread all the gold pieces between the sheets, and had then gone to bed, stripping herself, and had slept all night upon the money, taking a strange and ecstatic pleasure in the touch of the smooth flat pieces the length of her entire body" (306).

McTeague is thus a victim of the cultural mechanisms determining the behavior of others. These unleash in him forces from his own cultural past and that animal past always just beneath the thin layer of his social veneer. After some struggle, he sells his gilded tooth, symbol of that veneer. With surprising ease, he first "slipped back into the old habits" (243) of his original social self in his bachelor days, before Trina refined him further in marriage; then he sinks with her below even that level, to the squalor of Zerkow's rooms. But there are limits even to his toleration. Despite Trina's urgings, he will not sell his canary, symbol of his affiliation with an animal world that now must seem more friendly to him than the human and now become emblem of his own reduced condition. Like the bird in its cage, he is trapped by the past, that of others and his own. Appropriately enough, it is when he discovers that Trina has sold his concertina that he kills her. The concertina is a symbol of his connection to the animal world, but it is also a symbol of his uniqueness, his humanity. Deprived of the source of that uniqueness, the music that he plays to soothe the savage breast, the savage forces therein erupt in full, unrestrained form, and he beats her to death until "it became abominable" (318).

McTeague is thus reduced to the level of savage animal, or to as near that level as a human being can be. The cat's sensing his presence before he actually enters the room where he murders

Trina testifies to this fact. Thereafter, fittingly enough, he acts on an animal's sixth sense, a "brute instinct" (331) to warn him of danger as he escapes with the money with which Trina has committed adultery and returns to the condition of his youth in Placer County. He can sense that the veneers of his social self were mere projections of his original condition as the child of an "irresponsible animal." For "once it even occurred to him that there was a resemblance between his present work and the profession he had been forced to abandon" (328). In Placer County, Norris exclaims, nature is "savage, sullen, and magnificently indifferent to man" (322), but McTeague feels at one with it, "the still, colossal mountains . . . reflecting themselves in his own nature" (329). But if he reverts to the animal level, he is still a domestic animal, despite his savage attack on Trina, and even as animal still a part of the human world. Thus he is unlike Maria's flying squirrel, which can survive in the raw natural world once she lets him go. Rather, he is something like the canary in the cage. Like it, he cannot live in Death Valley. Like it, he must depend upon a human culture to sustain him. If that culture will not, then, like the bird, he must die.

The meaning of the novel's wall symbolism can now come into focus.[5] *McTeague* contains two literal barriers: the wall separating Old Grannis and Miss Baker and the fence separating the dogs, Alexander and the Scotch collie. There is one important parallel between these two "couples." The dogs, which bark ferociously at each other through the fence, get on amiably enough when they escape such separation. At the very moment of the dogs' escape and direct confrontation, Old Grannis and Miss Baker meet face to face and they too get along amiably. The moment is the turning point in their relationship that will permit them finally to enter a blissful marriage. What this suggests is that both man and dogs by fundamental nature have the instinct to live in harmony with their kind, but such harmonious relationships can be prevented by walls and fences; that is, by certain human creations. The larger meaning of this implication in the novel depends on the more specific meaning of these barriers and the nature of those separated by them.

A reader can deduce the following points from the situation of the old couple separated by their wall. Though sexual attraction can be one expression of the instinct to live in harmony with one's kind, it can of course also be a disruptive force—threatening to anesthetized women in dental chairs, for example. Consequently society creates restraints on the expression of sexual responses, restraints like those proprieties the older man and woman have so thoroughly absorbed. Hence, the wall both symbolizes social propriety and the larger human environment from which they absorbed it. When those proprieties are exaggerated by the environment of personal pasts and the insecurity that residence in Polk Street breeds, then the very forms that ought first to control sexual instinct and then lead to living in harmony (in marriage, for example) instead suppress sexual instinct altogether, if not the desire for companionship, and keep the two separate.

But that wall of propriety, thickened by insecurity and old age, at worst isolates Old Grannis and Miss Baker and makes them comic caricatures of young lovers. Their separation does not produce in them the vicious behavior that the fence creates in the dogs. The dogs become vicious because a fence, a human creation, is imposed upon the nonhuman world of pure instinct they represent and thwarts the normal expression of that instinct. However Old Grannis and Miss Baker may have responded to the thwarting of their instincts in the past (the narrator expresses ignorance of that past), it is clear what they have become. Instinct does not figure large in them. They have become purely social creatures of a human environment, as the dogs are not, and age has destroyed the sexual drive by which Norris represents man's animal self. They may experience a mild frustration from their wishing to live in harmony with one another while feeling they must remain separate, but the novel makes it indisputably clear that the thwarting of even this weakened sense of instinct is accepted by both. Had chance not intervened to permit a modest fulfillment, they would have remained in permanent and polite isolation.

But by virtue of their younger age, instinct is very much alive in the other figures of the novel, and in this regard they stand roughly between the dogs' world of nature and the world of purely social man represented by Old Grannis and Miss Baker, though some figures are closer than others to one or another of these poles. And when human barriers are erected to separate them from each other, they respond to the thwarting of their normal instinctual behavior to get along with their own kind with all the force of younger instinct; and hence they become as savage as the dogs do when separated by the fence. In the case of Trina and McTeague that fence becomes as sure a symbol of a social environment as the wall separating Old Grannis and Miss Baker. Circumstance intensifies Trina's sense of insecurity and warps her sense of thrift into miserliness, and both characteristics are derived from the environment of her German-Swiss background. Her miserliness is thus an expression of a background that becomes a fence isolating her from her husband because he does not share it and the trait in which it issues under these circumstances. Thereafter this fence transforms both partners into savage beasts, though of different kinds dictated by their different backgrounds. First, the very sexual forces that originally drew them together become vicious, McTeague's turning sadistic in response to the deprivation caused by Trina's miserliness, Trina's turning into masochism. Ultimately, however, her miserliness separates them sexually as well, with all the hideous consequences that follow.

The wall symbolism thus underlies one aspect of the novel's determinism, the environmental, and it interlocks with the sexual to create the nightmares in this novel. And the novel's larger structure supports its determinism in an interesting way reminiscent of the structure of Crane's *Maggie*. Juxtaposing a structure associated with a free-will axis to a deterministic one, Norris undermines the first with the second, thus expressing the novel's preferred philosophical vision. In the early chapters of *McTeague*, the outlines of an old-fashioned melodrama emerge. Such a melodrama depends upon stereotyped characters confronting clear-cut moral choices perceptible to reader as well as character within the melodrama. Virtue must triumph, evil must fail with consequent punishment. The cast of the stereotypes appears in *McTeague's* first five chapters, with the second presenting the temptation scene, McTeague struggling against his animal self before the anesthetized Trina. He is strong enough to leave the beautiful girl's innocence intact, though barely, settling for a kiss. Chapter 7, in which the characters gather together to hear the agent discourse on the wonders of the lottery, seems to strengthen the moral axis of this melodrama. The agent transforms the chance operations of the lottery into a beneficent force purposefully working for man's good: "Invariably it was the needy who won, the destitute and starving woke to wealth and plenty, the virtuous toiler suddenly found his reward" (99), and so forth.

This moral axis is enhanced by the treatment of character in the chapter. With Marcus Schouler acting as master of ceremonies, each figure responds to Trina's good fortune according to his humor. McTeague is confused, revealing his density; Marcus is "jolly," an assumed air that emphasizes his barely concealed jealousy. Maria uses the occasion to steal money from McTeague, and Zerkow, later told of Trina's good fortune, exclaims, " 'Oh, why couldn't it have come to me?' " (109). Finally, the old couple respond with characteristic shyness. Though characters are stereotypes, melodrama holds them squarely responsible for their action, and Norris's oblique references to original sin suggest that this may be the appropriate response to them. But he questions the concept of blame and thus forces the reader to reassess the meaning of those words like *sin* and *vice* that he employs. He forces him to see that such words are used to describe actions borne of forces over which man has no control.

The novel's other structure, its deterministic one, guides this reassessment. This structure follows the precepts for the construction of the naturalistic novel preached by Zola in his essay "The Experimental Novel," although probably Norris derived his structure from reading *L'Assommoir* rather than Zola's theoretical essay.[6] In his theoretical work, Zola declares that the novelist must act both as observer and experimentalist in order to introduce a "determinism" into the work. "The observer in him gives the facts as he has observed them, suggests the point of departure, displays the solid earth on which his characters are to tread and the phenomena to develop."[7] In his first chapter, Norris "displays the solid earth" of Polk Street in seven meticulously detailed paragraphs. In the first five he introduces his figures, whose characters are intrinsic to the development of subsequent phenomena. Fundamental to such development is the marriage of Trina and McTeague. Hence he permits a familiar kind of sexual determinism to run its course by the end of chapter 5, emphasizing the inescapability of sexual attraction with a concluding reference:

> "You loaf him?"
> "I don't know."
> Mrs. Sieppe set down the mousetrap with such violence that it sprung with a sharp snap. (75)

Thereafter, the experimentalist surfaces in Norris. He "introduces an experiment, that is to say, sets his characters going in a certain story so as to show that the succession of facts will be such as the requirement of the determinism of the phenomena under examination call for."[8] Chapter 6 concludes with Trina's winning the lottery shortly before her marriage. This chance event, the foreign element introduced into what otherwise appears as a familiar world to its inhabitants, begins the experiment. It acts as the catalyst for subsequent events, the "succession of facts" that demonstrates the underlying meaning of "the phenomena under examination," the determining force of culture in human lives. The novel's structure, with its symbols and its numerous parallelisms between subplots and central story, fulfill "the requirements of the determinism of the phenomena under examination."

The picture Norris paints is a grim one, depicting man as a mere pawn in the hands of Fate, comprehensible though its operations may be. But it is not a picture of unrelieved gloom. If many are destroyed, the inexorable process leading to their destruction brings Old Grannis and Miss Baker together.[9] William James, of course, found little comfort in such a view. The only compensation it offers for the pains of human existence is an aesthetic one. From this view it follows that because man has no power to alleviate life's pains, he should cherish its beauties, all the more so because, without freedom, he is as powerless to create beauty intentionally as he is to banish pain. Such a view, for James, encouraged decadence.[10] Because Norris never personally committed himself to the rigid determinism of his novel, he did not have to worry about its philosophical implications. It was left to the personally committed Theodore Dreiser to explore the ramifications of determinism in all their fullness.

FOUR

Dreiser's Trilogy and the Dilemma of Determinism

In "The Dilemma of Determinism," William James argues for a theory of indeterminism by arguing for the existence, not of man's free will, but of chance. He could well take the position that "the stronghold of the deterministic sentiment is the antipathy to the idea of chance," for to believe that something is "not controlled, secured, or necessitated by other things in advance of its own actual presence"[1] is to deny the fundamental premise of determinism: "For everything that ever happens there are conditions such that, given them, nothing else could happen."[2] If chance exists in the physical universe, then, it seems plausible to believe that man's freedom is a reality as well. Hence it is fitting that Dreiser, the only major American naturalist writer personally and explicitly committed to philosophic determinism, should have pondered the subject of chance during a lifetime that shows strong concern for understanding the ramifications of determinism.

In a section of his *Notes on Life* entitled "The Factor Called Chance," he writes that this concept may be "in most cases only another name for our ignorance of causes." He does grant it some status—it is not possible to know which spider's web will trap which fly—but he never abandons the rigid laws of cause and effect that in fact undermine the concept: "If it were possible . . . to know the exact operations of the entire universe in advance, [then chance would not exist]. But since such prevision is seemingly not granted to any life form, there intervenes the factor called chance."[3]

Although "chance" events do occur in Dreiser's novels—the Chicago fire that initially undoes Frank Cowperwood, for example—their existence is not meant to challenge the concept of determinism.[4] If Dreiser does not bother to explain the causes of the fire, he has good reason for the omission: he wishes to explain the forces which govern human character, not those issuing in the fire. But the very fact that elsewhere he should explore the subject of chance (and many others) in the context of determinism testifies to the firmness of his commitment to determinism and thus sets him apart from a writer like Norris. As a personally committed determinist, furthermore, Dreiser spent much of his career impressing his deeply held doctrine into the service of denying traditional religious and social beliefs, since these assume man possesses freedom of the will. Such denial did not blind him to another fundamental problem raised by his vision, the problem of how man can live with dignity and find order and meaning in a universe that proscribes his freedom. In his last years, he turned to a hazy mysticism, a personal development reflected in Berenice Fleming's study of Brahmanism in *The Stoic*, her own attraction anticipated by Solon Barnes's rejection of materialism and discovery of the spirit of love and purpose in nature and the universe in *The Bulwark*. In his quest for meaning, it would seem as though he abandoned his determinism, but this is not the case. There is a logical connection between these two apparently antithetical poles of his thought, the mechanistic and the "mystical," and the latter, rather than rejecting the former, embraces it.

This connection can be seen in the "trilogy of desire," if one is willing to set aside the usual view of *The Stoic*. The fact that the novel is incomplete has been elevated into a cardinal principle supporting established wisdom: that the work has no inner integrity and cannot be taken seriously as a thematic conclusion to the trilogy.[5] Such wisdom has not gone unchallenged. John J. McAleer has analyzed the trilogy to show that even *The Stoic* has an inner coherence and strong relations to *The Financier* and *The Titan*.[6] I will also leave established wisdom behind to show my own sense of the coherence of the trilogy.

Essentially one long novel, the trilogy possesses the unity of character, plot, and theme necessary to display the harmonious unfolding of Dreiser's thought. But the trilogy is of special value because it shows that the connections between the poles of his thought that gradually unfold depend upon his lifelong exploration of the implications of determinism. In the trilogy, Dreiser pursues those implications to the point where Berenice's conversion seems logical, even if abrupt because the action in this unfinished novel, though fully outlined, still needed further dramatic development. The trilogy, in other words, possesses an inner dynamic dependent on the unfolding of the intellectual premises of the first novel in the second, with the resolution of the philosophic problem raised by the second emerging in the third.

The goal of this chapter is to see how the first novel establishes a deterministic vision; how the second explores the implications of determinism to the point where it arrives at what William James called "the dilemma of determinism"; and how the third resolves that dilemma. Although each section of the ensuing discussion tries to stress the uniqueness of a single novel, the fact that the three novels are essentially one requires a good deal of jumping back and forth for purposes of clarity. The trilogy is a philosophical series of novels, and the meaning of a concept appearing in the second novel may well rest upon a premise established in the first; or the meaning of a subordinate line of thought in the second may require reference to the third in order to establish its full significance. This is the way of a philosophical work, and the critic must adapt to it.

The Financier

The Financier is an embodiment of *Dreiser's Law*, the term used by Dreiser's biographer, W. A. Swanberg, to explain Dreiser's early view of society. According to the first tenet of that law, "*beliefs held by the multitude, the bourgeois and their leaders, are likely to be wrong per se.*" The reverse is also true: "*Beliefs held by unconventionalists which fly in the face of orthodoxy are in all probability right.*"[7] This law explains Dreiser's attitude toward the two groups of characters in *The Financier*. Needless to say, no distinction is here made between narrator and author. A reader of Dreiser's essays and novels can see that no distinction exists.

Frank Cowperwood and Aileen Butler are the unconventionalists. They scorn the prevailing sexual mores embodied in conventional attitudes toward marriage and the Christian religious system sanctifying the social norm. "Aileen had no spiritual dread whatever. Cowperwood was without spiritual or religious feeling" (139).* In numerous ways Dreiser makes it clear that he is on "their" side, not that of their critics, who judge the central characters morally and legally for their transgressions against the laws of God and man. Dreiser's description of "the conventional mind" as "at best a petty piece of machinery . . . oyster-like in its functioning" (244), perceiving "nothing of the subtlety of life," reacting to interferences with "the placid flow of events" with a "grinding" that is "not unlike sand in a machine" (245), is one of several indications of his allegiance. Not only does he show contempt for this kind of mind, but also he exonerates Frank's and Aileen's behavior in terms that make moral condemnation of them irrelevant. Her "innate sensuousness" (87) and that "something chemic and hence dynamic" which in him was "clamoring for expression" (136) are mastering compulsions. As Dreiser states the matter in *The Titan*, Frank Cowperwood "could not control his own temperament any more than Aileen could control hers" (380).

Of course, no one has freedom in the trilogy, so even the moralists in its pages must be exonerated for their actions. Yet, given the pain they cause, or are forced to cause, one must wonder why Dreiser so clearly admires his principals. Why not shed tears over those to whom they are forced to cause pain? Two closely related answers to this question exist, one pertaining to the author's view of Cowperwood, the other to his views of society.

Cowperwood is strikingly like the "creative power" to which Dreiser alludes in his penultimate conclusion to the novel (501). This power, which expresses itself through nature, is central to Dreiser's determinism. For him, determinism meant that "the physical aspect of the world . . . is no more than a mechanism through which

*Theodore Dreiser, *The Financier.* Completely revised edition (New York: Boni & Liveright, 1927). I have chosen Dreiser's revision of the much longer 1912 edition for discussion and citation. It is about one-third shorter than the original, and I find that its greater compactness promotes a sense of the unity of the themes within the work.

something . . . expresses itself," that all things that exist and all events that occur "are mere manifestations of energy on the part of something that uses man as man uses a machine."[8] Like the creative power, Frank Cowperwood is a manipulator of men. His motto, "I satisfy myself," is a logical extension of this role, for the power pursues its own purposes (if any) for its own inscrutable ends. Of course Cowperwood himself is a pawn of that power, which is inaccessible to man, just as all other individuals, indeed all of nature, are its pawns. Nonetheless Cowperwood in his role as master manipulator is as close to a representation of that power as it is possible for a human to be. Since one cannot help standing in awe and admiration, if not reverence, before such a power, it is easy enough to transfer such feelings to its human likeness, the superman.

There is a second reason for Dreiser's admiration, and it can be found in a section of his *Notes on Life* called "The Theory that Life is a Game." There he asserts that the creative power has ordained that all things in nature must engage in contest, man included; for man has been endowed with vanity and pride as attributes necessary to play the game for victory. Chance and death give the game its intensity, as "each creature must contest with something else."[9] With such a view of life, one's sympathies do not necessarily go to the moral man, whose morality is either a projection of a temperament not quite fitted to play the game successfully, or a pretext for defeating a player with no moral pretensions. Men try to bet on a winner at the Derby. Do they sympathize with the horse that takes last place?

This view, a source of Dreiser's admiration for Cowperwood and Aileen, accounts for the two sets of characters in *The Financier*. By explaining their behavior according to "temperament," to "chemistry," and to "instinct," Dreiser allies Frank and Aileen to the world of nature, whereas other figures, due to their "lack of force" (135), are clearly a part of the social world, presumably accountable to its laws because there "the chemistry and physics of life" (147) are not large.[10] This division between "natural" and "social" characters is enhanced by the distinction between Aileen's chemical responses, based on physical law, which are the source of her decision to marry Cowperwood, and the canon law of the Catholic Church to which her Catholic father subscribes, and which is the source of his opposition to that marriage. And Dreiser's explanation of Cowperwood's finan-

cial dealings further emphasizes the distinction, for he sees Cowperwood as a victim of "that subtle chemistry of things that transcends
all written law and makes for the spirit and, beyond that, the inutility
of all law" (323). Men of nature, odd as it may seem, are the true men
of spirit. Others are men of the law, with its pale spirit. They are
social men.

This distinction is further enforced by the famous framework of
the book. The first chapter shows Cowperwood's sense of kinship
with the predatory lobster in the fishmarket, which becomes a
school for him as he learns the answer to the question, " 'How is life
organized?' " (5). If lobsters lived on squid, and men on lobsters,
then the answer to his question, "And what lived on men?" is self-
evident: "other men." This connection between human and animal
predators is confirmed in the first coda to the novel, "Concerning
Mycteroperca Bonaci," which implicitly associates Cowperwood
with the black grouper fish. Its markings changing so that it can
"strike unseen" (502), this fish is clearly like Frank Cowperwood in
his financial dealings with others and very much like the Cowperwood who, in his adulterous relationship with Aileen, displays the
same "power of simulation" (501) it possesses: "For purposes of social
success, in order not to offend, to smooth one's path, make things
easy, avoid useless criticism, and the like, it was necessary to create an
outward seeming—ostensibly conform. Beyond that it was not
necessary to do anything" (302).

Not only is Frank Cowperwood a product of nature, but he is
absolved of all responsibility for his behavior because of the
parallel between him and the black grouper fish and its relation to
the creative spirit. In this conclusion to the novel, Dreiser raises
several unanswered questions about that relationship, but they are
rhetorical ones only. For assuredly that spirit *does* will "that which
is either tricky or deceptive" (502); it does *not* "build this mortal
life in such fashion that only honesty and virtue shall prevail"
(501). Responsibility for Cowperwood's actions lies with the spirit, not with himself.

At this point in reasoning the distinction between "natural"
and "social" men breaks down, for the reader knows that "there
was no more escaping the greatness that was inherent in him
[Cowperwood] than there was for so many others the littleness

that was in them" (468-69). Their allegiance to conventional social codes reflects that "littleness," which is the mirror of a temperament produced in nature and is in itself one expression of the creative power. As a "natural conservator of public morals" (136), even Cowperwood's first wife, Lilian, is such an expression. Where all are victims of temperament, all belong to the world of nature, and hence all are pawns of, expressions of, the creative power.

Dreiser thus creates an amoral naturalistic axis for action rather than an ethical one in *The Financier*. A creative power wills a contest and creates the conditions for its enactment: the varying temperaments who engage in it. To emphasize the true impulses guiding men, he shows that even morality and legality are facades barely concealing the will to contest and to victory. The point is illustrated by the episode that the chance event of the Chicago fire initiates. Ultimately, the fire exposes Cowperwood's financial chicanery and places him at the mercy of Butler, Mollenhauer, Simpson, and those surrogates of the law who temporarily imprison him. All of these people essentially view Cowperwood's transgressions as "well within his human, if not his strictly legal rights" (259), but they use the law to subdue him in order to achieve a variety of personal victories and goals. Hence the truth of Maxwell Geismar's comment that for them, "ethics is a club, not a code, to finish him [Cowperwood] off."[11] And hence another truth: these men are much like the animal life to which Cowperwood is compared. They are impelled by the same impulses animating the lobster, the black grouper fish, and Cowperwood himself.

The action in *The Financier* thus logically leads to its penultimate conclusion, "Concerning Mycteroperca Bonaci." The novel answers the introductory question, "How is life organized?" The answer is provided by the structure of the action and by Dreiser's commentary, and it is brought out boldly by this first conclusion, which stands in relation to the novel much as the concluding triad of chapters in Henry Adams's *Education* stands in relation to the narrative preceding. That answer is delivered in Darwinian terms. Existence is a struggle, only the fittest survive, and the capacity to create illusions is part of man's equipment for survival. Like the black grouper, some men are fitted to be "an implement of illusion . . . a living lie, a creature whose business it is to appear what it is not, to simulate that with which it has nothing in common, to get its living by great subtlety, the power of its enemies to forfend against which is little" (502). And the greatest illusion of all is morality, for even moral men use it to engage in contest. Save for the very weakest, thus, predator and prey are not rigid classifications but roles that men play interchangeably, when circumstance and chance allow. As Dreiser reminds the reader, man's "feet are in the trap of circumstance; his eyes are on an illusion" (501). The trap is fashioned of temperament and "chance"; the illusion is morality.

If man was not made to know God, to love him, and to serve him, as the religionists would have it; or if man's highest expression of self, even in a godless world, is not to be found in ethical or moral behavior, then the second question that logically follows the first (How is life organized?) is this: What is the end of life? The question implies two others, one related to personal goals and the other to the larger end of existence itself. In answer to the first implied question—What is an individual's personal end or goal in life?—the determinist can only declare that it is whatever the creative power dictates for the individual. Dreiser said as much when he raised the question of what man should think of the creative power. "The mechanistic answer to that would be: we are to think what it chemically and physically constructs us to think, no more and no less."[12] If one's views of that power are dictated by it, one's goals will surely be.

Individuals cannot thus transcend their mundane selves to shape their lives according to principles derived from an absolute outside of man, but they can know something about nature, the visible expression of the creative power. Thus, though their private goals may be fated, they can answer the other implied question—What is the end of physical existence?—in larger terms, though not in the largest sense of all, the metaphysical one that would allow them to share divine knowledge. Dreiser makes this distinction clear in the following classic expression of his naturalistic vision:

> Knowledge can only be awareness of the laws of nature or life and of nature's skill in applying the same to the creation

of forms functioning within and according to its laws (The acquiring of knowledge is the beginning of wisdom). *Why* its laws came into being, man does not know. . . . *How* its laws came into being, he does not know but surmises, or has surmised, that they are *from everlasting to everlasting.* But that is a surmise. He does not know.[13]

From nature, if not from God, man can answer the question of the end of existence. And the man who believes that life is a game can only conclude that its end is victory, or, rather, the pleasure that victory brings. "For if this life game is not for pleasure," Dreiser writes in *Notes on Life,* "I fail to detect what else it is for."[14] And Frank Cowperwood is the very embodiment of the pleasure principle animating man; his motto, "I satisfy myself," a pure reflection of it. Cowperwood's larger-than-life appearance, of course, makes him seem an exception to human nature, and in some ways he is. Yet, at the same time, his portrayal merely brings out very starkly the impulse in all figures, though its operation may be concealed by a legal code through which some take their pleasure (Butler to revenge himself on Cowperwood, Mollenhauer to fleece him) or by a religious code through which Lilian achieves her temperamental need for stability.

The pursuit of pleasure as life's goal is a theme subdued in *The Financier,* subordinated to answering the question, "How is life organized?" But it is there in Aileen's disregard of her Catholicism brought on by her passionate response to Cowperwood, and in Cowperwood's pursuit of ever-expanding horizons of pleasure: "Wealth, in the beginning, had seemed the only goal, to which had been added the beauty of women. And now art, for art's sake—the first faint radiance of a rosy dawn—had begun to shine in upon him" (162). In *The Titan* this theme becomes dominant, but the point of view that life pursues pleasure receives thematic enrichment from Dreiser's view of illusion.

As a word, "illusion" appears in the penultimate coda to *The Financier,* and it is central to the meaning of its final one, "The Magic Crystal," with its grim forecast for Aileen's and Cowperwood's future: "Sorrow, sorrow, sorrow." Aileen's brilliant society will shine "in a mirage," her love elude as "a will-o'-the-wisp" (503). Her desires or illusions will not be fulfilled. As for Cowperwood, he will become "a soul that was as bereft of illusion as a windless moon" (503). He will see his desires as illusions because their fulfillment brings no pleasure. In *The Titan*, Aileen's prophecy is amply fulfilled, Cowperwood's less so there, though fully so in *The Stoic*. Nonetheless, the final coda of *The Financier* sets the terms for the central tension of *The Titan:* the pursuit of pleasure as opposed to the knowledge that the pursuit is futile, illusory, either because the goal is unattainable or, if attained, is unfulfilling.

The Titan

Life is a game, its end is pleasure, and *The Titan* portrays the highest type of victor and victory in this game. The participants' temperaments dictate their pleasures; circumstance determines their fulfillment. Since the trilogy is preeminently the story of Frank Cowperwood, he is the "circumstance" that looms large in the lives of Lilian, Aileen, and Berenice, the other major players in this game. And he, along with these first two women, is introduced in *The Financier* in a way that suggests a scale in the richness and diversity of temperaments allotted humanity and the corresponding pleasures that humans pursue. Dreiser seems to follow what Keats called a pleasure thermometer in his delineation of temperament and pleasure: the richer the temperament, the greater the pleasure. His figures are tropic, seeking pleasure as certain flowers seek the light of the sun, only the hardiest and most luxuriant capable of enduring it for long periods of time. Frank is one of the latter. His interaction with the lesser figures provides both the complexity and the progress of the trilogy as he moves away from lesser figures and their associated pleasures to Berenice and her pleasures.[15] In the process he causes pain, but in *The Titan* he also achieves an awareness of the goal of life consonant with Dreiser's own vision.

The growth of Frank Cowperwood in the trilogy is measured by his successive attractions to the women in his life. Each woman possesses a temperament fated to pursue certain pleasures, and in her turn each offers a new and larger pleasure to Cowperwood.

The women, save for Berenice after her conversion, are incapable of further growth beyond the stage they have attained when first introduced. Frank's movement from one to the other is a measure of his own growth, his development from lower to higher pleasures. Hence he is the only dynamic figure in the trilogy. Through the first novel and most of the second, Cowperwood's temperament develops and grows as instinctively and unconsciously as the banyan tree to which he is later compared. The first stage of the growth is through Lilian, whose "beauty measured up to his present sense of the artistic" (38). As "a natural conservator of the public morals," Lilian reflects her commitment to public mores in her worry that she is five years older than Cowperwood at the time they marry and in her shame of "the passion that at times swept and dominated her" after their marriage (136). She finds her pleasure in social institutions, home, and family, and her compensation for pain in religion. *The Titan's* early pages portray her after Cowperwood has left her for Aileen, and she is still the conventional Lilian handling her problems in a conventional way: "There must be a God. The Bible said so. . . . God would punish her [Aileen], no doubt. He must. So she went to church on Sundays and tried to believe, come what might, that all was for the best" (T, 30).*

Although he never comprehended the "palaver about the sanctity of the home" prior to his marriage (F, 52), Cowperwood "liked . . . the idea of self-duplication," and his early years are comfortable enough to make him conclude, "There was a good deal to this home idea, after all. That was the way life was organized, and properly so—its cornerstone was the home" (F: 61, 62). But that is the way life is organized for Lilian Semple Cowperwood, not for Frank Cowperwood himself. The height of her development is the beginning of his, and its next stage is marked by his involvement with Aileen Butler.

Aileen is "innate sensuousness" (F, 87), "the best that nature can do when she attempts to produce physical perfection" (F, 89), an *"objet d'art"* (T, 36). Unlike Lilian, who is ashamed of her passion-

---

*Theodore Dreiser, *The Titan* (New York: John Lane, 1914). All references to *The Titan* will be from this edition. From this point on, I shall insert an F, T, or S before a page number to identify the reference as to *Financier, Titan,* or *Stoic.*

ate impulses, Aileen possesses the "solicitous attitude . . . more often the outstanding characteristic of the mistress": "It appears to be related to that last word in art, that largeness of spirit which is the first characteristic of the great picture, the great building, the great sculpture, the great decoration—namely, a giving, freely and without stint, of itself, of beauty" (F, 173).

The initial reasons for Cowperwood's attraction to Aileen are, therefore, clear enough. In taking up with her he ascends the pleasure thermometer by discovering an "innate sensuousness" uninhibited by social strictures. In addition, she offers him enduring love, although his is only temporary. In *The Titan* she learns that "the sweet illusion which had bound Cowperwood to her for a time had gone and would never come again" (T, 200-201). Despite her every effort to control her emotions, she is fated by temperament to continue loving him and hence to suffer from his affairs with other women. She thus becomes an object lesson that "an enduring state of pleasure for anything is not contemplated by Nature as an essential portion of the career of man," as Dreiser puts the matter elsewhere.[16] The meaning of Aileen's situation is simple enough to understand. The crucial question raised by *The Titan* is why Cowperwood can find no enduring pleasure in Aileen.

The answer can only be that, if the goal of life is pleasure, Aileen does not offer the highest kind of pleasure attainable by man; and the temperament of a superman demands no less. "Joy must be innate in energy itself,"[17] Dreiser writes in *Notes on Life,* and Frank Cowperwood is distinguished by his capacity for joy, in its highest human terms translated into an appreciation of beauty. In this regard, Aileen is as deficient as Lilian before her. Lilian thought that "Frank was a little peculiar" (F, 64) for liking art, and Aileen "knew nothing of literature except certain authors who to the truly cultured might seem banal. As for art, it was merely a jingle of names gathered from Cowperwood's private comments" (T, 36). And this deficiency of Aileen's is symptomatic of a larger inadequacy that drives the beauty-loving Cowperwood from her. Cowperwood wishes to live his life as though it were a work of art, but Aileen's social ineptitude makes this impossible. A woman who arranges her husband's art works in her home so as to draw the remark " 'Your house reminds me of an art exhibit to-day' " (T, 71) is a woman whose social ambitions are destined to fail, as Cowperwood well knows: "Life had taught him how fortuitous must be the circumstances which could enable a woman of Aileen's handicaps and defects to enter that cold upper world" (T, 387).

Because Aileen does not fully satisfy Cowperwood's aesthetic sense, his love for her dies. The development of this theme of Cowperwood as artist is what distinguishes *The Titan* from *The Financier.* It appears in the early work, of course, but it appears as a theme subordinate to the central interest, an answering of the question, "How is life organized?" His sexual responses in the first novel take on aesthetic values—Lilian's body reminds him of "a figure on an antique vase or out of a Greek chorus" (F, 46), and of course Aileen is an *objet d'art.* Too, his role as financier is equated with the role of the artist: "All the knowledge that pertained to that great art was as natural to him as the emotions and subtleties of life are to a poet" (F, 8). Finance satisfies his love of beauty: "Instead of dwelling on the works of nature . . . he found a happy mean . . . whereby he could . . . rejoice in the beauty of life without interfering with his perpetual material and financial calculations" (F, 134). And of course after developing an interest in wealth and "the beauty of women," he turns to "art, for art's sake": "To the beauty of womanhood he was beginning to see how necessary it was to add the beauty of life—the beauty of material background—how, in fact, the only background for great beauty was great art" (F, 162). It is this subordinate theme that becomes major in *The Titan* as the artist, Cowperwood, moves from an instinctive love of beauty to a self-conscious awareness that its apprehension is man's highest pleasure. In a world divorced from God, beauty substitutes for divine truth. It becomes the only truth man can know with joy.

After a brief introduction providing a necessary transition between two novels, Dreiser immediately introduces the motif of art and artist in *The Titan.* As Cowperwood nears Chicago by train, he sees "an artistic subtlety which touched him." In his eyes, "this raw, dirty town seemed naturally to compose itself into stirring pictures." Dreiser asks for a laureate to sing the praises of "this Florence of the West" (T, 3, 4, 6). His love for Aileen quickly waning, Cowperwood is attracted most to artists, women like Rita Sohlberg and, later, Berenice. "Of all individuals he respected, indeed revered, the sincere artist." In fact, the reader learns what is only suggested in *The Financier,* that "the spirit of art . . . occupied the center of Cowperwood's iron personality." He cannot share art with Aileen, but he can with Berenice, for it is their "one god in common" so that "his mind was fixed on things beautiful as on a shrine" (T, 382, 440, 442). Toward the end of the novel, he suddenly becomes aware of the true end of existence: "At last he saw clearly, as within a chalice-like nimbus, that the ultimate end of fame, power, vigor was beauty, and that beauty was a compound of the taste, the emotion, the innate culture, passion, and dreams of a woman like Berenice Fleming. That was it: that *was* IT. And beyond was nothing save crumbling age, darkness, silence" (T, 470).

Dreiser's naturalistic vision of Cowperwood, indeed, depends upon the theme that he is an artist and that the artist creates beauty as his highest pleasure. A passage from each of the first two novels can explain why. In *The Financier,* the reader is told that Cowperwood "admired nature, but somehow, without knowing why, he fancied one could best grasp it through the personality of some interpreter, just as we gain our ideas of law and politics through individuals" (F, 64). Why he prefers an artistic interpretation to the raw material can be inferred from his description in *The Titan.* There he is not simply a connoisseur of art but a practicing artist, one who is "relentless . . . in hewing life to his theory—hammering substance to the form of his thought" (T, 503).

Frank Cowperwood prefers the art work to the raw material that it interprets because in it, the artist puts "nature under foot" and "conforms things to his thoughts," to borrow some phrases from Emerson's *Nature* (1836). The result is congenial to Cowperwood's temperament because he does the same, though on a larger scale. As financier-artist his medium is not the canvas but society itself, and therefore he goes beyond the artist in the scope of his creativity, a fact that is perfectly natural for a superman. As superman he cannot be content to master a portion of his environment, but the whole. And, of course, as superman, his environment is human society, much as the lobster's, the squid's, and the black grouper's environment is the ocean. To master his environment he must become a financier, for only financial relationships give body and form to the whole of it. Hence he becomes one of that band of men who "grow until, like colossi, they bestride the world, or, like banyan-trees, they drop roots from every branch and are themselves a forest—a forest of intricate commercial life, of which a thousand material aspects are the evidence" (T, 472). Hence too the significance of the business aspect of the novel, Cowperwood's attempt to gain fifty-year franchises for his street railway lines. Newspaper criticism of him is in the spirit of the governor's view that the issue is "the ideals of one man and the ideals of men" (T, 485). The superman tries to hammer the substance of the whole, human society itself, to the form of his thought, and this emphasis in the novel successfully unites the themes of artist and financier whose unity some critics have called a failure.[18]

The theme of the financier as artist explains a passage in *The Stoic* describing Cowperwood's response to the beauties of nature on a pleasure trip in Scandinavia. He sees it as beautiful, and he admires the control exhibited by a skipper directing his whaling yacht through the waters, but he nonetheless finds that "the thing that impressed him most about this entire northern scene was the fact that it represented such a sharp and socially insignificant phase of a world that really had no need for any such temperament as his" (S, 223).* His artistic nature must have society for its material, for giving form to this medium is the greatest possible challenge to his aesthetic power. Nature can be left to lesser artists. And in another way he is superior to the conventional artist. He can maximize his pleasure in a way unavailable to other artists because he can live within the art work of his creation. Keats may wish to be drawn into the urn, but he can only do so imaginatively. Not so Cowperwood—by virtue of his humanity he can live within his medium. To do so with greatest pleasure, however, he must live there harmoniously. He must be in the foreground of

---

*Theodore Dreiser, *The Stoic* (New York: Doubleday, 1947). Subsequent references to *The Stoic* will be from this edition.

his picture, with society his backdrop, and only the proper woman can regulate his affairs so that together they live within the general harmony of the social picture.

In appearance "the true society woman, the high-born lady, the realization of that ideal" (T, 348) represented by the grandes dames whom Aileen could not equal, Berenice is also a connoisseur of art and, as dancer, sculptor, and painter, its practitioner. Hence she becomes his "pole-star" (T, 465), for Cowperwood recognizes her potential and his need. That potential is made explicit in *The Stoic*. In the second chapter, the reader learns that Berenice "desired not so much to express herself in a given form of art as to live so that her life as well as her personality should be in itself an art form" (S, 6-7). And Cowperwood knows her value in equally explicit terms, for he believes she can use "her independence and force . . . to achieve temperamental and social perfection" for them in London (S, 92).

The pursuit of this highest kind of pleasure, the beauty of life lived as art, makes Cowperwood a superman. Conventional artists may mimic his artistic skills, but they lack the force to try to hammer the substance of an entire society to their thought. Yet even the superman has his limitations, for Cowperwood loses his battle for the franchises in *The Titan*. Problems of the sort raised by his loss led Dreiser to explore another implication of determinism, introduced explicitly in the case of Aileen.

For Dreiser, Aileen poses the problem of what compensations for the pains of human existence are available within a deterministic system. In *The Titan*, he asks of her plight: "What shall life say to the loving when their love is no longer of any value, when all that has been placed on the altar of affection has been found to be a vain sacrifice? Philosophy? Give that to dolls to play with. Religion? Seek first the metaphysical-minded" (T, 185). For a person like Aileen, there clearly can be no compensations. She sees through an illusion, her belief that Cowperwood's love for her will endure, yet she is fated by temperament to suffer without compensation because of her enduring love for him. Frank Cowperwood also suffers—he fails in his effort to get his franchises— but he is luckier than Aileen, for his temperament permits him to find compensation in illusions of beauty; in art and in beautiful women.

Ultimately even Cowperwood's compensations fail to satisfy him, however, as *The Stoic* makes clear. To see why and thereby to understand the link between the emphasis on aesthetic experience in *The Titan* and the shift to the differing emphasis on ethical action in *The Stoic,* one must examine Dreiser's private meditations on the subject of compensation.

Central to these meditations is the concept of illusion.[19] Dreiser uses it in three basic ways. First, it is a belief at variance with the structure of reality. Religious belief is one example; Aileen's belief in enduring love another. He also uses it in reference to art, an illusion because a human creation, a fiction. As such, art is an illusion of an illusion, for Dreiser uses the word ontologically as well. Nature itself—man included—is an illusion because it is only the temporary garb of its wearer, a permanent and enduring energy called the creative power which expresses itself in the world of flux. And this concept, illusion, is intrinsic to the inherent grimness of Dreiser's views, just as it becomes the source of his ultimate salvation.

In his view, life is a matter of luck, one's sum total of pleasures and pains dictated by temperament and chance. Because man is trapped in that "material seeming . . . which . . . is itself an illusion" (F, 502), even the most miserable of men cannot take legitimate comfort from the ultimate compensation for pain when all else fails, a belief in God's goodness. This is so because for most of his career Dreiser insisted that, although the creative power manifests itself in the vale of illusion, its intentions (if any) remain forever unknowable. He saw this situation as one part of life's tragedy.

Not only is man separated from his ultimate source, but his situation is worsened in another way. Even in a godless world, ethical action has been traditionally viewed as the highest good. God may not reward men for the pursuit of ethical goals, but the knowledge that one has contributed to the betterment of others' lives helps to compensate for life's pains. But Dreiser's determinism denies that men can act freely in ethical fashion. His fated selves do only what they can, not what they ought. Describing man's double plight in this way in "The Essential Tragedy of Life," Dreiser exclaims, as well he might, "Herein lies the pathos."[20]

In fact, the inability to find compensation in God never disturbed Dreiser till the end of his life, but man's status as a will-less machine caused him pain. In his *Notes on Life,* Dreiser writes of Einstein: "He will begin by asserting that Free Will is a myth, and in the very same breath assert that man should abolish war. But without Free Will—how?"[21] His essential humanity desired an ethical view of life calling for purposive action for the betterment of the human condition, but his determinism denied his finding compensation for life's pains in ethical action; for such action could only be "ethical" if it were willed, and hence morally superior to other kinds of actions and their attendant compensations. In a world where no action is willed, none can be given ethical priority.

Robert Elias discovered this fact when he interviewed Dreiser. Working with Elias's notes, Swanberg wrote: "Elias found him likeable but illogical. If man was a will-less machine, what was the point in Dreiser's sociological activities and his insistence on the freedom of the individual?" But Dreiser's own determinism dissolves the contradiction: "About determinism and human helplessness, he said of course he was helpless personally and the efforts he made for social equity were not of his own volition but things that he had to do because the forces that moved him required him to."[22]

Trapped in a deterministic world, the man who recognizes that he cannot purposefully alter the world one whit or find any compensations beyond those fated him might well become a pessimist. But despite strong streaks of pessimism, Dreiser's nature was essentially optimistic. His determinism denied man the ability to act purposefully, just as it denied him the knowledge of transcendent meaning and purpose. But his naturalism declared that laws of nature were accessible for all to see and verify, and so Dreiser finds philosophic compensation in the unalterable operations of what he sees as the primary law governing the system of illusions called nature, the equation inevitable.[23] He gives it expression in the conclusion to *The Titan,* and his senti-

ments imply not just an acceptance but an affirmation of Cowperwood's disappointing failure to get his franchises, an affirmation
growing from an acceptance of a larger need, the need to sustain a
universal balance:

> At the ultimate remove, God or the life force, if anything, is
> an equation, and at its nearest expression for man—the
> contract social—it is that also. Its method of expression
> appears to be that of generating the individual, in all his
> glittering variety and scope, and through him progressing
> to the mass with its problems. In the end a balance is
> invariably struck wherein the mass subdues the individual
> or the individual the mass—for the time being. (T, 550-51)

A law that operates to balance opposites is a logical adjunct to
Dreiser's view of life as a game. If the essence of life is contest,
then life necessarily possesses two basic features. First, it must
have opposites. In the game of life, there can be no winner
without a loser, and hence no joy without pain. Lilian must suffer
for Aileen's good, Aileen for Cowperwood's, and Cowperwood
for society's. Its second feature is that life must always remain in
an unstable equilibrium. No victory can ever be so complete that
the contest is permanently ended; for if the game were over,
existence itself could not be. Instead, man would enter the stable
equilibrium of what Dreiser refers to in *The Titan* as "Nirvana!
Nirvana! The ultimate, still, equation" (T, 551). Life as contest
resists Nirvana and demands instability. As he describes it in his
conclusion, "For, behold, the sea is ever dancing or raging"
(T, 551).

The equation inevitable, therefore, is the principle within the
game that guarantees its continuation by prohibiting any victory
so complete as to end all contest. It is the law that describes the
actual operations of all elements in nature, and even illusions, in
the sense of mistaken beliefs, function accordingly. Moral views
may falsely assume in man a freedom he does not possess, but
their application to Cowperwood in the newspapers and the
courts restores the balance between the individual and the mass.
Dreiser makes this point clear, too, in his conclusion: "In the
meantime there have sprung up social words and phrases express-

ing a need of balance—of equation. These are right, justice, truth, morality, an honest mind, a pure heart—all words meaning: a balance must be struck. The strong must not be too strong; the weak not too weak. But without variation how could the balance be maintained?" (T, 551).

Without joy *and* pain, joy could not be; ultimately, existence could not be. The law is so central to his thought that in his *Notes on Life* he invests it with religious authority: "So, if there is no god, no surveying and controlling intelligence, there is yet this universal balancing and proportioning of positive against negative, or what may seem good to one against what may seem evil to it and vice versa."[24]

One can now see that Dreiser finds compensation for the pains of human existence in the larger natural process itself. Life for life's sake! he in effect exclaims, and affirms for both pain and joy. In his essay of the same name, he makes it crystal clear that the equation inevitable is his compensation, and he uses language that shows his kinship to Cowperwood:

> In truth, somewhere in the scheme of things is implanted a love of beauty and order as well as their contraries, which can only find expression via equation, and this it is, chemical, inherent awareness of it no doubt, which eases the ache of existence for us all (God, man, devil). For if life loves change, movement, difference, contest, it also plainly loves their contraries, for these exist, and we could not know the one without the other.[25]

Such sentiments, of course, place Dreiser in league with the artist, Frank Cowperwood. Dreiser affirms the importance of oppositions in life for the sake of life itself; and Cowperwood's valuing the harmony of opposites in art thus translates Dreiser's philosophic view into aesthetic terms, for Cowperwood's zest for art is one expression of his zest for life. In addition, his zest for love and finance, for life as lived as opposed to life as interpreted as art, carries Dreiser's philosophic vision into the story on the level of concrete action. Without experiencing and causing pain, Cowperwood cannot have the highest kind of pleasure. He thus is a clear illustration of Dreiser's own philosophic commitment, and

Dreiser seems to have him in mind when he writes in "The Equation Inevitable":

> Art, the love of life for itself, is nothing more than a synthesis of many equations whereby many lovely harmonies and their opposites are expressed or implied. Hunger, balanced against satiation, creates more beauty. Life builds and wills far beyond the ken of man or his companion animals, and all that he can know is the chemic thrill of life, its joys, the necessity of equation and so-called fair play, or rhythm and balance. For, behold, life is ever dancing and does not will to be still.[26]

Dreiser's thought in his essays and his *Notes on Life* thus shows that he was forced to confront what William James called the dilemma of determinism, a dilemma, according to James, "whose left horn is pessimism and whose right horn is subjectivism."[27] Dreiser yearned for an ethical view of life in his role as social crusader, but his determinism forced him to the verge of pessimism on this score, for individuals were trapped by their fated selves and could only do what they could, not what they ought. If men could not through freely willed conduct make a world with abundant evils a better place to live, then Dreiser had to find a way to make such a world reasonably habitable, if he was to avoid pessimism.

His response to the problem closely follows the pattern James observes in "The Dilemma of Determinism," a fact that testifies to the philosophical rigor of Dreiser's mind. If men do *seeming* evil (moral judgment is irrelevant to Dreiser's hard determinism), they also do *seeming* good; and the existence of the good is dependent on that of the evil. "For, behold, the sea is ever dancing or raging." But the determinist is still left with what James calls "the judgment of regret."[28] If good cannot exist without evil, why regret the existence of the evil? Dreiser's judgment of regret is not pronounced in *The Titan*, but he clearly does regret Aileen's suffering, if not Lilian's, and he seems to include even her in his compassion in the novel's conclusion when he intones the consequences of Cowperwood's behavior: "The lives of two women wrecked, a score of victims despoiled" (T, 552). In a determined world, the judgment of regret is itself necessitated, but it is also philosophically erroneous. Since evil is the necessary condition for good, one ought not to regret the evil.

In handling his judgment of regret, Dreiser adopts that very subjectivism which James declares is the only alternative to pessimism for the determinist intent on making his world reasonably habitable.[29] The regret may be philosophically wrong, for the seeming evil was unavoidable and has a positive role to play— Cowperwood is "caught at last by the drug of a personality he could not gainsay" (T, 552)—yet the regret itself emphasizes to its holder how precious is that which has been destroyed. Without the regret, one could never know the qualitative value of love.

In the conclusion to the novel, Dreiser does not speak in direct terms about the value the existence of evil has for heightening consciousness, nor does he mention Aileen by name, yet surely the novel's closing words contain this view and pertain to Aileen, among others: "In a mulch of darkness is [*sic*] bedded the roots of endless sorrows—and of endless joys. Canst thou fix thine eye on the morning? Be glad. And if in the ultimate it blind thee, be glad also! Thou hast lived" (T, 552). There are several meanings in this passage which, taken together, reveal Dreiser's subjectivism. The mulch of darkness sprouts both joys and sorrows, and Aileen experiences both, for she has metaphorically seen the light and been blinded by it. The proper response of the determinist celebrating the equation inevitable is to rejoice, for the blindness has its utility. As Dreiser notes in "The Necessity for Contrast" (*Notes on Life*), "Life . . . must have both ignorance and wisdom, good and evil, morality and immorality . . . for it to function at all as the thing we call life." Without the blindness, light could not be. And blindness has a further utility, for it serves the purpose of knowledge. In the same section of his *Notes,* he writes, "We are only aware of heat because of the possibility of contrasting it with cold, light because of darkness, and so on." Finally, without contrast, value cannot be, for one can only value one moment over another through contrast: "The things that count to any man . . . are the contrasts of this moment . . . his past moment and his next one."[30] Rejoice in the blindness, in other words, for it makes one appreciate the light. The passage's utilitarian levels of meaning thus compound the subjectivism of the last, the value of blindness. For if the darkness is indispensable to the existence of the light, one must value it as well as its opposite.

But even in the trilogy, finally, the subjectivist solution to the dilemma of determinism did not satisfy. James complained that it ultimately led to aestheticism and decadence.[31] In *The Stoic,* Dreiser felt that it led to a restlessness born of an utter loss of meaning in life. He had certainly touched on the problem in his *Notes on Life,* in that part called "The Problem of Progress and Purpose." Commenting that "you, and almost every other person in life, will agree that life without a purpose is meaningless,"[32] he concludes: "But see how this works out. Your non self-evoked, non self-created purpose or desire, a thing not originated by you but forced upon you by life, proves very often (not always) a delusion, sometimes a trap, which does for you completely."[33]

In *The Stoic,* Frank Cowperwood illustrates the kind of trap that ensnares man when his purpose in life is preordained rather than freely chosen. That very purpose which is supposed to give life meaning becomes, under this condition, the factor denying it meaning. Judging by what appears in *The Stoic* and is absent from the earlier novels in the trilogy—a concern with endowing life with meaning proceeding from ethical conduct in a deterministic world—one can fairly say that Dreiser's other self, the social crusader, at last demanded a union with the determinist that would not sacrifice the crusader's own autonomy.

The Stoic

The lives of Dreiser's characters can have no meaning because their selves are fated. Because this statement seems at variance with the obvious relish for life displayed by Cowperwood in the first two novels of the trilogy, some further explanation is needed. If one thinks of life as having meaning in some cosmic sense, then it is clear that from Dreiser's point of view, his characters do not possess such meaning, because it can be derived only from knowing and following divine mandates, to which they have no access. For most of his career Dreiser declared that man cannot even know whether or not the creative power is intelligent or purposive, much less know of its possible design; so characters who think life has cosmic meaning are deluded. Frank Cowperwood is not one of them. He recognizes the cosmic meaninglessness of his life, fleetingly in *The Financier,* more forcefully in *The Titan.* In the first novel, he gazes at the stars after his imprisonment, thinking "of the earth floating like a little ball in immeasurable reaches of ether," which made "his own life [appear] very trivial" (F, 468). This theme is resumed in *The Titan.* As Cowperwood watches Berenice stroke a fledgling sparrow, the thought comes to him "with great force, how comparatively unimportant in the great drift of life were his own affairs when about him was operative all this splendid will to existence" (T, 393). And in *The Stoic,* this sense of his triviality is translated into the problem of life's meaning, Cowperwood's central problem in that volume. After Cowperwood learns of his imminent death and sails for America, Dreiser tells the reader that "once on the boat, Cowperwood felt alone, spiritually alone, at last admitting to himself that neither he nor any man knew anything about life or its Creator" (S, 247).

This is a sad conclusion to Cowperwood's career, for it is reasonable to assume that he was now aching for some cosmic justification for his existence. Earlier in the novel, at Canterbury Cathedral with Berenice, he envies what he thinks of as her youthful ability "to be so thrilled, to be so deeply moved by color, form, the mystery and meaninglessness of human activity!" (S, 138). Presumably he has lost just enough of his relish for life to require some larger justification for his existence, and this view is borne out by Berenice's concluding thought about Cowperwood, "that his worship and constant search for beauty in every form, and especially in the form of a woman, was nothing more than a search for the Divine design behind all forms" (S, 305).

But there is a second sense in which life can have meaning, what Paul Edwards calls the terrestrial sense. From this angle of vision, the principal thoughts and actions that constitute a person's life become meaningful if they are united into a purposeful pattern and inspire the individual with that satisfaction commonly associated with purposeful action. As Edwards makes clear, a life need not have cosmic meaning in order to have terrestrial meaning; but as he also makes clear, no life can be viewed as possessing legitimate meaning of either kind without freedom.[34]

Cowperwood may be a superman, but he shares the common lot of Dreiser's characters insofar as his life cannot be considered meaningful in even a terrestrial sense. He has a goal, and he pursues it with vigor; but both the goal and the means for its pursuit (means that dictate the nature of the goal) are functions of his fated self. Dreiser's earlier quoted comment on "non self-evoked, non self-created purpose" confirms this fact; and, indeed, he calls all goals and purposes illusions precisely for this reason. They exist simply to assure the continuity of the game that is the life process.

If the lives of Dreiser's characters must be seen as meaningless when observed from without, this fact need not cause them personal distress so long as they are unaware of their enslavement. Or, even if aware, they might like Dreiser take refuge in beauty, affirm that life is, or can be, worthwhile, if not meaningful. In *The Stoic,* Cowperwood becomes aware of his own position and follows the latter route. But Dreiser no longer felt the subjectivist solution to the dilemma of determinism satisfying, for how else explain the novel's conclusion, Berenice's repudiation of a life of pleasure and beauty in order to work for the betterment of the lot of the poor! Dreiser finally demanded meaning from life, meaning to be found in ethical action, and he prepares for this view in his portrayal of Cowperwood.

That the problem of meaning becomes urgent for Cowperwood in *The Stoic* has already been noted, but not the way in which the problem is thrust on him. The specific terms that the problem takes are of special interest. In his life with Berenice, Cowperwood has achieved as much of the beauty of life as circumstance permits (Aileen refuses him a divorce), yet he must continue to pursue his business life as a financier. He is caught in a vicious circle, experiencing the pleasure of the achieved goal of a financier, beauty, while forced to play a game whose end has already been achieved. This conception of Cowperwood dominates the novel throughout, right through the moment when, knowing he is going to die, he reflects on his entire past life.

Early in the novel, he shows that he is dimly aware of his predicament and dissatisfied with it. Before they leave Chicago for London, where he will resume his financial operations, Cowperwood tells Berenice: " 'What I would prefer to do . . . now that I have you, would be to loaf and travel with you, for a time, anyhow. I've worked hard enough. You mean more than money to me, infinitely more. It's odd, but I feel all at once as though I've worked too hard all my life.' " Berenice's reply: " 'You've been like some big engine or machine that's tearing full speed somewhere, but doesn't know exactly where' " (S, 11).

Her comment is significant because it reveals the true position of the fated self in a determined world, and Cowperwood becomes more clearly aware of this when he expresses amazement to DeSota Sippens, another successful businessman, that "we can get so excited over it"—that is, the pursuit of financial affairs—when "neither of us can do much more than eat a little, drink a little, play about a little while longer" (S, 113). Sippens replies as though he were Dreiser himself: " 'I look on it all as some sort of a game that I'm here to play. . . . And I guess that's the answer: to be doing something all the time. There's a game on, and whether we like it or not, we have to play our parts' " (S, 113–114).

Frank Cowperwood still experiences pleasure, but even the experience of it is fated, and this knowledge blunts the pleasure and emphasizes the problem. He wonders again about his financial dealings: "But now, here he was. And what was it all about? What was he to get out of it, other than the pleasure with Berenice, which, had she willed it otherwise, he might have found in a more peaceful way" (S, 154). If one's fate is a happy one, one can value life for its own sake, call life worthwhile, but one cannot quite escape the anguish that is the common lot when one learns the meaninglessness of existence. Cowperwood's reflections after he learns of his impending death bear out the truth of this observation. He reviews his life—"the men, in the main so helpful, the women so entertaining." He thinks of "this lovely hour with Berenice, here by the Thames, and this pleasant lawn that spread before them." And he feels "the fleeting beauty of life and its haunting poignancy." The very thought of death "had a tendency to emphasize the value of all he had been and enjoyed."

Yet such comfort is small; for "he could only consider the poetic value of this hour, and its fleetingness, which involved sorrow and nothing but sorrow" (S, 230). *The Stoic* thus fulfills the concluding prophecy of *The Financier:* "Sorrow, sorrow, sorrow." Death, the ultimate pole of a polarity without which existence cannot be, enhances the poetic value of the hour; but if the beauty is there and felt, so is the meaninglessness. Subjectivism is not enough.

It would be bad manners to pursue what has already been acknowledged, the weak literary quality of the later part of an action that Dreiser was fleshing out even on the day before his death. This is a matter which was beyond his control. But the framework *is* there, and one can explain its logic.

The problem of the fated self is central to this framework, as it is to the trilogy at large. Man must have freedom if he is to achieve significant meaning of any kind in life, but he can obtain freedom only by escaping the fated self. Short of renouncing his determinism (and Dreiser never did),[35] no such escape seemed possible. But a way out of his dilemma opened in Dreiser's last years as his view of the creative power changed. Earlier he thought its character unknowable, for all man could know is its expression in nature; but late in life he saw greater implications in such knowledge. Adopting an Aristotelian approach to nature, he played a variation on the Thomist theme for proof of the existence of an intelligent God: "I see motion; I infer a mover." Dreiser in effect said, I see artistry, so there must be an artist intelligent enough to create the design. Elias notes that the intelligence of the artist did not immediately suggest that the power was good,[36] but even on this point Dreiser relented. His own sense of unity with nature became sufficient evidence "that the unity of the creative force must be good and that there was involved with it a kind of love."[37]

Elias records the shift to account for the aged Dreiser's exalted view of man: "As *a part of* nature he and his will were tinctured by the aesthetic color and swept up in the universal grandeur of the vast and amazing scheme before the idea of which one could only stand in reverent gratefulness for being alive."[38] But in *The Stoic,* a further implication to Dreiser's changed view of the creative power appears. Even as *a part of* nature, man can escape from his fated self, and Dreiser could now see this other implication in man's unity with nature. As a part of nature man must possess some part of the power that manifests itself in every single aspect of nature. And that part which he possesses must be consistent with those attributes distinguishing him from other creatures in the animal world; for each of the multiple aspects of creative power expresses itself by creating unique things and unique species in nature. In the animal world, man is distinguished by his higher intelligence and by his awareness of concepts like choice and freedom, though his fated self cannot freely exercise that intelligence to make free choices in a vale of illusion. Therefore that part of the power which he possesses must have something to do with the core of his uniqueness, his intelligence and his very awareness of the freedom resident in power itself—must indeed be part of its intelligence and freedom. And that part constitutes a second self whose status is other than the fated one's—that very self, in short, which Emerson celebrates in *Self-Reliance*.

Indeed, such thinking logically proceeds from Dreiser's earlier thoughts on the self. Individuality, he had declared, was a myth. One man could never know another, much less himself, because he cannot know "the forces which are making and operating or driving us and which same we do not even know ourselves."[39] These forces are reducible to mechanical stimuli in the natural world to which the mechanism called man reacts. A true self, Dreiser thus suggested, could only be an autonomous one. When he reached the point where he could distinguish between the self fated by forces created by the creative power and the self that participates in that power's freedom, the question became, How activate that second self?

He must have thought of the possibilities inherent in Cowperwood's sense of his own triviality in *The Financier* and *The Titan*, for in *The Stoic* he links Cowperwood's sense of personal triviality to the problem of meaning and freedom, and through Berenice he makes a recognition of one's personal triviality a precondition for escaping the fated self. Only by recognizing that self's triviality can one see that its existence is a myth, an illusion, and by so much is one liberated from it and the illusions that it pursues.

But there is a second condition to be fulfilled before true selfhood can be attained. One must recognize that one is a part of nature and learn those other implications of this recognition already spelled out, that men possess part of the power of the creative spirit. In *The Titan* Berenice already possesses the feeling of unity with nature that Cowperwood never achieves. As she strokes a fledgling sparrow whose mother stands by, watching, Cowperwood notes that the "splendid will to existence" in nature that inspires his own sense of triviality is not only "sensed by her," but that she feels a part of it. "It was not so much bird-love as the artistry of life and of herself that was moving her" (T, 393). When he asks how she knows the bird's mother feels no fear for its offspring, she replies, " 'Do you think the senses of the world are only five?' " (T, 394), showing by her response that she has an extra sense linking her to the natural world. She stands in contrast to the Cowperwood of *The Stoic*, who feels out of place in nature on a boating trip to Scandinavia; and she therefore is the likely candidate for attaining true selfhood in the conclusion to the trilogy.

She does so through Brahmanism. Although Dreiser came to respect all religious forms as possible avenues to reaching the creative spirit, not all would do for the trilogy. In a work exploring the ramifications of determinism, Brahmanism was the logical choice, because it permitted him at the same time to retain his determinism (he never abandoned the doctrine) and to transcend it in a world view much like the one he had held all along. For both views, the earthly realm, the realm of nature, is a realm of illusion and enslavement. If Dreiser's sense of enslavement does not come from selves fated to be reborn in an eternal cycle of reincarnation, it does come from selves fated to follow the illusions of nature so long as they remain alive.

Hindus do find freedom from the vale of illusion, however, and they do so through the discovery that they have personal access to the realm of Brahman;[40] through the discovery, that is, that the core of the self is in fact Brahman. Dreiser could draw on this view in *The Stoic* because, as discussed earlier, his view of the creative spirit had changed. He was now in a position to respond to the demand for meaning that had gradually emerged in the determined world of the trilogy. By permitting Berenice both escape from the illusion called individuality and access to the insight and freedom of a self that is part of Brahman, Dreiser provides the freedom without which meaning cannot exist while retaining the vale of illusion that is the world of determinism in which most people live.

In his portrayal of Berenice after Cowperwood's death, Dreiser keeps his focus sharply on the problem of the fated self, to show that it is the central problem of his trilogy and of his mechanistic philosophy. Before Berenice picks up her copy of the *Bhagavad-Gita*, she is troubled by a critical article that "tended to single her out as an opportunist" in her relations with Cowperwood, a view violating her self-image. "For as she saw herself . . . she was wholly concerned with the beauty of life." The passage recalls Dreiser's view that one individual can never really know another, for individuality is a myth. But if her public image is not her true self, neither can her self-image be. She does not utter such a thought directly; but the passage from the *Bhagavad-Gita* that she reads immediately after the offensive newpaper article speaks for her adequately enough. It begins: "Part of myself is the God within every creature" (S, 275).

When Berenice wishes to escape the scenes of her life with Cowperwood, she has a strong practical reason to do so—bad publicity; but Dreiser fashions the terms of that need so as to anticipate the solution to the central problem of the trilogy. After she decides to go to India, she reveals one of the factors in her decision. She recalls that Dr. James, Cowperwood's physician, advised some of his patients to visit a Hindu Swami to relieve their physical and mental distress: "For, as he had noted, there was something about the limited thought of the self that was lost in the larger thought of the not self that brought about forgetfulness of self in the nervous person, and so health" (S, 277).

The dichotomy between self and "not self" thus sets the terms for Berenice's release from the bondage of her fated self. In India she learns the two conditions essential for escape. The first is a lesson in nonattachment, a concept stressed several times by her guru (S, 290-291). Such a lesson is equivalent to a lesson in the triviality of the self fated to pursue nature's illusions, and hence a lesson in its own illusory nature. Thereafter she learns the falseness of the "idea of separateness" (S, 295), for her guru asks, "Is not the whole universe yourself?" (S, 297).

This discovery is of great importance. Her acknowledgment of her oneness with the universe is equivalent to an acknowledgment that she is part of nature and yet, paradoxically, free from the illusion of nature and the self that is a part of it. For Brahman is in all of nature, and so her sense of unity with it allows her to discover the truth of that line from the *Bhagavad-Gita,* "Part of myself is the God within every creature." Hence she is in a position to renounce that self which "worshipped beauty in all its forms" and so was beauty's slave. Thereafter she achieves her true identity with its "pure knowledge" and "perfect freedom" promised her by an earlier reading of the *Bhagavad-Gita.* She can thus return to the determined world of fated selves as a free soul.

In this way Berenice becomes the true stoic in this novel, though Cowperwood's centrality in the trilogy would suggest otherwise. Yet Cowperwood is only superficially a stoic, for he fits the commonplace meaning of that word, one who is indifferent to life's pains and joys. Cowperwood's lot has been mainly one of joys but, in the end, though he still experiences pleasure, he must remain philosophically indifferent even to his joys, because they provide his life merely with poetic value, not with meaning. His restlessness indicates that he endures pleasure much as others endure pain, while Berenice becomes the stoic in a more precise sense of that word. In her subsequent life working for the poor, she becomes stoical in the ethical sense that she "does not shrink from doing what is disagreeable," nor does she "long to do what is agreeable" (S, 191), so long as she can translate her divine illumination into concrete ethical action.

Berenice's need to translate divine wisdom into ethical action shows an Emersonian view of religion. In his poem "The Problem," Emerson states his respect for the churchman but stoutly maintains: "Yet not for all his faith can see/Would I that cowled churchman be." There is more than one way to contact God, just as there is more than one way of utilizing the freedom and truth that such contact brings. If one religious form does bring divine illumination, furthermore, what remains important is the illumination, not an unswerving loyalty to the form that provided it. Emerson wore out Unitarianism to go his own way, and there is every evidence that Berenice uses Brahmanism to achieve freedom without feeling any necessity to remain bound to the essential concern of the Brahman, the experience of divine illumination and emancipation from self.[41] Her reflections on India reveal her puzzlement that "a country could have evolved such a noble and profoundly religious philosophy of life and yet, at the same time, have evoked and maintained such a low, cruel, and oppressive social system" (S, 300), and thereby show how American a Brahman she is. That puzzlement also shows that through her Dreiser uses Brahmanism to reconcile what he for so long thought was irreconcilable: his humanitarianism and his determinism. If Berenice had to achieve cosmic meaning in order to gain the terrestrial meaning in life that impels her to work for the poor in New York City, it is clear which level of meaning she finds primary. For her, as for Dreiser, the cosmic is but the condition to gain that freedom without which life could not have a level of meaning that becomes indispensable: the terrestrial.

In viewing Dreiser's development into an American Brahman, one can best recall the truth of William James's comment on the dilemma of determinism. "Remark how inevitably the question of determinism and indeterminism slides us into the question of optimism and pessimism, or, as our fathers called it, 'the question of evil.' The theological form of all these disputes is the simplest and the deepest, the form from which there is the least escape."[42] At the last, "the question of evil" became too much even for the committed determinist. If Dreiser did not seek refuge in the faith of his fathers, the Catholicism of his youth, in his own way he returned to "the simplest and the deepest . . . form from which there is the least escape." But he could never have made his way even this far without finding freedom in a second self. Still, had he not found it, his lot would not have been quite so bad: he would have had aesthetic vision as compensation. Dos Passos could not find even this much comfort when he pointed to the vacuum within society's self.

FIVE

Dos Passos
and Society's Self:
Manhattan Transfer

Dreiser explored well the problems of the fated self aware of its condition, aware especially that it could experience no sense of meaning, whether of a cosmic or a more limited terrestrial kind. That self, like all the selves that comprise society, was a part of the continuum of nature and, as such, but an expression of the creative spirit controlling all of nature. But if nature was man's cross for Dreiser, it also became for him man's salvation; for by recognizing one's connections with nature one could find within the personality another self that shared the energy and intelligence of the spirit. His work thereby points to another view of nature in American literary naturalism, one far more benign than those views of it appearing in "The Blue Hotel," *The Red Badge of Courage,* or *McTeague.* Society may still be a part of the continuum of nature, but society now becomes more destructive to the individual than nonhuman nature.

That shift appears strikingly in the pages of *Manhattan Transfer,* where Dos Passos portrays various forms of alienation (the most important of which is self-alienation) and traces its cause to the social organization to which industrial capitalism gives rise.[1] No Marxist, he does nonetheless embrace an economic determinism that operates in the novel within the matrix of the dynamic progress of a capitalist economy.[2] Prominent references to this progress order the three parts of the novel. Early in the work a real estate agent boasts that "we are caught up . . . on a great wave whether we will or no, a great wave of expansion and progress," and his touting New York as the "second city in the world" (15) echoes what a headline announces at the beginning of the chapter.* References to the beginning of World War I punctuate the second section, and there Martin Schiff protests the effects of growing economic consolidation: "But good God hasnt a man some rights? No, this industrial civilization forces us to seek a complete readjustment of government and social life (263). Individual protest is, of course, to no avail, and in the third section Dentsch, a businessman, proudly but cautiously announces the completion of a process in which the center of economic exchanges passes from London to New York. " 'America . . . is in the position of taking over the receivership of the world. The great principles of democracy, of that commercial freedom upon which our whole civilization depends are more than ever at stake' " (288).

Against this background the novel reveals one form of its economic determinism, the effects produced by a capitalistic economy, appropriately represented by the stock market, on the lives of nations, institutions, and individuals. On the international level, it alienates nation from nation by fostering warfare, as several references testify. Joe Harland, the former wizard of Wall Street, advises the labor organizer Joe O'Keefe that America will enter the war on England's side, O'Keefe's Irish hostility to England notwithstanding: "You follow the stock quotations and . . . don't let em fool you with all this newspaper talk about strikes and upheavals and socialism" (238). That is, the stock exchange, not the threat of socialism or social upheaval, will determine those countries with which America will choose to ally itself and those from which America will alienate itself. And Congo Jake asserts that the war is fought "so that workingmen all over wont make big revolution. . . . Too busy fighting. So Guillaume and Viviani and l'Empereur d'Autriche and Krupp and Rothschild and Morgan they say let's have a war" (227). The point of view reflects Dos Passos's own feelings at the time. As he recalled them later: "Capitalism was the sin that had caused the war; only the working class was free from crime."[3]

*John Dos Passos, *Manhattan Transfer* (Boston: Houghton Mifflin, 1925 and [Sentry Edition] 1953). The page numbers in my text also apply to two other editions: Harper and Brothers (New York, 1925) and Grosset & Dunlap (New York, 1925).

If the stock exchange decrees that nations alienate themselves from others through warfare, it is logical that it should ordain groups within such nations to follow suit. In its position at "the center of things," a phrase used frequently in the novel, it by its very nature generates widespread social strife, for action in its service demands manipulation and exploitation, as the narrative makes clear through its portrayal of a pattern of social warfare. Joe Harland illustrates the connection between the economic structure and two major groups alienated from each other, business and labor. Reduced to the level of a night watchman for a contracting firm, the former Wizard of Wall Street reads a headline mentioning such conflict: "CONTRAC- TORS PLAN LOCKOUT TO ANSWER BUILDERS' STRIKE." Juxtaposed to the headline is his momentary reverie of his past in which he "saw himself in a dress-suit wearing a top hat with an orchid in his buttonhole" (190). The former exploiter is now one of the exploited, and surely his memory of a past social self recalls the demand on that self to extract maximum advantage from "the bears" when he played "bull," to use the parlance of the stock market. Lest he forget, Gus McNeil drives home the character of the economic system as it reflects itself in business–labor relations when he asserts that in a time of financial panic caused by war, the contractors have the upper hand: "I'll tell you one thing though the lockout is a wonderful thing for the contractors. Wont be no housebuildin with a war on anyway" (225).

Even legitimate contest in the political arena becomes a function of the economic center. The association between the two realms is expressed through the complex relations between Dentsch and Blackhead, business importers, on the one hand, and on the other by Gus McNeil, the representative of Tammany Hall, and by a lawyer- turned-politician, George Baldwin, who decides to run for office on a spurious Reform ticket. In his appeal to Baldwin to run for office, Dentsch links the two realms by identifying "the great principles of democracy" with "that commercial freedom upon which our whole civilization depends" (288). The political contest thus becomes an economic one, each corrupt party vying for influence to gain the big money and thus to satisfy the financial ambitions of its member politicians. In this regard, the political contest mimics the war be- tween the bootleggers and the hijackers. The shady dealings of the political arena thereby merge with the franker contest for the same end between groups legally alienated from a "respectable" social world that demands their services during Prohibition.

That the economic system fosters not just group alienation but alienation of individuals from each other is so obvious as to need little further commentary. As children Jimmy Herf and his cousin Maisie play "stock exchange," a game of the bulls and the bears. When Maisie bids too high for a stock, her cousin calls her a fool and draws this reprimand from her: "Don't you know that God says in the Bible that if you call anybody Thou fool you'll be in danger of hellfire?" (107). Her question misses several points. In his own way Jimmy has been moral because helpful, but to be helpful in this game is to advise individuals how to take competitive actions that will indeed alienate them from others, for this game is indifferent to moral concerns. And this game writ large will later alienate him not only from the social structure but also from those relatives of his who represent it, his uncle and his other cousin, who derides him as a dreamer and hence a failure. Ironically, in war, itself caused by the stock exchange, he is drawn together with Ellen in marriage because presumably the war gives them a common, if temporary, ideal, the protection of democracy. But in peacetime the true character of that democracy emerges as one that encourages alienation of individuals from each other. Ellen dissolves their marriage so that she can pursue her own career without the burden of a husband-reporter who cannot make the money she desires.

The influence of the economic structure on society does not necessarily argue for a philosophic determinism that denies the existence of man's faculty of free will. Rather, it seems to argue only for the existence of what Sartre once referred to as "statistical determinism." In the days when he regarded Dos Passos "as the greatest writer of our time," he wrote of *1919*:

> We get a glimpse of an order beyond the accidents of fate or the contingency of detail, an order more supple than Zola's physiological necessity or Proust's psychological mechanism, a soft and insinuating constraint which seems to release its victims, letting them go only to take possession of them again without their suspecting, in other words, a statistical determinism.

These men, submerged in their own existences, live as they can. They struggle; what comes their way is not determined in advance. And yet, neither their efforts, their faults, nor their most extreme violence can interfere with the regularity of births, marriages and suicides. The pressure exerted by a gas on the walls of its container does not depend upon the individual histories of the molecules composing it.[4]

One can adapt this view to the relation between the economic structure and individuals within it as portrayed in *Manhattan Transfer*. The economic structure creates the conditions that will assure, from a statistical point of view, the alienation of individuals and groups. From this point of view, large numbers of individuals in such a society will join groups that will compete with and alienate each other, just as large numbers of single individuals will alienate other individuals. The statistical view thus allows one to see the shape and character of society as determined even while permitting the existence of individual freedom. Elmer, Anna Cohen's Communist boyfriend, best describes that shape and character when he exclaims, "Cant you see we're in the middle of a battle just like in the war?" (331).

One can see other ways in which this view orders the novel. Still accepting the notion that these characters possess free will, one can see that the economic structure possesses a dynamic that makes it the agent alienating individuals from itself, even those who wish to be a part of it. The factor called chance on which the system rests decrees that some individuals must be losers in the game of stock exchange. Chance exists because the stock market's operations embrace a far-flung network of domestic and international factors beyond the control of individuals, groups, and nations. It is a self-regulating mechanism that makes individuals feel like passive pawns.

The novel contains several references to chance, but the most instructive one in the present context is Joe Harland's remarks on it. He attributes his past good fortune to wearing a special necktie, his impoverishment to his loss of it. Hence he is reduced by chance to a statistic, another business failure in the world of Wall Street. So, too, is the apparently contented Dentsch, who seems to be content with the system but nonetheless loses his importing business in an economic slump. Bud Korpenning is also such a statistic, in life as well as in death. The moment before his suicide, this refugee from rural upstate New York, who never manages to rise much above the level of a tramp, fantasizes himself as a prosperous part of the system, richly dressed and driving to his wedding ceremony at "the center of things" in a magnificantly turned-out carriage. He thus shows his emotional commitment to that system's values even as he is about to become one of its casualties, another statistic measuring the suicide rate among the individuals for whom the system has no role. For it decrees the existence of a faceless mass, a lumpenproletariat, many needles in the haystack (Bud refers to himself as one of them), since it cannot accommodate full employment and a decent life for all. Chance and circumstance dictate who shall be a member of this group, and who even as such a member will be able to survive its awful anonymity.

This motif of the indifference of the system to individual want or individual need is important because it points to the essence of Dos Passos's naturalism. From a statistical point of view one might harmonize determinism and freedom in *Manhattan Transfer*. But in presenting the most essential form of alienation, Dos Passos creates a harmony between freedom and determinism that is specious, because freedom of choice becomes thoroughly meaningless. For all figures must experience alienation from the self through the agency of society as the price for engagement in society in any way and on any level. Herf's experience illustrates the terms of man's predicament. To develop selfhood one traditionally became sufficiently engaged in society to translate the self into the social world, but the effort now leads to alienation from self. To escape from this situation Herf exercises the only freedom available to man by choosing between "one of two unalienable alternatives: go away in a dirty soft shirt or stay in a clean Arrow collar" (365-366). But then Jimmy Herf immediately asks in this, his final fantasy, "But what's the use of spending your whole life fleeing the City of Destruction?" For escape does not lead to selfhood. As *USA* makes clear, the city is America; indeed, it is the Western world.

The fact that Herf can make even this choice, however, seems to argue against determinism in the novel. The way out of this conundrum lies in understanding the fuller meaning of alienation from the self in relation to determinism.[5] It is a condition akin to the popular view of schizophrenia, which sees two radically different selves in one individual, though the popular view in fact does not quite apply since it permits both selves to take charge of the person now and then and therefore grants each a level of development that society denies the true self of persons, in the naturalistic view of Dos Passos. Dos Passos thus has a dual view of the self similar to that of Bergson, who divided the self into the shadow, or social, self and the durational, or true, self from which it was all too easy to become divorced. Bergson insisted that the social self was determined, and that only the durational one was free; hence, acts of the will performed by the social self were determined by society, whereas acts performed by the durational self were free because they were self-determined.[6]

Dos Passos's dual view of the self thus explains why characters who exercise their will are conscious of the fact that they do not experience the freedom that its "free" exercise brings. Examples of this phenomenon abound. After her divorce, a suitor of Ellen's declares his intentions: " 'I waited until you were free, didnt I? And now here I am.' " She replies, " 'We're none of us that ever . . . I'm just numb' " (267, Dos Passos's ellipsis). Her later protests make the reader aware that social alternatives to the life into which she ultimately settles cannot overcome the problem of alienation from the self and its consequent feeling of a lack of freedom. " 'I'm so sick of all that stuff,' " she declares. " 'Oh just everything like that aesthetic dancing and literature and radicalism and psychoanalysis. . . . I guess I'm growing up' " (343). Her "growing up," of course, entails her becoming the mechanical doll (399, 375, 300) that is the sign of her alienation from self, but those who cope with the problem in the other ways she mentions fare no better. Tony Hunter is cured of his homosexuality through psychoanalysis, only to go on the vaudeville circuit with the actress California Jones. He thus replaces one social mask or self with another, exchanging the image of the maladjusted actor with the heterosexual or "adjusted" one. Jojo and Cassie immerse themselves in the arts, leading a life dedicated to art for art's sake; but such a life entails adopting a pose—the romantic in agony— that is as spurious a representative of the true self as the social selves to which it is supposed to be superior. Radicalism, even of the syndicalist variety espoused by Martin Schiff, requires the development of a class consciousness that hardly represents, much less fulfills, the demands of the durational self, as Martin's attempted suicide indicates. That even these alternatives, largely disapproved by society, fail to help individuals overcome the problem of alienation accentuates its pervasiveness in the society at large, as Ellen's resigned acceptance of the condition illustrates.

Freedom of the will for the social self is thus meaningless to its possessor because an individual wishes that faculty to be exercised by a truly representative self, as frequent testaments to alienation from self in the novel indicate. For the acts born of a durational self, and the self that would develop through them, would be radically different from the ones chosen by and working in the service of the social self. The jump between one kind of freedom and the other is a quantum one, quantitatively so great as to reduce the exercise of the "free" will enjoyed by the social self to the reality of sheer determinism by simple force of contrast.

This view of kinds of freedom further clarifies an apparent philosophical inconsistency within the novel. On the one hand, characters clearly do make choices, as Jimmy Herf does when, in conclusion, he chooses "one of two unalienable alternatives" (365). On the other hand, Dos Passos treats his material in such a way as clearly to introduce environmental determinism into his novel. The fragmentation of the novel into a myriad of shifting scenes represents individuals as what Blanche Gelfant calls "discontinuous states of mind and feeling,"[7] and reduces them to functions of their environment. Such philosophical inconsistency, however, best conveys Dos Passos's view of the condition of man in society. "No two men are alike any more than two snowflakes are alike," he later wrote.[8] Man's potential freedom lies in developing a unique self whose acts are free because self-determined. His problem is to prevent society from metaphorically kidnapping his unique self by enforcing on him an alien social self.

Jimmy Herf and Ellen Thatcher best exhibit the terms of the problem. As children, they fear kidnappers. They also sometimes try out selves, he as "the head waiter at Delmonico's" (79), she as "Elaine of Lammermoor" (54). As an adult Herf rejects the self of a businessman, tries out the self of a reporter, and finally rejects society altogether. Their choices are functions of latent durational selves either seeking expression in the outside world or attempting to avoid the continued violation of their own intrinsic nature by society. Their problem is that once a social self is adopted, their childhood fears are realized; their authentic selves are metaphorically kidnapped because society will not permit any freedom sufficient for a social self to become a vehicle for expressing the durational one. And Dos Passos emphasizes the rupture between the two by placing the most important choice Jimmy Herf faces at the end of the novel, thus calling attention to the nature of that choice. In the end, Herf, still seeking authentic self-expression, must choose between adopting a social self denying such expression or abandoning the environment that demands its adoption.

What emerges after its adoption is a Hobbesian self with Hobbesian liberty: "the absence of all the impediments to action that are not contained in the nature and intrinsical quality of the agent."[9] This Hobbesian self is a social self that is fully a product of its environment, while the self that grows in Bergson's duration is never permitted development. The novel mainly stresses the gap between the two selves by applying the Hobbesian view of liberty of self to that social self and translating that view into pure determinism, which must be called pessimistic philosophic determinism because of the very totality of Dos Passos's Hobbesian vision of that self.

Dos Passos uses several methods to convey his view of self in society. The most impressive is his use of imagery, which at first appears conventional in employment and type but which soon manifests the fact that the novel was written with consummate skill and out of a youthful sensibility—the sensibility that is always in a privileged position for conveying the disillusionment that follows the thwarting of the drive for self-expression. Dos Passos's sensitivity emerges in his tasteful selection of appropriate images to convey his theme; his great talent emerges through his astonishing sense of subtlety in integrating those images into the texture of this Joycean text.[10]

The opening pages are an example of a conventional employment of conventional imagery to support the major theme, the deterministic view that selves are social products. The imagery of labels appears here in a variety of ways. At Ellen's birth, her mother exclaims of the newborn child, " 'But it hasn't any label on it.' " (She fears that " 'it's not mine.' ") " 'I'll label it right away' " (7), replies a nurse. The point is clear: Ellen will be given a self by society at the cost of her personal identity, just as others associated with subtler label imagery will be denied authentic selfhood. One man tells Bud Korpenning, " 'It's looks that count in this city' " (5), and another advises him that he needs a union card (24). An otherwise inconsequential figure, Bertha Olafson, supplements this theme, the need for a social self, when she tells her husband they must move to Riverside Drive: " 'Your position demands it' " (41). Status rather than selfhood is achieved and is alone achievable in this society, and hence figures don different labels to identify their varying social selves, Ellen becoming Helena and Elaine as her career develops; Congo Jake, the successful bootlegger Marquis des Coulommiers and, finally, the wealthy Armand Duval of Park Avenue.

But the imagery of labels is supported by a subtler use of imagery designed to show the environment invading the psyche, destroying both those who resist its encroachments and those whose imaginations it enslaves by harnessing those imaginations to unfulfilling ideals—money, beautiful women, prestige, and the Success that their possession symbolizes. This line of imagery and associated motifs stems from a central symbol for the environment that invades the psyche: the Great Lady on a White Horse, the Danderine Lady who represents the meretricious fictions devised by a civilization to ensure its own perpetuation. Her long hair recalls Godiva and explains her larger significance. Godiva saved Coventry by riding naked through its streets on condition that no one look at her. Peeping Tom, who did, was struck blind. In this novel Godiva is gaudily clothed in the trappings of her civilization. All look at her, and all are struck blind.

This motif of blindness ripples through the novel like the light imagery with which it is associated. Clearly figures like Uncle Jeff Merivale and his son James have been blinded by the value of success, as attested by James's ironic tribute to wife, mother, and flag, which made his Ten Million Dollar Success possible. As representatives of society, such types subscribe to and encourage the dissemination of the fictions represented by the Danderine Lady in order to ensure the perpetuation of the social norm. Such ensuring comes in a variety of types and at high cost to the psyche. When Stan first sees the

Danderine Lady, he alters a jingle to fit the spectacle: this woman with " 'rings on her fingers' " and " 'bells on her toes' " will " 'cure dandruff wherever it grows' " (143). Stan is obviously not blinded to the vulgarity of the complex of values she represents, and in this sense his imagination is hardly enslaved by her. But his total being is enslaved in another way. As the scion of a wealthy family, he cannot escape the demands of the business civilization she symbolizes. His social self is thus inseparable from her, to the detriment of a durational self that seeks aesthetic expression in an architectural career. The conflict born of the enslavement of the social self and the suppression of the durational one dominates his being; even before his death "his mind went on jingling like a mechanical piano" to testify to one way that the Danderine Lady can invade the psyche:

> With bells on her fingers and rings on her toes
> Shall ride a white lady upon a great horse
> And she shall make mischief wherever she goes . . . (252)

The Danderine Lady is thus within Stan's psyche in the sense that she induces conflict in him, and she represents a destructive light that blinds him in the sense that this conflict drives him blind drunk. How blinding a force she becomes is seen as he muses on her while spreading about his room the kerosene that will ignite and engulf him in flame: "The only man who survived the flood rode a great lady on a white horse" (253). But the severity of Stan's conflict denies the possibility of his riding and thus controlling her. For him, the only figure who escapes the flood is "longlegged Jack of the Isthmus," but Stan's legs are not long enough to straddle the gap between his two selves, and he is destroyed.

Dos Passos treats his imagery adroitly to show that Stan's destruction is inevitable. The impressionistic introduction that opens the novel describes the anonymous men and women leaving the ferry for Manhattan as figures pressing "through the manuresmelling wooden tunnel of the ferryhouse, crushed and jostling like apples fed down a chute into a press" (3). In the center of the novel the broken boxes, spoiled cabbageheads, orangerinds, and the green spume of the waves licking at the ferry in the first introduction reappear as Stan leaves the ferry to go to his death by fire. Stan thus carries into the center of the story the prediction inherent in the deterministic metaphor of the introduction by becoming one of those apples being fed down the chute to the press. Significantly, the images of the boxes, cabbageheads, and rinds are associated with light, for gulls fly above them in a "whitening light" and "a million windows flashed with light" (251) as Stan leaves the ferry. By creating this association, Dos Passos gives his imagery the determining power of Henry Adams's lines of force. The ferry conveys people to a destination where they are attracted by destructive social lines of force imaged by the light, which becomes a fire. An admirer of Whitman,[11] Dos Passos would make crossing Brooklyn ferry not a journey to expanded selfhood but a trip to self-destruction.

The central image of light flashing in the windows as Stan goes to his death draws together earlier parts of the novel, just as it points to later parts as well. It recalls the blindness motif associated with Bud Korpenning's earlier death, just as Stan's song about the flood recalls Bud's death by water. (Dos Passos seems to suggest that either the flood or the fire next time will get men.) Before he drops to his death in the waters beneath Brooklyn Bridge, Bud fantasizes himself a success, driving to his marriage at "the center of things" in clothing and carriage bespeaking a glittering prosperity with Maria Sackett, a childhood sweetheart with whom years earlier he had imagined "how we'd come to New York City an git rich" (123). The four horses that draw their carriage are white, like the Danderine Lady's. As Bud fantasizes, "the sun has risen behind Brooklyn. The windows of Manhattan have caught fire. He jerks himself forward, slips, dangles by a hand with the sun in his eyes. The yell strangles in his throat as he drops" (125). In his own way Bud has been blinded by the illusions of the Danderine Lady. Certainly he has not pursued the big money, for he has barely survived in New York. But his imagination has been enslaved by her in a more pathetic fashion. Her values provide him with the only compensation, albeit in fantasy, for the pains of his existence. They thus blind him to the source and cause of his misery, a materialistic culture that, upholding the same values, is blind to his condition and to itself as the cause of it.

Both Bud Korpenning's death and Stan Emery's draw together light or fire imagery within a framework of fantasy to show how the environment can invade the psyche, but there is a slight difference in emphasis between the two episodes. In Stan's case the imagery functions to show that the environment is destructive because it suppresses authentic selfhood and thereby gives rise to an intolerable internal conflict. In Bud's case it functions to show that the environment is destructive because it neutralizes conflict by enslaving his imagination and blinding him to the real cause of his misery. In a later part of the novel, this imagery gives a more dramatic focus to the meaning of Bud's plight, because it shows that even those who are politically aware cannot escape the situation of this very simple man.

Anne Cohen's career is central here. She is, after all, the lover of a Communist radical opposing the system, and is very much influenced by his ideas. Yet she too has internalized the environment symbolized by the Danderine Lady, a fact that first becomes manifest after she returns from a dance and sinks into reverie: "*Somebody loves me, I wonder who* . . . [Dos Passos's ellipsis]. The tune is all through her body, in the throb of her feet, in the tingling place on her back where he held her tight dancing with her" (275). The environment is literally within her, structuring her natural sexual responses in the clichéd rhythms and words of a pop culture. By getting within the psyche, the culture guarantees its own perpetuation even by people who are conscious enough of its oppressive reality to wish to alter it. Anna's Communist boyfriend preaches the need for radical change, but an interchange between the two reveals that his imagination is as enslaved as hers:

> "Oh," said Anna looking up at the sky, "I'd like to have a Paris evening dress an you have a dress suit and go out to dinner at a swell restaurant an go to the theater an everything."
> "If we lived in a decent society we might be able to . . . [Dos Passos's ellipsis]. There'd be gayety for the workers then, after the revolution" (358).

Thus, even as Communists Elmer and Anna maintain an allegiance to goals whose pursuit by others is responsibe for their own plight. A subsequent fantasy of Anna's confirms this fact: "Elmer in a telephone central in a dinnercoat, with eartabs, tall as Valentino, strong as Doug. The Revolution is declared, The Red Guard is marching up Fifth Avenue. Anna in golden curls with a little kitten under her arm leans with him out of the tallest window" (397). Hollywood and the Revolution thus converge in fantasy, and she dreams of "Elmer, loving as Valentino, crushing me to him with Dougstrong arms, hot as flame, Elmer" until "the white tulle shines too bright" (398) as this seamstress for Madame Soubrine accidently sets the fire that horribly disfigures her. In larger terms, one can explain the significance of the event by noting that the environment provides the means to neutralize her discontent. She is aware of the dreariness of her life, but her enslaved imagination finds escape from that reality in public fictions. In this way the environment claims her for its own and destroys any selfhood that might challenge its authority. As Ellen Thatcher puts the matter to calm customers aware of an accident: " 'Madame Soubrine asked me to tell everybody that it was nothing, absolutely nothing. Just a little blaze in a pile of rubbish' " (398). Like others, Anna is a victim of the light that blinds and the fire that burns.

Not only does Dos Passos use imagery to show the environment invading the psyche; he reverses its function to spatialize the self by extending it into the environment. To grasp the fuller meaning of using this method the reader must remember that, though Dos Passos may treat his characters impersonally, they are nonetheless capable of experiencing personal suffering. They are or become aware of their conditions, as their various confessions of alienation attest, and this awareness is at once the source of their suffering and of their special feelings about themselves and others as being quite literally spatialized. Their expression of such feelings generates another striking line of imagery in the novel.[12] Such imagery abolishes the distinction between environment and individual and promotes the novel's determinism. When a character links his own humanity to the inanimate objects that the human world creates, after all, he suggests that his own self is as much a social product as these objects are. To repeat, Bud Korpenning thinks of himself as a "needle in a haystack" (17).

That cliché takes on a profound meaning because it is part of a larger pattern of spatial references dramatizing the plight of the self. Just before his death, Stan exclaims, "Kerist I wish I was a skyscraper" (252). Metaphorically his social self is indeed a skyscraper, for it is a function of the environment which that building represents. Hence he wishes to be a literal one to escape the torture that his knowledge of the existence of a more representative, though undeveloped, self inflicts. Jimmy Herf dreams that "the arm of the linotype was a woman's hand in a long white glove," and that "the linotype was a gulping mouth with nickelbright rows of teeth" (329). A marriage to his wife has been replaced by marriage to a machine that represents the cold self she has become to him. Through both her rejection and the machine's demands, he is devoured. In his final fantasy Herf once again views Ellen in spatial terms, terms reminiscent of Stan's, for he sees the many faces, hence social selves, of Ellen trapped and staring from the windows of a skyscraper.

If imagery is the vehicle used to spatialize the self into its environment and to permit the environment to invade the self, then it is appropriate to use an image to suggest the overall condition of human social selves: the humble image of the fly. Like Bud Korpenning, flies are mere nuisances, easily swatted out of existence. Like Ellen's many selves, they are ultimately all alike—in the case of human selves, because they are all social products. Like the many figures of this novel, they are attracted to light. Like these same figures, they are prisoners, unable to pass through the windowpane through which the light shines. Flies carry germs the way these figures carry parts of their culture. They infect each other with their germs as surely as the Danderine Lady infects others with the attractions of her "culture." They travel through space and are spatial objects, just as these figures travel on ferryboats and become little better than objects—or flies.

In his treatment of flies as in his treatment of other imagery, Dos Passos again shows his genius. In this case, his genius consists in his introducing the trivial and making it appear to exist only as part of the fabric of ordinary life, but then gradually giving depth of meaning to the inconsequential. So flies at first appear here and there as just a feature of the humdrum reality of life whose oppressiveness Dos Passos portrays so well. As he has a shave in a barber shop, Bud Korpenning stares "up at the ceiling where four flies made figure eights round a red crêpe-paper bell" (16). Ellen's hypochondriachal mother, in bed as usual, also stares "at the ceiling watching the flies buzz teasingly round the electriclight fixture" (22). Jimmy squeezes a fly "into mashed gray jelly between finger and thumb" (96). Much later Ellen awakens from sleep with "red buzzing in her eyelids" and "sits up shaking her head to get rid of a fly blundering about her face" (240).

But long before Ellen's dream, the ordinary fly has already begun to assume some depth of meaning in these pages. Shortly after Jimmy squeezes the fly, it becomes significant as an image of the human condition. He dreams he is on a yacht, and he sees approaching "a fly the size of a ferryboat" (98). A dark man calls to him to jump,[13] though he resists (till the end of the novel, when he leaves Manhattan). The fly that he crushed will have its revenge, becoming the social mechanism, the ferryboat of the novel's first page that disgorges people into that "manuresmelling" tunnel through which they are fed.

The logic of imaging society as a large fly becomes clear later when individuals identify themselves or others with this insect. By the novel's end, Jimmy Herf feels that "life was upside down, he was a fly walking on the ceiling of a topsy-turvy city" (351). Subsequently, Martin Schiff shouts at his friends in a restaurant, " 'You are all bored, bored flies buzzing on the windowpane. You think the windowpane is the room. You dont know what there is deep black inside' " (361). Of course, "deep black inside" is the economic center, which reduces individuals to the condition of flies. If the ferryboat of Jimmy's dream is a large fly, the fly called Society that creates the selves of these individuals, then clearly the individual is just a small fly, a smaller version of Society; for the novel thoroughly obliterates the distinction between the social environment and the individual self by reducing the self to its environment.

Jimmy attempts to escape such reduction by leaving New York, so it is Ellen who becomes Martin Shiff's symbol of social man, the fly buzzing at the windowpane. In Jimmy's final reverie, he sees her reflected in the many windows of a skyscraper: "Ellie in a gold dress, Ellie made of thin gold foil absolutely lifelike beckoning from every window" (365). Her social selves have become those very "flies buzzing on the window pane" of which

Martin Schiff spoke, driven there by that "deep black inside" which Martin associates with death; for shortly afer he makes his remarks he threatens to commit suicide by running into "the sincerity of black," the East River. And those remarks stand as bleak commentary on Ellen's fate. She is society's prisoner because she is society's self.

The second and more obvious way in which Dos Passos conveys his view of self in society is through his familiar treatment of character—his use of what has been aptly called the "narrative collage."[14] The self that is spatialized is by and large inert, as incapable of continuous growth as a man-made object like a doll or a needle. Changes in such objects do not evolve from within but are imposed from without. For this reason the collage method is appropriate. The reader views those disconnected states of consciousness which are the characters for brief moments in a sequence whose units are widely scattered throughout the work. He sees what first they are, then what they become, with the disparity between the two often dramatic. The method thus shows the careful reader the kind of trauma the characters undergo, a suppression, as it were, of an incipient authentic self whose growth is halted by the imposition on it of society's self. The same device works to show that society's self is just that, a social product, not a natural outgrowth of original selfhood. If this "narrative collage" does not entirely eliminate will from the novel, it deflects from it sufficiently for the reader to see that change in character cannot be attributed to conscious choices of individuals but to their environment, whose presence is as pervasive as the mechanical symbols that dominate the work.[15]

The kind of change characters experience is most easily witnessed in Ellen, whose career extends from her birth through her "maturity." As a child Ellen dreams of becoming Elaine of Astolat, an idealized woman who dies for love. Subsequent glimpses of her show the loss of that self by an adult who pursues a theatrical career, marries and divorces a homosexual, falls in love with a man who burns to death in an alcoholic stupor, marries Jimmy Herf and divorces him to become the doll-wife of George Baldwin. Because the reader sees no evolution in Ellen's consciousness, he is left with a sense of a sharp contrast between two selves; and the same literary technique responsible for this effect forces the reader to blame society for the development of her alien self, the suppression of her true one.

What can easily be overlooked in a novel whose literary method requires close, careful reading is that in all his principal figures Dos Passos maintains the distinction between what a character is (or might be) and what he becomes at the hands of society, even those characters who make their first appearance in the novel in far more advanced form than Ellen's. At heart an anarchist even earlier than when he expresses such sentiments directly before the war, Congo Jake is swept into the system to become a bootlegger. Jeff Merivale, Jimmy Herf's uncle, first appears as a fairly ordinary young man who just "got a raise" and expresses no ambition other than to marry. In his next appearance he has become the successful businessman fearful of being " 'run out by a lot of damn foreigners' " (101) and spouting the platitudes of a business civilization: " 'And dont forget this, if a man's a success in New York, he's a success' " (119). Gus McNeil emerges on the scene as a simple fellow who is " 'goin to go out West, take up free land in North Dakota or somewhere an raise wheat' " (46). Chance intervenes: he is injured in an accident, collects money in a subsequent lawsuit, and thereafter appears as a Tammany Hall politician. Even major figures who first appear as highly developed social selves possess some unrealized potential that lies dormant beneath the packaged social self. A conniver from the beginning, George Baldwin nonetheless confesses to Ellen his alienation from self prior to their marriage. Dentsch, who seems well attuned to the business world until his business fails, seems to reveal the glimmerings of a better self in the moment of his business's demise: "To his surprise he found the gray drawn lines of his face cracking into a smile. . . . 'Well Serena,' he said with a trace of jauntiness in his voice, 'this is the end of my business career' " (372). And perhaps the beginning of a personal life? one is tempted to ask, though Dos Passos in fact never permits such development for his characters.

The third way in which Dos Passos advances his view of self in society is through his famous use of newspapers in his narrative. Newspaper stories characteristically omit that personal consciousness which one usually regards as the true identity of the figures whose actions they report. So if a character in the novel is mirrored in a newspaper story, such a juxtaposition emphasizes that the character has as single-dimensional a self as the figure in the story, the very self that in other ways Dos Passos reduces to a product of its environment. Furthermore, when Dos Passos juxtaposes events and moments in the lives of his characters to newspaper events, he spatializes his characters' lives by equating episodes in their lives with events external to them. This equation then transports the character's action out of a chain of causation in his personal life and makes it but a small link in a vaster chain of causation in the public world represented by the newspaper. Thus the characters' actions come to appear not *self*-generated but caused instead by the social forces in the huge world outside the self.

The effects of mirroring of character and displacement of cause appear early in the story: the story of young Nathan Sibbett's act of matricide, which Bud Korpenning reads in the newspaper while he is getting a shave in a barbershop, is the mirror image of Bud's act of patricide (16–17). Bud's fragmentary recollection of the murder of his father is on a par with the fragmentary newspaper account of Nathan's murder of his mother, so Bud and Nathan possess about the same amount of selfhood. This kind of effect—giving Bud a newspaper rather than a personal identity—certainly supports Claude Edmonde Magny's statement that "Dos Passos's characters do not have their own inner rhythm; its place is taken by the objective, mechanical rhythm of social facts, which replace at every moment the personal time, the 'lived time.' "[16] And perhaps she had something in mind like displacement of cause when she wrote that "it is social time, external time, that will carry them along in its inexorable unfolding."[17] For Bud's act of patricide is not only mirrored in the story of matricide but also juxtaposed to headlines reading "RELIEVE PORT ARTHUR IN FACE OF ENEMY" (17). So Bud's bloody personal conflict with his father is but part of a larger international conflict; his act but part of a larger causal world of historical forces producing international conflict: in this case the Russo-Japanese War. The cause of Bud's act is to be found not within himself, therefore, but in that "great wave of expansion and progress" (15) mentioned earlier, a historical wave producing momentous events that will make the history books, as Bud's act of patricide surely will not.

The example of Bud is but one of numerous examples of these two effects in *Manhattan Transfer*. Their repeated appearance in this volume; the repeated appearance of these effects through the more formal devices of Newsreel, Camera Eye, and Biography throughout the three volumes of *USA*; the sheer scale of repetition of such effects explain what the self is in Dos Passos's pages. It is a product—a product of present social forces, but not of present social forces alone. It is also a product of past social forces, and this historical dimension in the novel's determinism introduces another of Dos Passos's major points, that the Hobbesian self has not always existed but has been produced by a larger network of forces transcending the immediate locale and moment of *Manhattan Transfer*.

Manhattan Transfer may be a story of New York City, but the forces that hold its characters in thrall are hardly confined to Manhattan. Dos Passos takes pains to show that if his characters are mere drops in a wave, the wave has inundated other places as well, as demonstrated by his juxtaposing newspaper headlines to the private experience of Bud. The total effect of such juxtapositions is to give spatial extension to the movement of the wave of which individuals are a part—to extend it from New York City halfway across the globe to Russia. But those same juxtapositions give the wave a larger historical dimension, in which the present moment is seen as part of the wave of the past. For the trend that these characters illustrate has its source in the rise of that industrial civilization, now a century old, which Martin Schiff blames for disrupting both private and public life. The conditions for alienation did not exist in that Jeffersonian past which several critics have noted as Dos Passos's primary point of reference. The national principles associated with Jefferson exalted individualism, what Dos Passos calls "freedom lived."[18] But the rise of industrial capitalism diverted the course of American history and caused man to lose contact with his true essence, that selfhood whose development earlier historical conditions permitted and the Founding Fathers' principles guaranteed. Such a loss, as Dos Passos presents the matter, is tantamount to moving from a world that one could view as free to one that can only be viewed in terms of pessimistic social determinism.

In *Manhattan Transfer*, Jimmy Herf is the primary spokesman for Dos Passos's historical perspective. He arrives in New York from Europe on the Fourth of July, hears an orator read the Declaration of Independence, and is told that his grandfather was killed fighting in the Revolutionary War. As a young man he recalls "the embattled farmers [who] stood and fired the shot heard round . . . " (232) at the outbreak of World War I, and he abandons New York thinking of Patrick Henry's famous phrase (402), among other things. His life in New York, of course, attests to his disillusionment with the ideals of the American past embodied in such words,[19] the same kind of disillusionment that Ellen expresses when, reduced to a "walking talking doll," she exclaims, "Care for what, for what; the opinion of mankind?" (400). She thus carries into the story the historical vision represented by the anonymous old man, characterized as a "broken doll in the ranks of varnished articulated dolls," who gazes at Broadway and sighs, " 'I remember when it was all meadows' " (249). When it was indeed all meadows, the patriotic words that these figures recall in their disillusionment were meaningful. Now they are as empty as the characters themselves, as Jimmy Herf indicates in his own sigh, "If only I still had faith in words" (366), and as Ellen attests in her rejection of all words signifying ideals as " 'just words' " before she turns to the task of " 'getting back into the center of things' " (267).

Because it is a cliché, the repeated use of this last phrase in the novel seems only to contribute to the theme of the meaninglessness of words and their associated ideals. It does this, of course, but at the same time it is charged with greater meaning. For in *Manhattan Transfer* there are three centers of things: a personal, a historical, and an economic center. The historical center appears in references to the American past, and that center fostered the development of a personal one, an individual's authentic selfhood. But the present, economic center suppresses the personal center, fills the vacuum with a social self indistinguishable from it, and reduces the individual to the level of Hobbesian man. Thus Dos Passos sees the emergence of Hobbesian man as a relatively new historical phenomenon, and his vision of the central problem of modern man is indeed a relatively new one, though his vision has historical antecedents.

In the nineteenth century the problem of the relation of the self to society first makes its appearance as a dominant concern of English and American literature; but though the self frequently cannot be realized in society, writers do permit it some expression within severe social limitations. Wemmick can draw his bridge against the world and fulfill himself in his own little world with his father. Huck may have internalized society's code to the point where he experiences guilt for helping Jim, and he may resent society sufficiently to leave it, as Jimmy Herf does. But he can and does act meaningfully in his relationship with Jim and thus gives expression to a self beyond the reach of society. The very totality of the conditioning effects of society on the individual sets Dos Passos's vision apart from Dickens's or Clemens's—or Keats's or Wordsworth's, for that matter. Or, rather, one should say that Dos Passos brings the nineteenth-century vision of man in society to that determinism which is its logical conclusion. Man's true self is potentially free, he says, and one's awareness of it can give man sufficient freedom to abandon society; but once in society, there can be for man no authentic self-realization because no escape from a social self reducible to the environment is possible.

This emphasis on the subject of selfhood can easily be missed by a cursory reading of a novel employing the methods of the "narrative collage." At first it seems like the usual novel about the sensitive American poet confronting the wicked world of American Philistines.[20] Herf, after all, has pronounced literary inclinations and complains of the inadequacy of American life for failing to support aesthetic expression as he reads *Jean Christophe*. But after his mother addresses him as " 'my little dreamer' " (81), the reader comes to recognize that Herf's plight—even if tentatively accepted as an American one only—is the plight of all the figures in the work, for all are dreamers. Earlier discussion indicates that the novel contains a marked emphasis on dreams and reveries in which a wide variety of characters participate. In addition to those already mentioned, other figures show themselves as dreamers. " 'Dreamin' again Cassie' " (161), her boyfriend Morris says to her. Ed Thatcher speaks of the kind of girl he hopes his newborn daughter will be (9). Phil Sandbourne encounters disaster trying to fulfill a fantasy inspired by a beautiful girl's glance. Most people in this novel are dreamers, a point Ellen Thatcher makes when she says, " 'I think that this city is full of people wanting inconceivable things' " (262).

The problem for the dreamers of *Manhattan Transfer* is that they seek to translate an authentic self into the outside world, though the world turns their very capacity for dreaming against them by giving them dreams that inhibit selfhood. Hence, the novel's real dichotomy is the self against the world, and when the world wins, the true self loses; and individuals experience alienation from self. The enduring quality of the novel, indeed, stems a good deal from its subject of self-alienation, a condition that has been a central preoccupation of thinkers in all disciplines for quite some time now, and one still attracting literary concern.

Nor did Dos Passos view the condition as essentially an American one. Alfred Kazin was no doubt right in stating that Dos Passos's is "the protest of a mind whose opposition to capitalism is no greater than his suspicion of all societies,"[21] though the promise of America made the appearance of the problem here all the more disillusioning for the intensely American Dos Passos. The historical vision of *Manhattan Transfer*, indeed, suggests that the world is a network and that the problems faced by America are not necessarily exclusive to it.

And what of solutions to those problems, or at least to the central one? Does Dos Passos offer one? Long after writing *Manhattan Transfer*, he expressed a concern to reverse "the trend towards individual serfdom into a trend towards individual liberty," and added, "the first prerequisite is a fresh understanding, untrammeled by prejudice or partisan preconceptions, of the institutions we live in."[22] Reading *Manhattan Transfer* is that prerequisite. The novel offers that understanding. It pinpoints the source of the problem, and its naturalistic vision implies the condition that must be met before man can overcome the central problem of self-alienation.

The cause of the problem lies in an industrial civilization that, the novel indicates everywhere, has blotted out the harmony of nature's cycles, although here and there man can still perceive them. A series of introductions to chapters traces the cycle of the day in terms reminiscent of Eliot's "Preludes": "Morning clatters with the first L train down Allen Street" (129). The noon sun "shines like a dandelion on the toe of each new-shined shoe," then "spirals dimly into the chopsuey joint" (144). As the day ends, "the sun's moved to Jersey, the sun's behind Hoboken" (169). These juxtapositions of nature and society reach their climax in Jimmy Herf's exclamation: "*Express service meets the demands of spring. O God to meet the demands of spring. . . . Chockful of golden richness, spring*" (352).

The contrasts in this reverie created by Whitman's admirer have their meaning. Man is a part of nature, in Whitman's sense of the matter, for man is, or can be, an expression of that vital impulse which manifests itself throughout the material world. But in divorcing man from nature and its automatic cycles leading to nature's renewal, civilization has divorced man from the vital impulse and that durational self which is at once its best human expression and also the source of human renewal. Clearly Dos Passos's characters seek such renewal, albeit unsuccessfully. Anna Cohen sees "April . . . coaxing unexpected colors out of the East Side streets" (357) as she goes to complain to friends of her pennilessness. Before Ellen buys a new dress, she first buys a bunch of arbutus and presses it to her face: "May woods melted like sugar against her palate" (395). For Whitman's disciple, however, such renewal is possible only in a society that permits man to sing a song of his true self—a society that restores him to nature, that is, and thereby permits the development of that self which is his as an endowment of nature and whose expression alone can fulfill "the demands of spring." Dos Passos did not render such a society, though Steinbeck suggested how one might come into being. Nor did Dos Passos render a version of a second self, though to him, as to Whitman, its existence was certain. It was left to Steinbeck and to Faulkner, each with his own vision of that self, to fill this gap.

SIX

Steinbeck
and Nature's Self:
The Grapes of Wrath

Both Dreiser and Dos Passos saw the self as a product of mechanisms and hence incapable of freedom, and both postulated the existence of a second self beyond the limitations of determinism. Dreiser arrived late at the notion and, borrowing it wholesale from Brahmanic thought, barely tested its meaning, save to see it as the source of man's freedom. Although Dos Passos never developed a version of such a self, he early found its existence and suppression the cause of man's misery and, in elaborating on that theme, he was able to enlarge a cluster of themes and attitudes associated with a second self—in particular those associated with its relationship to society and to nature. In *The Grapes of Wrath*, Steinbeck renders his version of a second self in man and brings to mature development that cluster of themes and attitudes. Significantly, he brings them to maturity within a framework of determinism and so harmonizes authentic freedom and determinism in a way that Dos Passos never could do, since the second self, the true source of man's freedom, remains forever an embryo in his pages.

The interchapters of Steinbeck's novel create a network of interlocking determinisms through their emphasis on the operations of abstract, impersonal forces in the lives of the Oklahomans. Chapter 5 is especially effective both in capturing the poignancy of the human situation created by such forces and in pointing to the kind of deterministic force underlying the others in the novel. In one fleeting episode a nameless Oklahoman who threatens the driver of a bull-dozer leveling his house is told that armed resistance is futile, for the driver acts in the service of the bank, and "the bank gets orders from the East." The Oklahoman cries, "But where does it stop? Who can we shoot?" "I don't know," the driver replies. "Maybe there's nobody to shoot. Maybe the thing isn't men at all. Maybe . . . the property's doing it" (52). Or at least the Bank, the monster requiring "profits all the time" in order to live and dwarfing in size and power even the owner men, who feel "caught in something larger than themselves" (44, 42).*

The vision that appears here has a name: economic determinism. This view does not say that man has no free will. One might indeed find among a group of bank presidents a corporate Thoreau who prefers jail (or unemployment) to following the demands of the system. It merely asserts that most men charged with the operation of an economic structure will act according to rules requiring the bank's dispossession of its debtors when a disaster renders them incapable of meeting payments on their mortgaged property. Far from denying free will, such determinism fully expects and provides for the willed resistance of the Oklahomans. The police take care of that. Nor is this vision without its moral component, though neither the police nor the owner men can be held individually responsible. "Some of the owner men were kind," Steinbeck writes, "because they hated what they had to do, and some of them were angry because they hated to be cruel, and some of them were cold because they had long ago found that one could not be an owner unless one were cold" (42). These anonymous men are not devil figures but individuals performing functions within a system, so the work indicts the system rather than individuals who act in its service. In the case of the Oklahomans, the indictment is founded on a fundamental irony: societies, designed to protect men from nature's destructive features—here a drought—complete nature's destructive work, ex-pelling men from the dust bowl into which nature's drought has temporarily transformed their farms.

But the expulsion of the Oklahomans is not the only inexorable

*John Steinbeck, *The Grapes of Wrath* (New York: Viking, 1939). All references are to this edition.

consequence of the operation of economic force. These men, women, and children who "clustered like bugs near to shelter and to water" (264) automatically create in their camps a society within the larger society, acting according to the same instinctual dictate that initially made the Joad family, seeking self-preservation, seem "a part of an organization of the unconscious" (135). "Although no one told them," the families instinctively learned "what rights are monstrous and must be destroyed" (265)—the "rights" of rape, adultery, and the like—and which must be preserved. Instinct welds the group "to one thing, one unit" (272); and the contempt, fear, and hostility they encounter as they traveled the highways "like ants and searched for work, for food" reinforce the bonds of group solidarity by releasing an anger whose ferment "changed them . . . united them" all the more (388, 385). Here is the basis of that much-remarked-on shift in the novel from farmer to migrant, from "I" to "we," from family to group.

This emphasis upon the spontaneous development of a social group is not limited to the interchapters; but it is there that Steinbeck notes not only the inevitability of its development but, more important, the concurrent emergence of a group consciousness and the inevitable future consequences that its emergence entails. Economic determinism thus spawns responses that are biologically determined. Of course the scope of Steinbeck's biological determinism is sharply limited. He states with certainty but two simple facts: that the "anlage of movement" (20) possessed by the oatbeards, foxtails, and clover burrs of chapter 3 has its counterpart in the anlage of "two squatting men" discussing their common plight, and that the realization of the potential in such anlage is inevitable. As the narrative voice proclaims to the owner men: "Here is the anlage of the thing you fear. This is the zygote. For here 'I lost my land' is changed; a cell is split and from its splitting grows the thing you hate— 'We lost *our* land' " (206). Thus, forces that destroy one community create another by stimulating the communal anlage inherent in instinct, which sets the primary goals of life—in the Oklahomans' case, survival.

But in a novel that so beautifully portrays society as a system of interrelated forces, there is more to the matter than what has just been described. If economic determinism breeds biological determinism, biological determinism in turn spawns an inevitable social conflict that in time becomes an historically determined sequence of events with predictable outcome. Although there are references to it elsewhere, chapter 19 most clearly transforms this economic determinism into an historical one. It describes armed Californians, who earlier had stolen land from Mexicans, guarding the stolen land. Following the pattern of the Romans ("although they did not know it"), "they imported slaves, although they did not call them slaves: Chinese, Japanese, Mexicans, Filipinos" (316). Later appear the dispossessed Oklahomans of the East, "like ants scurrying for work, for food, and most of all for land" (317). When the slaves rebel, Steinbeck, using repetition, emphasizes the cause-effect relationship between the migrants' condition and their rebellion against it. "The great owners, striking at the immediate thing, the widening government, the growing labor unity; . . . not knowing these things are results, not causes. Results, not causes; results, not causes. The causes lie deep and simply" (204). And that he believes these causes compel the appearance of the effect proceeding from them—that is, believes the causes determine that effect's emergence—becomes clear in chapter 19 when he associates "the inevitability of the day" (325) when the owners must lose their land with their violent temporizing: "Only means to destroy revolt were considered, while the causes of revolt went on" (325).

But now some observations about the relation of the interchapters and the plot of *The Grapes of Wrath* are needed in order to show that Steinbeck's determinism can embrace freedom of the will because his literary structure creates a statistical determinism. The interchapters display the growth of a group consciousness controlled by instinct's response to the dynamic of economic forces. This emphasis is carried into the story in a variety of ways, most notably through Ma's insistence on keeping the family together. But in the story proper, instinct does not rule each person with equal power. The instinctual power that drives the group in the interchapters is unequally distributed among its individual members. Granpa's resistance to leaving Oklahoma testifies to the power of age to overcome the instinct to survive. And age is not the only force limiting the role of instinct in individual lives. Attached to his land, Muley Graves refuses to leave it in order to depart for California. He makes a choice that reduces him to "a ol' graveyard ghos' " (71) living by night as a trespasser on land once his own. Noah finds the hardships of the journey greater than the comfort derived from the group and leaves, last seen walking by a river into the greenery of the surrounding countryside to an unknown future. Connie, angry that he did not remain to work for the bank (and thus aid in the Oklahomans' dispossession), abandons his pregnant wife Rosasharn.

In the plot, then, free will plays a major role. Even those who remain with the group make numerous free choices to assure its survival, as Ma's words about the need to get to California testify: "It ain't kin we? It's will we?" (139). This emphasis on choice and free will sets limits on the rule of instinct, limits that avoid reducing the individual to the level of a will-less animal, a mere pawn of instinct. Man's possession of instincts roots him in nature, but he is different from other things in nature, as Steinbeck makes clear by describing in chapter 14 man's willingness to "die for a concept" as the "one quality [that] is the foundation of Manself . . . distinctive in the universe" (205). And this emphasis on man's uniqueness in nature, so inextricably related to his will, in turn limits the scope of the novel's historical determinism, which is based on Steinbeck's biological determinism. Even in the group that will give history its future shape, there are individuals who will depart from the historical patterns which that group is aborning.

Seen in this way, Steinbeck's determinism does not at first sight seem a far cry from Dos Passos's, at least insofar as the economic base that underlies their respective deterministic outlooks issues in a statistical determinism for each writer. But Steinbeck's interchapters are a technical innovation that create a significant expansion and difference of vision, first appearances notwithstanding. Steinbeck gains two major advantages from them. First, by creating this preserve for rendering abstract social forces, he releases a considerable number of other chapters—his plot chapters—for portraying characters as developing states of consciousness rather than as those fragments of force which they seem to be in *Manhattan Transfer*. He thereby can *emphasize* the existence of free will in his novel. Just by making freely willed decisions the basis of his statistical determinism, in other words, he gives will a role more prominent than the one it plays in Dos Passos's work, where chance prevails and will is nugatory.

The second advantage is of far greater importance because it shows Steinbeck's idiosyncratic way of harmonizing determinism and freedom. In addition to portraying abstract forces operating on a grand scale in space and time, those chapters also are instrumental in showing the change in the group from an organism biologically determined by instinct and externally determined by social forces to an organism that achieves rationality and hence a freedom of will capable of transcending the bonds of determinism.[1] The interchapters are indispensable because they dramatize Steinbeck's belief that a group is a living organism possessing a life of its own independent of the individuals who comprise it, and the implementation of that view is a part of the novel's genius.

Steinbeck clarifies his view of a group in *The Sea of Cortez*, a collaboration of sorts (see below, p. 219), where in a passage specifically written by him he uses marine analogies to explain his sense of the normal relation of an individual to the group of which he is a part:

> There are colonies of pelagic tunicates which have taken a shape like the finger of a glove. Each member of the colony is an individual animal, but the colony is another individual animal, not at all like the sum of its individuals. Some of the colonists, girdling the open end, have developed the ability, one against the other, of making a pulsing movement very like muscular action. Others of the colonists collect the food and distribute it, and the outside of the glove is hardened and protected against contact. Here are two animals, and yet the same thing. . . . So a man of individualistic reason, if he must ask, "Which is the animal, the colony or the individual?" must abandon his particular kind of reason and say, "Why, it's two animals and they aren't alike any more than the cells of my body are like me. I am much more than the sum of my cells and, for all I know, they are much more than the division of me." There is no quietism in such acceptance, but rather the basis for a far deeper understanding of us and our world.[2]

This quotation stresses the individuality of the group and the uniqueness, apart from it, of its component elements. In the following quotation Steinbeck introduces an added dimension in the larger animal, here a school of fish:

> And this larger animal, the school, seems to have a nature and drive and ends of its own. . . . If we can think in this way, it will not seem so unbelievable . . . that it seems to be directed by a

school intelligence. . . . We suspect that when the school is studied as an animal rather than as a sum of unit fish, it will be found that certain units are assigned special functions to perform; that weaker or slower units may even take their place as placating food for the predators for the sake of the security of the school as an animal.[3]

Biology thus seems to confirm the eternal copresence of the one and the many. Applying the thrust of the thought of this passage to the relation of the human individual to his group, one can account for this phenomenon, the purposiveness of the larger animal independent of the individuals composing it, only by assuming that individual men have a dual nature, both a group identity and a personal one independent of it but not necessarily in conflict with it.

More must be made of this observation, but in order to do so precisely, it is necessary to restate the earlier relation established between interchapters and plot, using now not the language of determinism and free will but language taken from Steinbeck's quotation above. The content of the interchapters and the content of the plot of *The Grapes of Wrath* relate to each other as the larger animal (the migrant group) to the individuals composing it. The plot portrays members of the school in their rich individuality, whereas the interchapters show the formation of the larger animal that they compose, a formation that takes place both on a de facto level (by virtue of circumstance, a physical group is formed) and on an instinctive one, which endows the animal with life. By virtue of the instinct for self-preservation, in the camps twenty families become one large family, sharing a single instinct. The animal can come to life on this instinctual level because the animal's anlage is in the separate family, the basic unit through which man fulfills his needs, and the instinctual sense of unity is strengthened by a common set of threatening circumstances issuing in shared emotions: first fear, then anger. In this condition, the "school intelligence" directing its drives is instinctual alone, and hence the human group is more like the school of fish to which Steinbeck refers. Guided solely by instinct, the human group-animal achieves a measure of protection from a hostile social environment, but with instinct alone, it can no more transcend the social determinism of the body politic than the turtle (which in the novel symbolizes it in this condition) can transcend the machinations of the drivers eager to squash it. Chance alone can save the group or the turtle as both walk, like Tom, one step ahead of the other, living from day to day.

But the group changes, and in this respect the plot goes one step further than the interchapters, which halt with the fermenting of the grapes of wrath. For the plot shows the emergence of a rational group consciousness, first in Casy, then in Tom, whose final talk with his mother, representing the principle of family, discloses that his own consciousness has transcended such limitations. In fact it is mainly in Tom that the group develops a head for its body; for he survives the murdered Casy, and he was from the beginning more clearly a member of the de facto group than Casy, who owned no land. And by stressing how the animal that is the group achieves rational consciousness and (hence) freedom, Steinbeck harmonizes freedom and determinism in his most important way. The group determined by instinct and circumstance in the interchapters achieves both rational self-awareness and freedom in the person of a member who substitutes the consciousness of a group for a private consciousness and thus gives the group access to the faculty of human will. Tom thus enables it to move from instinct to reason and to that freedom which reasoned acts of the will provide. By having the group consciousness mature in the plot section of his novel, Steinbeck thus unites it to the interchapters structurally and harmonizes his novel philosophically.

And he provides a triumph for the group within the context of determinism, for their attainment of rational group consciousness is itself a determined event because such potential is inherent in the species. Their achieved freedom of will as a group thus is the final term of a socially determined sequence of events that leads to the group's creation, and the group's exercise of it to attain its ends fulfills the historical determinism of the novel. Yet this is not the only hope in these pages, for the prospective triumph of the group provides hope for the triumph of the individual as a whole person.

The Grapes of Wrath is the story of the exploitation of a dispossessed group, and it is difficult not to feel that it will always engender sympathies for the dispossessed of the earth wherever and whenever they might appear. But the novel's indictment of society for what it does to individuals should have an equally enduring appeal; for here its message goes beyond the conditions of oppressed groups and addresses individuals in all strata of complex societies. The condition of individual Oklahomans in fact is an extreme representation of the condition of social man, and in the capacity of individual Oklahomans to change lies the hope for social man.

The migrants' achievement of rational freedom speaks for more than freedom for the group. It tells readers of a vital difference in kinds of freedom. Steinbeck has written, "I believe that man is a double thing—a group animal and at the same time an individual. And it occurs to me that he cannot successfully be the second until he has fulfilled the first."[4] Only the fulfilled group self can create a successful personal self; only freedom exercised by a personal self in harmony with a group self can be significant.

This aspect of the novel's vision depends upon Steinbeck's fuller conception of an individual's two selves. One is his social self, definable by the role he plays in society and by the attitudes he has imbibed from its major institutions. The other is what is best called his species self. It contains all the biological mechanisms—his need for sexual expression, for example—that link him to other creatures in nature. And by virtue of the fact that he is thus linked to the natural world, he can feel a sense of unity with it in its inanimate as well as its animate forms. But the biological element in this self also connects him to the world of man, for it gives him an instinctive sense of identification with other members of his species, just as the members of other species have an instinctive sense of oneness with their own kind.

The species self thus has connections to nonhuman and human nature, and Steinbeck refers to the latter connection when he speaks of man as a "group animal." He views a healthy personal identity as one in which the species self in both its aspects can express itself through the social self of the individual. But society thwarts, or seeks to thwart, the expression of that self. It seeks not only to cut man off from his awareness of his connections to nonhuman nature, it seeks also to sever him from the group sense of oneness with the human species that the individual's species self possesses. Ironically, therefore, purely social man loses a sense of that unity with others which society presumably exists to promote.

The novel's social criticism rests on this view, and its emphasis on grotesques, purely social beings cut off from their connections to nature, both human and nonhuman, portrays an all-too-familiar image of modern man. In too many instances, by imposing mechanical rhythms on human nature, society creates half-men. Its repeated attempts to distort the individual's identity is emphasized by numerous dichotomies between social demands and instinct. Tom tries to comprehend the meaning of his imprisonment for killing in self-defense. Casy tries to understand the meaning of his preaching sexual abstinence when he cannot remain chaste himself. And the point is made by the basic events that set the story moving. A mechanical monster, indifferent to the maternal instincts of the Ma Joads who exercise their species selves in the interest of family solidarity, expels families from their land. The social mechanism thus tries to thwart the demands of the group aspect of the self to remain together. And the same mechanism is responsible for sowing what has become a dust bowl with cotton, rendering it permanently useless for agriculture, thus showing its indifference—nay, hostility—to the connections with nature that the species self feels.

This suppression of the species self is not rigorously foreordained for every individual, and hence the novel's determinism does not rest on the universality of its occurrence. Ma's personality remains undistorted from the novel's beginning to its end. Her intense commitment to the family proceeds from a very live species self; and though she must enlarge her vision to include more than her family, her insistence that Casy join the family on its westward exodus and numerous demonstrations of her concern for others outside her immediate family bear witness that her vision is not all that limited to begin with. But such suppression is nonetheless widespread, and indeed a sufficient number of people must be transformed into grotesques if social structures are to perpetuate themselves. They thereby make many men grotesques and subject all men to economic determinism. Thus the attention to grotesques is part of the pattern of economic determinism in the novel; such determinism can only prevail under conditions guaranteeing with statistical certainty that society can distort man's nature.

The novel singles out two social institutions that assure the creation of grotesques: religion and the law. Lizbeth Sandry is the major representative of a grotesque created by religion. Her intolerance of dancing represents her intolerance of sex, and such intolerance displays religion's warping influence on human instinct. She arouses Ma's ire by warning Rosasharn, "If you got sin on you—you better watch out for that there baby" (421). Her religious views, importing a supernatural mandate into the realm of nature, impose on natural behavior value judgments (like "sin") designed to thwart the normal expression of the species self. This divorce between her social and species selves, indicated by her views, makes Lizbeth Sandry much like one of Sherwood Anderson's grotesques, as all social selves alienated from the species self must be.

Uncle John and Connie's wife, Rosasharn, carry into the family Lizbeth Sandry's fanaticism. Uncle John's felt sense of guilt over his wife's death impels him to blame all the family misfortunes on what he takes to be his sin: his failure to summon a doctor when she complained of physical ailments. His exaggerated sense of sin fails to take into account his own human nature (his natural fallibility) and circumstance; for his reluctance to call a doctor doubtlessly depended on strained finances. His compulsive references to that sin make him as much a grotesque as Lizbeth Sandry, his grotesquerie compounded by his need for wild drinking bouts to escape the sin.

Not only does he become a grotesque, but his obsession with sin blinds Uncle John to the true cause of the family's misfortunes and so shows that religion can indeed be an opiate of the people useful for sustaining an unjust social structure. In this sense Rosasharn is like him, for she has been affected by Lizbeth Sandry's sense of sin. Of course, Rosasharn's sense of sin does not transform her into the grotesque that Uncle John has become. It illustrates that selfishness noted by other critics, for throughout most of the novel she thinks only of herself and her unborn baby, to the total exclusion of the problems of other people. But her view of Tom's killing a deputy, which is one illustration of her selfishness (she shows concern only for her baby, not for her brother), also points to the larger consequences of Uncle John's obsession with sin. She tells Tom, "That lady tol' me. She says what sin's gonna do. . . . An' now you kill a fella. What chance that baby got to get bore right?" (537). Like Uncle John's explanation for family misfortunes, her view of the real-enough threat to her unborn child deflects the source of that threat into a theological realm inaccessible to man, the realm of the devil who tempts man's fallen nature to sin, rather than assigning it to the realm of the accessible and the real, the social forces responsible for the deaths of Casy, the deputy, and her own child.

If religion enforces a split between man's two selves, suppressing one and thus deforming the other, so do most social institutions. Hence the law motif is central to the novel, law being the second (and more important) institution that Steinbeck indicts in his defense of the self; for it is law that holds society's other institutions together and, supported by police power, gives them their governing authority.

References to the law appear in a variety of contexts, but their meaning is best embodied in the opposition between law and fundamental human needs, those " 'got to's' " (191) to which Casy refers that compel men to say, "They's lots a things 'gainst the law that we can't he'p doin' " (608). Burying Granpa, for example, in defiance of local edict. But there are more important illustrations of how the law thwarts the expression of man's nature, even when it does not manage to distort it. Tom finds no meaning, at the novel's outset, in a system that imprisons him for killing in self-defense, and he discovers the true meaning of the system only after he kills the deputy who murders Casy—a nice bit of symmetry that illustrates his growth in awareness as he perceives, like Casy, that his second killing is also an instinctual response, one of self-defense against the true assaulter, the system, which so thwarts man's instinctual life that it leaves him no choice other than to strike back. This line of meaning is echoed by others: by Ma, who says of Purty Boy Floyd, "He wan't a bad boy. Jus' got drove in a corner" (501); by the nameless owner men who tell the tenants early in the novel, "You'll be stealing if you try to stay, you'll be murderers if you kill to stay" (46). And it is implicit in Tom's own position at the beginning of the plot: to leave the state violates the conditions of his parole, yet to stay means to break up the family and to face unemployment and possible starvation.

Under such circumstances, it is not surprising to discover that the true prison in *The Grapes of Wrath* is the world outside the

prison walls, the real point of Tom's story of a man who deliberately violated parole to return to jail so that he could enjoy the
"conveniences" (among them good food) so conspicuously absent
in his home (36). "Here's me, been a-goin' into the wilderness like
Jesus to try to find out somepin," Casy says. "Almost got her
sometimes, too. But it's in the jail house I really got her" (521). He
discovers his proper relationship to men there because it is the
place of the free: of men who exercised the natural rights of
nature's self only to be imprisoned by the society that resents their
exercise. And in fact he can see how the law violates self because
he has already seen how religion does. Without the revelations of
the wilderness, he would not have had the revelation of the
jailhouse; the first is indispensable to the second. Together, they
make him the touchstone for understanding the novel's philosophy of self and for measuring the selves of the novel's other
characters.

Just as the species self is the ultimate source of freedom for a
group, it is the same for an individual. If man can recognize that he
is a part of nature by virtue of that self's existence—if he can affirm
for this aspect of a naturalistic vision—he can liberate himself
from the condition of being a grotesque and, in recognizing his
oneness with others, escape the tentacles of economic determinism as well. This is the novel's philosophy of self, and Casy's
life is its lived example, both in his thought and in his practice.

Casy has arrived at the vision that man is a part of nature in the
novel's opening pages, the discrepancy between his religious
preachment and his sexual practice prompting his withdrawal
from society to go to the hills in order to comprehend his true
relation to the world and leading to his Emersonian sense of
connection with nonhuman nature: " 'There was the hills, an'
there was me, an' we wasn't separate no more' " (110). Casy has
thus found his deepest nature, that self which is connected even to
nonhuman nature, and so he has taken the first vital step toward
his liberation. In his way of recovering this self, Casy should be
measured less by Emerson than by Thoreau, who went to the
woods " to drive life into a corner" and discovered that "not till we
are lost . . . , not till we have lost the world, do we begin to find
ourselves, and realize where we are and the infinite extent of our

relations" (*Walden*, chapters 2 and 8). For Thoreau, as for Casy and Steinbeck, a true knowledge of the relationship between one's self and the external world can only be derived from an empirical study of the structure of physical reality. Such empiricism imparts the knowledge that man does relate to the whole and inspires, in Steinbeck's words written elsewhere, "the feeling we call religious," the sense of unity between self and outside world that makes "a Jesus, a St. Augustine, a St. Francis, a Roger Bacon, a Charles Darwin, and an Einstein."[5] Writing of his own interest "in relationships of animal to animal," Steinbeck later gave a clue to the general source of the religious vision at which Casy has arrived at the beginning of *The Grapes of Wrath*:

> If one observes in this relational sense, it seems apparent that species are only commas in a sentence, that each species is at once the point and the base of a pyramid, that all life is relational to the point where an Einsteinian relativity seems to emerge. And then not only the meaning but the feeling about species grows misty. One merges into another, groups melt into ecological groups until the time when what we know as life meets and enters what we think of as non-life: barnacle and rock, rock and earth, earth and tree, tree and rain and air. And the units nestle into the whole and are inseparable from it.[6]

Any reader of "Song of Myself" would know instantly what Casy and Steinbeck mean. This sense of relationship inspires reverence not for an unknowable God outside of nature but for knowable nature in all its forms; for if one feels united to "the hills," one is clearly in a position to take the next step and feel reverence for nature in its animate forms, and especially in the form known as the human species to which all men belong. And Casy has clearly taken this step as well, as his subsequent remarks on the holiness of man testify. "I got thinkin' how we was holy when we was one thing, an' mankin' was holy when it was one thing." Such human holiness and the consequent sense of human solidarity it engenders come from each man feeling he is "kind of harnessed to the whole shebang" (110), to all of nature. In finding his deepest self, then, Casy has run against the grain of his old social self to embrace a naturalistic religious view which, from Steinbeck's angle of vision, more surely inspires that sense of brotherly love preached by Christianity than Christianity does. A passage from *The Log from The Sea of Cortez* aptly represents the religious view of the novel:

> Why do we so dread to think of our species as a species? Can it be that we are afraid of what we may find? That human self-love would suffer too much and that the image of God might prove to be a mask? This could be only partly true, for if we could cease to wear the image of a kindly, bearded, interstellar dictator, we might find ourselves true images of his kingdom, our eyes the nebulae, and universes in our cells.[7]

By descending into his species self, Casy abandons the arrogance of social man who thinks of himself only in terms of his distinctiveness in nature. Specifically, he abandons his social self as preacher and the limitations which it imposes on creating significant relationships with the world outside. As a preacher he necessarily divorced himself from his species self, with its instinctual need for sexual expression, because of Christianity's sexual ethic. Or, rather, since in fact he did act on these instincts, it is more accurate to say that the Christian sexual ethic cut him off from the knowledge that his species self is his better self. Not only does it promote a sense of connection with nature which a Christian sense of man's uniqueness denies—more important, it promotes a sense of connections with all of mankind suppressed by Christianity's parochialism, its division of the world between those who possess the truth and those who live in outer darkness.

Casy's reverence for nature (which also inspires a reverence for human life) allows him to escape character deformations visible in other figures in the novel. Such reverence is markedly absent in men who use their cars to try to run a turtle down, just as it is absent in Al, who swerves his car to squash a snake. When Al becomes "the soul of the car" (167), of course, he is helping his family in their and his time of need, and to that extent the promptings of his species self are very much with him. But its larger sympathies are blunted because the social means by which he is forced to help his family, the automobile on which he must rely, tarnishes him with the taint of "mechanical man," a phrase Steinbeck uses to describe the social man divorced from his species self, and thus accounts for his squashing the snake. In the car he loses contact with that aspect of the species self which reveres life in all its forms, and by so much he becomes a warped victim of society.

Casy escapes this kind of warping because he has established a relationship to the whole, to nonhuman nature. But he also escapes the warping of an Uncle John or a Lizbeth Sandry because he is empirical in establishing a relation to the parts, to the members of the human community which must be man's first concern, as he makes clear when he says, "I ain't gonna preach" and "I ain't gonna baptize":

> I'm gonna work in the fiel's, in the green fiel's an' I'm gonna be near to folks. I ain't gonna try to teach 'em nothin'. I'm gonna try to learn. Gonna learn why the folks walks in the grass, gonna hear 'em talk, gonna hear 'em sing. Gonna listen to kids eatin' mush. Gonna hear husban' an' wife a-poundin' the mattress in the night. Gonna eat with 'em an' learn. . . . All that's holy, all that's what I didn' understan'. All them things is the good things. (127-128)

Like Thoreau, Casy has reason to believe that most men "have *somewhat hastily* concluded that it is the chief end of man here to 'glorify God and enjoy him forever' " (*Walden,* chapter 2). But his empiricism, not oddly at all, makes him accept in others the very religious view he has already rejected, for such might prove to be the true expression of another's nature. Here he is best measured by Emerson, the Emerson who proclaimed, "Obey thyself," when he tells Uncle John, "I know this—a man got to do what he got to do," or when he says of Uncle John's obsession: "For anybody else it was a mistake, but if you think it was a sin—then it's a sin" (306).

And he follows Emerson in another way. Casy's interest in the parts shows that, like Emerson, he cannot rest satisfied with a religious "high," the feeling of oneness with "the all" that he has already experienced at the novel's opening and that Emerson experienced as "a transparent eyeball" (*Nature:* 1836). Like Emerson, he must translate the insight derived from that experience into ethical terms on the level of practical action. Having concluded that the devil whom most men should fear is society ("they's somepin worse'n the devil got hold a the country" [175]), he not surprisingly discovers the level of practical action by which he can relate to them in a prison, whose inmates are there mainly " 'cause they stole stuff; an' mostly it was stuff they needed an' couldn' get no other way. . . . It's need that makes all the trouble" (521). Since society cannot provide man's basic needs, Casy will help to secure them and, in the process, he brings his species self into relation with men by adopting a social one that permits its expression. He becomes a strike organizer.

Casy's new personal identity is thus an expression of a larger self which, as Emerson knew, can be realized in a diverse number of concrete social forms, though such self-realization earns the world's displeasure. Members of the family who remain in the group thus move toward that larger self when they abandon older views of theological sin as a causal factor in human affairs and approximate Casy's newer view in their words and actions. Uncle John displays this movement, his escape from the ranks of the grotesque, when he floats Rosasharn's stillborn baby to the town, admonishing it to "go down in the street an' rot an' tell 'em that way" (609), just as Rosasharn does when she breastfeeds the old man in the novel's closing paragraph. Her gesture acknowledges the truth of Uncle John's words, that the sin that killed her baby was social and not theological in origin. The same gesture shows her overcoming a solipsism engendered by her pregnancy by enlarging the sympathies of her species self to embrace more than the child that society denied her. That gesture, finally, is the perfect one to signal the awakening of nature's self, the self growing from that human biological nature which mothers and fathers the species.

The novel thus suggests the desirability of a society based not on absolutes imported supernaturally into nature by systems derived from a priori thinking, but one whose institutions accommodate themselves to subjective absolutes. In this way Steinbeck's novel expands the naturalistic vision of *Manhattan Transfer.*

It develops the theme only subordinate in the earlier novel: man and nature are one, not two. But *The Grapes of Wrath* is also a logical and satisfying conclusion to naturalism prior to Dos Passos. If man's connections to nonhuman nature seemed a source of savagery for Crane, nonetheless, at the last, nature in "The Open Boat" was just nature—a vast system for man to interpret for his own benefit, could he but escape the complicated social fabric to see that the primary purpose of societies is to aid him in creating such interpretations. Even in *McTeague,* brute nature is not entirely without its redeeming values: it alone provides McTeague with the sixth sense to flee the city that so twists the lives of the people in Norris's pages. Because the novel is so completely deterministic, however, nature is not used as an avenue of escape. In its form as sexual drive, it instead contributes to McTeague's destruction. But for Steinbeck, nature did become a viable avenue of escape when he developed a religious vision based on the feeling resulting from empirically ascertainable knowledge, the knowledge that man is related to the vast system called Nature. This vision is implicit in Dreiser's view of a creative spirit, but unlike Dreiser, Steinbeck postulates no unknowable purpose in this spirit possibly running at cross-purposes to man's own. He escapes the tentacles of determinism that hold Dreiser's men and women in thrall because he does not unravel the Hobbesian dilemma; because he does not reduce consciousness to temperament or instinct; because he instead makes consciousness in the service of man's instinct the center of man's freedom. Like Emerson, and Dreiser at the last, he assumes that if nature's spirit has purpose, man as part of it can give it expression and direction by realizing his own purpose. To attain knowledge of this ability is to begin to meet the demands of spring.

SEVEN

Faulkner and Naturalism's Selves: *The Sound and the Fury*

Viewing *The Sound and the Fury* as part of the naturalistic movement is to the mutual advantage of the novel and the movement. The structure of the novel comes to make a good deal more sense when it is seen as an outgrowth of American literary naturalism, just as the coherence of the movement becomes more readily visible when the novel is seen as an enrichment of it. As part of that tradition, the novel represents a second line of development away from determinism in naturalism, so a few words recalling the larger context are in order.

One major development in American literary naturalism is a movement *toward* hard determinism. This constitutes a movement away from the soft determinism of Crane, in which man retains the appearance of freedom while in reality his willed actions or the self in "control" of them are products of conditions beyond the control of the individual. Such illusions of freedom disappear in the hard determinism portrayed in *McTeague* and the first two volumes of Dreiser's trilogy, but this determinism yields to Dos Passos's conception of two selves, one determined, the other potentially free but denied development. Dos Passos sees this potentially free second self both as a Whitmanesque self, a part of an impulse innate in all of nature, and at the same time as the source of any individual's personal identity and freedom.

Thereafter, Steinbeck works with determinism and the potential freedom of a second self by displaying a group's movement from determinism to authentic freedom through the liberation of a second self in man, a species self whose liberation brings not only freedom to a group but fulfillment to individuals. In his conception of a species self, Steinbeck thus emphasizes the connections to nature that Dos Passos's second self has.

Through the influence of Bergson on Faulkner, *The Sound and the Fury* represents a second line of development from Dos Passos's conception of selfhood. *The Sound and the Fury* portrays the two selves whose existence Bergson postulates as a response to and partial escape from determinism in *Time and Free Will*. These selves are literal counterparts of those of Dos Passos. Bergson's shadow self, a social product lacking freedom, is a spatialized self because it is a product of spatialized time, the time of clocks and watches, and so it parallels the quite literally spatialized social selves of Dos Passos. The self that grows in Bergson's durée or inner time is for Bergson the source of man's true individual identity and freedom, that self which is suppressed by society in *Manhattan Transfer*. If Benjy is witness, man's second self still has its roots in nature, but Faulkner subordinates Steinbeck's view of that self to emphasize its value as the source of individual identity, a fact to which Quentin Compson bears witness.

In *The Sound and the Fury*, Faulkner works with each of these selves either in their "pure" form or in the complex interactions by which they manifest themselves within a single individual. Each section of the novel portrays a self springing out of the naturalistic tradition. In the order of selves portrayed, Faulkner shows a progression from the bedrock human consciousness of Benjy to more developed consciousnesses. Viewed as an outgrowth of the naturalistic tradition, therefore, the structure of the novel makes much more sense, because it explains why Faulkner sections the work as he does. He organizes it to show his conception of a movement climaxing in ideal selfhood by drawing on views of the self that he inherited from naturalism.

Seen from this same perspective, the novel is not only enriched by the tradition; it also enriches the tradition. Specifically, it explores further dimensions of selfhood inherent within that tradition. To do so Faulkner first abandons the determinism of naturalism for parody.

He endows both selves of naturalism with freedom but parodies each when presenting either one in its pure form, whether the pure shadow or social self hitherto considered determined or even the "pure" durational self, which for Bergson as for Dos Passos is the source of man's identity and freedom. Through the substitution, Faulkner delivers his silent commentary on the possibilities and liabilities of being such pure selves. But he also leaves parody behind, and when he does so he explores the possibilities for achieving inner tranquility and tragic stature within the framework of those conceptions of the self inherited from naturalism. The last section, quite properly called the Dilsey section, points to the possibility of attaining inner tranquility within a naturalistic world, while the second section, Quentin Compson's, points to the way of attaining tragic stature in that world.

Since tragedy has always been the highest of all literary forms, at least this side of epic, Quentin's section will be discussed last here. *The Sound and the Fury* is not a tragic novel, and a refusal to let the novel's ordering of its sections dictate the order of the discussion below does not constitute an attempt to turn it into one. This departure from the novel's ordering of its sections will give Quentin's section an authority derived from a sense of ascending rank of greatness not among sections of a single novel but from an ascending rank of greatness between novels—between, that is, *The Sound and the Fury* and *Absalom, Absalom! Absalom, Absalom!* is a tragedy. The Quentin Compson of *The Sound and the Fury* not only plays an essential role in creating that tragedy; he also shows how the selves of naturalism, his very own selves, can attain the tragic dignity and tragic stature they assume in *Absalom, Absalom!*

Faulkner fashions Benjy's character according to Bergsonian concepts that tell the reader what Benjy is *not* and therefore point to what he is as well as what he might have been. He conveys what Benjy is not through parody. To oversimplify the matter, Benjy is a parody of what he might have been, a developed human being. Parodies of course deflate through comic exaggeration, and that is why the foregoing statement, even though true, is oversimplified. For if Faulkner's intention were simply to parody the normal human being, his effort would be pointless and he would be as witless as the idiot who is the vehicle of his parody.

But if parodies deflate through comic exaggeration, they also can be more affirmative. They can point to important aspects of the thing parodied and thus exalt even as they mock. Certainly this is the possibility to look for when an author employs an idiot to convey his parody. Everyone knows that in literature idiots, like fools, need to be taken seriously—at least in part. If life *is* a tale told by an idiot, then the idiot may be speaking well even as "he speaks somewhat wildly" (to borrow a phrase from Emerson's "The Poet"). This is the case for Benjy. In parodying what Benjy might have been, Faulkner conveys his view of human potential. In using this method to tell the reader what Benjy is, Faulkner shows his fundamental compassion.

Benjy might have been Bergson's developed self in both its dimensions, the durational and the social. Instead, he is but a parody of a durational self, lacking both the depth of individuality that such a self confers and the freedom with which to express it. He is a primal human consciousness, the bedrock on which more developed consciousnesses are formed and, according to the Bergsonian vision of man as a part of nature (on which this parody is based), he is on the dividing line between the human and the animal worlds, distinguishably human but nonetheless a part of the animal world as well.

One sign that Benjy is on that dividing line is that he lacks freedom. Though this deficiency recalls a deterministic interpretation of what it means to be a part of nature, Benjy's deficiency is of course not the consequence of his being part of nature but of his idiocy, for Faulkner's vision, like Bergson's and Steinbeck's, permits the development of freedom within the natural world as an attribute of nature. But Benjy's very failure to develop in this regard is portrayed through a parody that shows that if his potential for freedom is imprisoned by his condition, his prison is ultimately a human one.

To see that Benjy is a parody of a durational self, it is necessary to recall briefly Bergson's view of duration and then to introduce a couple of related concepts that were not relevant to the discussion of Bergson in chapter 2.

Duration is the "continuity of the past in the present,"[1] "a flowing, irreversible succession of [psychic] states that melt into each other to form an indivisible process,"[2] a "quality" rather than a "quantity,"[3] "the form which the succession of our conscious states assumes when our ego lets itself *live,* when it refrains from separating its present state from its former states."[4] Intuition tells man that "reality is true duration, change or movement itself, not a succession of changing states or things that are ever passing out of existence, but movement in being and therefore indivisible."[5] But reason separates these states by projecting durational time into space. The psyche's state at three o'clock is viewed as separable from a different state at half-past three, rather than seen as containing the earlier state from which it is inseparable. By so much does reason spatialize one's psychic life by identifying it with the physical objects, the clock's hands, and by so much does one conceal the flow of durational time by separating that flow into units in space. Bergson explains the effect of reason on man's apprehension of durational time in this way: "We set our states of consciousness side by side in such a way as to perceive them simultaneously, no longer in one another, but alongside one another; in a word, we project time into space, we express duration in terms of extensity, and succession thus takes the form of a continuous line or a chain, the parts of which touch without penetrating one another."[6] Through reason, thus, man leaves the world of pure succession, in which psychic states whose movement constitute duration melt indistinguishably one into the other, and enters a world of mathematical succession, what Bergson calls "simultaneity," which separates states into "before" and "after" and thus gives them a spatialized order of succession, that chronological movement in time which defies the notion that all man's past psychic states exist "in one and the same instant" in a present state that is itself forever in the process of becoming.[7]

Reason thus gives rise not only to a conception of time different from the true time in which man lives, it gives rise to a second self, that social self living in the habit world of society and space which conceals the durational self of unfolding psychic states in durational time. As a consequence, "we are now standing before our own shadow."[8] But Benjy has not yet developed that shadow self which so obsesses Quentin. Because his reason has not developed, his self seems like a purely durational one, his time merely the merging of one psychic state into another without sense of that chronological time by which reason gives order to the world.

To experience duration is to experience a "quality, that which consciousness reaches immediately and which is probably what animals perceive," rather than to experience a "time that has become quantity by being set out in space."[9] The form that the experience of durational time takes, thus, rather than the experience of quality in itself, is the crucial factor that separates man from the animals. Here Bergson's distinction between habit memory, which man shares with the animals, and pure memory is instructive. Both man and the animals possess the former, "motor mechanisms created by repetition" to realize the basic goal of life, a "correspondence to environment—adaptation, in a word—"[10] and in man such memory takes on a human social form as he is conditioned by his environment to follow routines. Thus, Benjy must visit the gate daily and the cemetery weekly. He tolerates little departure from routine, wailing when Luster deprives him of the flowers that he places in two jars, and similarly hysterical when Luster takes him to the left rather than the right of the monument at the novel's end. The form his habit memory takes seems distinctively human, dependent upon his perception of the proper arrangement of humanly created buildings to which routine has accustomed him. But because animals as well as men share habit memory and can be similarly conditioned, even to humanly created objects, this in itself is not the distinctive feature of Benjy's humanity. It is because he possesses pure memory, which man alone has, that Benjy has one foot in the human world and thus is on the dividing line between the human and animal kingdoms.

Pure memory "records, in the form of memory-images, all the events of our daily life as they occur in time."[11] These memory images, which are not confined to visual ones alone (for Caddy smells like trees), wash back and forth in Benjy's limited consciousness as they are called up by his perceptions of the external world. Because he is an idiot and cannot grow in consciousness, his stock of such images must be limited to those available to the limited past of a three-year-old. And as a three-year-old he cannot enlarge that stock with fresh perceptions of the present external world, for an increase of such fresh perceptions demands a growth in consciousness that his idiocy prohibits. He is thus trapped in a parody of the durational self, for he is deprived of the ability of that self to be forever in the process of becoming.

There is a paradox here. The development of that very rationality which is responsible for cutting man off from his true self and developing a shadow one is the prerequisite for the continuing development, albeit on an unconscious level, of his true self. As soon as man spatializes time and the self, he is in danger of losing his true source of freedom, that vital self whose development can continue beneath the veneer of the civilized, spatial one. Yet the development of such a shadow self is the penalty man must pay for his freedom, which proceeds from the continuing development of a fundamental self beneath the shadow one. Although the shadow self obscures it, that self is accessible to man through the exercise of intuition which restores him to a true knowledge of it.[12]

Benjy has reached the threshold of spatialization, but he cannot take the crucial step across. He has a sense of space, for he must have order among the objects that occupy it, as testified by the conclusion to the novel, in which he is pacified only when "cornice and facade . . . post and tree, window and doorway, and signboard [are] each in its ordered place" (401).* But even domestic animals have such a spatial sense and require such an order, so Benjy is not far removed from them in this regard. Like them, Benjy lacks an intellect and cannot spatialize time; consequently he lives in a chronology-less world without past and future. Furthermore, he lacks intuition, though at first it does not appear so. He can smell death, and Roskus avers he knows more than he appears to. But in Bergsonian terms, intuition is "instinct that has become disinterested, self-conscious, capable of reflecting upon its object and of enlarging it indefinitely."[13] Clearly Benjy cannot meet this standard.

Finally, the sure sign of his bondage is the inability of his "durational" self to become. The developing man's durational self always contains the whole of the past in a present that continually flows into the future. No two psychic states can ever be the same, since a future state always contains elements of a past that were not present in prior states. State two can never be like state one, for it contains state one as well as other elements that constitute its own being, and for the same reason state three cannot be like state two. Benjy's psychic states, though they flow back and forth, are dammed up and cannot flow

*William Faulkner, *The Sound and the Fury* (New York: Random House, 1954). The copyright page reads, "The text of this edition . . . is reproduced photographically from a copy of the first printing." Quotations from the novel (and the Appendix) are from this edition.

into the future. Hence they are repeatable in every detail, governed by his sensory responses to the world. The same memory images—firelight, Caddy's eyes, her veil, her perfume's fragrance—accompany representations of his past psychic states called into being by sensory stimuli. Those states are in a sense at the mercy of space. He has not spatialized time sufficiently to develop a shadow self, but whatever selfhood he has is called into being by the spatial world assaulting his senses. Hence he is as much determined by the senses as rational man, according to Bergson, can be determined by the intellect, which creates spatial time and the shadow self.

As a parody of a durational self, Benjy also parodies Bergsonian freedom. In an ideal Bergsonian world—one without shadow selves, only durational ones—Benjy might at first sight be considered truly free, for his actions (his howling, for example) seem to bear the imprint of Bergsonian freedom. "We are free," Bergson writes, "when our acts spring from our whole personality, when they express it, when they have that indefinable resemblance to it which one sometimes finds between the artist and his work."[14] The personality he has in mind is that durational self "which lives and develops by means of its very hesitations, until the free action drops from it like an over-ripe fruit."[15] But though Benjy seems to meet this standard, his freedom is really only that "spontaneity of the life of the senses"[16]—the phrase is Maritain's, Bergson's strong critic—which even animals share, and Bergson viewed true freedom as something more than this by calling the free act "a synthesis of feelings and *ideas*" (emphasis added).[17]

Thus Benjy's apparent freedom reduces itself to animal spontaneity. He requires as a fundamental sign of the developing durational self that faculty which cuts man off from it, an intellect. As he is, he remains only the embryo of a human psyche, which is, like an animal's, "the prisoner of mechanisms."[18] He stands as witness to Faulkner's fundamental realism, his refusal to exclaim, "O for a Life of Sensations rather than of Thoughts!", as Keats did in his famous letter to Benjamin Bailey. Such a life would be the life of an animal, or an idiot. For the same reason he stands as guard against the temptation among readers—especially among youthful readers—to misinterpret the meaning of the condition of Dos Passos's selves. If those selves testify that a Jason is no ideal self to which to aspire, and if they also testify to the desirability to express the durational self, then Faulkner makes it clear that one cannot be a durational self alone. Wordsworth and other romantics may have idealized idiots and imagination and, along with Keats, denigrated Keats's "sole self" and reason, but the realistic Faulkner sees that these too are indispensable to *self*-expression.

But Faulkner does not employ parody simply to show that he is hard-nosed about the human condition. At the same time that he parodies Benjy, he shows that Benjy has the precious seeds of selfhood, even if they will never grow. Faulkner thus permits the reader to see that this "prisoner of mechanisms" has a humanity that shines through the prison, appearing in those memory images which man alone possesses. They make Benjy capable of a joy and suffering that are distinctly human. He is capable of joy, for he could enter sympathetically into the durational self of Caddy, as she entered his own, and thus form memory images of his association with her. He can experience the pure, reasonless pleasure of sharing the quality of the durational lives of Dilsey's congregation and their visiting minister, for their voices leave him "rapt in his sweet blue gaze" (370). But for the most part he is distinguished by his capacity for human suffering, that suffering attributable not to the pain his habit memory inflicts when his environment is disturbed, but to the pain arising from his possession of a purely human faculty, pure memory and the memory images it records.

Faulkner tells the reader in his appendix, added much later,[19] that Benjy does not recall the physical person of Caddy, nor does he recall the literal pasture once he is at Jackson. He remembers "only the loss of her" and "only its loss" (423, 424), and it is the memory of loss that his memory images depict. Idiot though he is, he thus participates in the human experience and becomes the prototype of all of suffering humanity, and more. Standing as he does on the dividing line between two worlds, he is also the expression of suffering in the nonhuman realm as well. Perhaps for this reason Faulkner stresses his bellowing in the last part of *The Sound and the Fury*, once in human terms as the sound of "all time and injustice and sorrow become vocal for an instant by a conjunction of planets" (359), again, and more movingly, in terms that embrace the world beyond the human, as "the grave hopeless sound of all voiceless misery under the sun" (395).

———

If one cannot be purely a durational self without becoming an idiot, one cannot be purely a social self without becoming as mechanical as an electric eye on a billboard, and as blind. Dos Passos creates spatialized selves to indict society for enslaving the individual. Faulkner parodies the spatialized self to indict the individual who enslaves himself to society. Faulkner's two parodies thus work against sentimental impossibility and hardheaded possibility. If Benjy testifies that it is impossible to be solely a durational self this side of sanity, Jason testifies to the dangers inherent in the very real possibility of becoming only a social self. Not all of Faulkner's social selves are comic or trivialized, for the parody of Jason prophesies Thomas Sutpen and his Design in *Absalom, Absalom!* But in this case Faulkner does trivialize it through parody in order to point to the importance of retaining the durational self as the seat of individuality, value, and freedom.

This parody of a social self is conveyed through self-revelation. For the most part, Jason in his monologue unwittingly reveals a self that exhibits traits that serve three overlapping functions: they act to show the status of the self as spatialized, they transform the monologue into a parody of the social self, and they act as indictments of that self. In a novel of multiple narrations, it is impossible to avoid comparing and contrasting the principals, and that process also helps to illuminate the way in which details serve the three functions mentioned.

One can begin best by using the principle of contrast to explain an omission from Jason's narration that a reader might find odd if he is depending on Bergsonian landmarks to aid him in identifying the nature of Jason's self. Jason's obsession with clock time suggests that he is the very shadow self that Bergson sees as a product of spatialized time, so at first it seems strange that Faulkner endows him with no consciousness of his shadow. In fact, in the final section of the novel Faulkner seems to take pains to emphasize Jason's ignorance of it. As Jason pursues his niece in a futile effort to recover his lost money, the narrator observes that "the running shadow patches were not the obverse" (382); that is, Jason's shadow is not before him so that he can see it.

There is, however, a persuasive explanation for this omission. Faulkner omits shadows from Jason's consciousness to contrast him sharply to Quentin. Quentin's preoccupation with his shadow demonstrates his own awareness of a distinction between his two selves, the durational and the social; or, to put the matter in another way, such awareness permits him to give the symbolic value of a social self to his shadow. Since Jason possesses no durational self, no such distinction can exist for him. Hence, by denying him a consciousness of his shadow, Faulkner in fact employs the principle of contrast among speakers to emphasize Jason's purely shadow existence.

In other ways the principle of contrast emphasizes Jason's existence solely as a shadow self lacking a durational one. The void at the center of Jason's being is revealed most tellingly by the contrast between his brother's and Dilsey's apprehension of bells, the symbol of time, and his own. For Quentin, bells signify both chronological and durational time. His dual relationship to them signifies the existence of dual selves within him. Much the same can be said of Dilsey. She has a shadow self that lives in clock time, for she always knows the precise time of day when the chimes of her clock sound. But she also has a durational self. She refuses to permit the chimes of her clock to converge with clock time, and thus she demonstrates her allegiance to the pure music of the chimes and to that Christian sense of time which their sound symbolizes to her—a kind of time that suggests the quality of her durational self. For Jason, on the other hand, bells have only a single value, the utilitarian, a fact that accounts for his indignation when Parson Walthall tolerates pigeons fouling a courthouse clock rather than permit their destruction: "What does he care what time it is" (308), he exclaims. Jason's inability to relate to the bells in any sensitive way signifies his existence as a shadow self only.

The last section confirms this meaning extracted from the principle of contrast by rendering the nature of Jason's self through images that intertwine time and space. There Jason is defeated by his niece Quentin in his pursuit of the money, and Faulkner associates a description of Jason's defeated self with a bell striking the half-hour. As Jason hears the bell ring, he sits in his car, "his invisible life ravelled out about him like a wornout sock" (391). Out of context the adjective "invisible" misleadingly suggests the existence of a durational life in Jason, but in context this possibility vanishes. His life is invisible to those passersby leaving Easter Sunday services because they cannot know his situation, that his selfhood depends solely on the money he has lost. His self thus fittingly unravels in space, for the shadow self is a function of that spatialized time which is the only meaning the bells have for Jason.

Jason's existence as the shadow self who is society's self is finally confirmed by his (thwarted) social ambition, that desire for the bank job he never received, and by commercial and materialistic concerns that have always been the standard fare for portraying and criticizing social man. But Jason is more than a social self, more than a shadow self. He is a parody of a social self.

The substance of his narration contributes to the parody by making the narration itself a parody of a literary form. Jason complains. He complains about everyone and everything, a feature that so pervades his narrative that to cite all his complaints would be tantamount to quoting the narration in its entirety. Because the narration is a long string of complaints, it recalls the literary form called a complaint. The traditional complaint, however, usually appears in one of two forms, both of which become intertwined here.[20] In the first, a young man complains of unrequited love for a lady, for whom he would give the world. Jason's complaint parodies this form of the tradition by inverting it. Not only does he distrust the entire female sex, but he specifically complains against a woman (his niece Quentin or, what is for him interchangeable, her mother Caddy) for depriving him of a position in a world he loves, the position of bank job to which he refers compulsively throughout the narration.

The second form of the complaint is a complaint against one's position in the world. It is usually limited in scope; a complaint about insufficient money, for example. But Jason feels spurned by the world in a massive way, and the massiveness of his complaint against the spurning generates the parody of this second tradition. Jason values the world's opinion so greatly that he is obsessed by his public image, and thus his complaint against the woman who deprived him of status in it unites the two forms.

To see the parody of this second tradition, it is necessary to see the scope of his feeling rejected by the world, a scope so wide that one critic finds it akin to "the furthest stages of paranoia."[21] Jason's sense of rejection goes beyond his sense that he is a victim of family members and the other groups he mentions. He feels vicitimized by all of society, here represented by government at every level: the local ("those grafters in the Mayor's office": 243), the state (the politicians won't fix the roads: 297), and the national ("them up there in Washington": 292).

That is just the human world spurning Jason, however, and Jason's sense of rejection goes beyond that world. Birds clearly have left their droppings on him (309)—little wonder that he fears to go out without a hat—and even the vegetable world seems against him. When he first pursues Quentin and the circus man he complains of "briers and things grabbing at me" (301). The personification must be intentional, both on Faulkner's part and Jason's, for shortly before, he remarks: "I happened to look around and I had my hand right on a bunch of poison oak. The only thing I couldn't understand was why it was just poison oak and not a snake or something. So I didn't even bother to move it" (300). Things are bad, and they can only get worse. And do.

When even the nonhuman world turns on its lover, parody results. And the parody bears another name, which becomes clear if one keeps in mind the character of the speaker as well as the substance of the narration. The man awful enough to permit Caddy only a glance at her baby through a carriage window as he drives around the square; the man who burns complementary tickets to the circus before Luster, who wants to attend but does not have the admission fee; there is a name for such a man, and it appears in the opening words of his narration and in the echo of those words towards the end of his complaint: "Once a bitch always a bitch, what I say" (223, 329). Jason is the "bitch," and his series of unrelieved complaints aptly show him "bitching." Thus parody is wrought to a fine point as the traditional male in the literary complaint becomes the male "bitch" of vulgar expression and the complaint itself his vulgar "bitching."

The parody of the literary form called the complaint carries over into the last section of the novel, in which the resolution of the action also points to one major meaning of the parody as well. In a complaint the speaker often seeks divine intercession on his behalf; but this complainant seems to sense that if even the non-human world spurns him, then the infinite compassion and mercy of the divine world has its limits, too, and that world draws the line at Jason. Hence he treats even the heavens as his enemy rather than his friend as he calls out while trying to regain his money, "And damn You, too, . . . See if You can stop me" (382). If the very churches he passes in his pursuit of Quentin and the money are each seen by him as "a picket-post where the rear guards of Circumstance peeped fleetingly back at him," then perhaps the world outside of nature is not to be trusted either. From his point of view, the resolution of the action seems to confirm his suspicions. But from the reader's point of view justice of the kind commonly called poetic is done. A con man is outconned.

The resolution points to one major meaning of the parody by suggesting the first way in which the shadow self can be indicted. If suicide is a crime, then the shadow self can be accused of it, for this spatialized self is *self*-defeating. The resolution supports the truth of Job's statement to Jason: "Aint a man in dis town kin keep up wid you fer smartness. You fools a man whut so smart he cant even keep up wid hisself" (311-12). "Hisself" is Jason, as Job makes clear. The shadow self may feel spurned by the world, but it defines itself through worldly values and so counts on some measure of control over it to give it selfhood. When that control fails, it lacks the resources of the durational self to find interior values untouchable by the world of time and space and so fittingly unravels into space "like an old sock." Selves who live solely by the world are easily destroyed by the world. For the reader of *Absalom, Absalom!* that meaning becomes writ large in the career of the man Rosa Coldfield calls a "walking shadow": Thomas Sutpen.

What the shadow self does not possess, it cannot recognize in others, and so the parody indicts Jason for another limitation. Not just true freedom from the world, but authentic individual identity apart from it are to be found in the durational self, which is forever developing in duration, enriching its possessor in the process—even in the process of suffering. But the shadow self lacks the self to acknowledge this identity in others. Its opening remarks thus reveal the special nature of this deficiency. The phrase *"once* a bitch *always* a bitch" (emphasis added) associates a static view of time with an abstract view of self and thus emphasizes Jason's inability to apprehend the flow of Caddy's durational self, which Quentin is able to perceive. For Jason the self is unchanging, "once" and "always" the same, frozen in time and hence easily definable in a single word.[22] This view is true only of the shadow self, and Jason's life is living testament to its truth. His mother tells him that gasoline "*always* made you sick . . . *Ever since* you were a child" (296, emphasis added). Once again, the reader sees that Jason's description of Caddy better describes himself.

The parody shows more deficiencies than simply that the shadow self is *self*-defeating and unable to acknowledge the source of selfhood in others; it shows that the shadow self is plainly and simply blind, though in the metaphoric rather than the literal sense of that word. One image in the novel provides a comprehensive understanding of this fundamental deficiency that makes Jason so massively flawed that he becomes a parody. The image central to the work is the eye—in the final section of the work an eye is literally illustrated, drawn into the text as a picture. For Jason this eye has only its billboard value as a symbol of a growing Mottson. His shadow self is blind to the rich complex of values that the eye as image holds for Quentin and Dilsey—not to mention Benjy, who is so conscious of Caddy's eyes. Clearly Jason cannot see in any such depth, and so the eye on that sign in the novel's last section raises the larger question of what social man can see.

What social man can see is what Jason can see, and his vision is perfectly consistent with the status of the self that does the seeing. Jason can only see objects in space divorced from the durational values they have for others, and he sees even his human others in pretty much the same terms as objects because he is unconscious of their durational lives. His exclusively spatial sense is sharply revealed by the precision of his statement that he "was within sixty-seven miles of there [Memphis] once this afternoon" (305). With such a pronounced spatial sense, it is not surprising that he defines others in literal spatial terms. He identifies people with places. Benjy belongs to Jackson, the state asylum. He tells his mother that after her death, "I'll sure have him on number seventeen that night" (276). Similarly, he frames his niece in a spatial field of vision. "I think I know a place where they'll take her too and the name of it's not Milk Street and Honey Avenue either" (276). The name of it is Beale Street, Memphis's red-light district, to which he alludes in the closing words of his narration. Jason's sense of space, too, generates the primary action of his section, his pursuit of his niece Quentin. His central focus of vision at the beginning (as at the conclusion) of the action is the town square. It is appropriate that what violates his sense of decorum ("my mother's good name") is his spying Quentin's and the circus man's appearance in this public space; for the self committed to space and space's time is the social self committed to social values. Like Benjy, Jason must have "each in its ordered place," and he translates physical space into social terms to sustain his own felt need for social order, affronting the inner sanctity of others in the process. And this commitment to space and the stable social order with which he associates it emerges most clearly at the end of the novel. Jason jerks the reins of the horses so that they will draw the carriage to the right of the monument in the square rather than the left, and he does so in the interests of silencing Benjy's howling and thus to attain that "peace and quiet" which is the sole value he attributes to Caddy's slipper. The "bitch" cannot tolerate the idiot, and so it would seem as if the selves that they represent are utterly alien to one another and cannot grow or act in concert with each other. That statement, however, is true of the dual selves of other naturalists. It is only true of Faulkner's *parodies* of such selves. These very parodies suggest the need to be both selves by showing the inadequacy of being either one alone.

Benjy and Jason represent extremes of selfhood, the one a parody of the durational self, the other a parody of the social or shadow self. Dilsey represents a healthy harmony between these two selves. One may legitimately infer the existence of a durational self in Dilsey from her sympathy for Benjy. Without a durational self, she could never establish a rapport with the only self he has, one "durational" in nature. The sure sign of a harmony between this self and a shadow one is to be found in that relationship to her clock mentioned earlier. She knows the chronological time of day, and she gives it the respect it deserves by performing her duties faithfully according to it. So she does have a shadow self, one that lives according to the practical demands of the clock. But she never leaves another dimension of time behind. By not permitting the chimes to converge with clock time she honors that pure music of the bells that Bergson explains is the best way of imaging an apprehension of duration. Needless to say, to apprehend duration is to live from the self so easily obscured by the spatialized shadow self. Dilsey's relation to her clock thus shows the harmony of her selves.

The description of the setting of the black church that Dilsey attends shows that she is not alone in reconciling a durational with a shadow self: "The whole scene was as flat and without perspective as a painted cardboard set upon the ultimate edge of the flat earth, against the windy sunlight of space and April and a midmorning filled with bells" (364). Because it lacks depth and perspective, the scene is much like a primitive painting of the sort Grandma Moses has popularized in America. As Cleanth Brooks has pointed out,[23] Faulkner is no primitivist. His description of the church does not act as commentary on some supposed primitive nature of the worshipers within; the verbal picture acts, rather, as a metaphor to represent a different, nonprimitive kind of black identity and points to the reality accessible to its possessors. The scene contains space, of course, but because it is without depth, a sense of it is reduced. The description therefore suggests that the black worshipers do possess those shadow selves which inevitably grow in spatialized time, but its deemphasis of space also suggests that they are not so shackled to such a self that they fail to be in contact with their durational being.

For the blacks, space is replaced by Bergson's pure sound, the "midmorning filled with bells" in this description, those very bells which later are still ringing "from the direction of the section known as Nigger Hollow" (377) and filling the air "high in the scudding sunlight in bright disorderly tatters of sound" (380) as Jason pursues his niece in space. That sound replaces space for the blacks shows their apprehension of durational time. Furthermore, since these are church bells, magnified versions of Dilsey's chimes, those selves of theirs which grow in duration possess the qualities associated with people who believe in Christian time.

Events within the church confirm the significance of its description and of the sounding of the Easter church bells. The largely black congregation (Benjy is the only white there) is at first disappointed that the visiting preacher "sounded like a white man" with a voice "level and cold" (366), for such a white social self has lost contact with the enduring reality of self and of God whose expression they seek. But soon their disappointment vanishes as the music of his voice fills space as surely as the church bells do: "The voice died in sonorous echoes between the walls. It was as different as day and dark from his former tone, with a sad, timbrous quality like an alto horn, sinking into their hearts and speaking there again when it had ceased in fading and cumulate echoes" (367). Words become music and the distance between the congregation and the minister vanishes, a mere illusion of space, as they are absorbed into his own voice. In such merger, these durational selves transcend the bondage of space and language to mingle with each other like Donne's angels in pure air: "And the congregation seemed to watch with its own eyes while the voice consumed him, until he was nothing and they were nothing and there was not even a voice but instead their hearts were speaking to one another in chanting measures beyond the need for words" (367).

In this description the reader sees from two perspectives what it means to live in Christian time. From Faulkner's point of view the blacks have transcended chronological time by moving into duration and thus awakening their durational selves committed to a sense of Christian value and time. This kind of transcendence is apparent because it is the "chanting measures" of the minister's voice that spark this religious ecstasy. When words become music, when a sermon becomes a rhapsody, then the emphasis on music signifies the awakening of selves that apprehend duration as the ear apprehends musical notes blending into each other (the parallel is Bergson's).[24] These awakened selves apprehend each other in the same way. As Dilsey sheds tears showing her rapport, Benjy sits "rapt in his sweet blue gaze" (370). Even his own "durational" self responds to a flow of words whose musical movement rather than literal meaning is of special importance here.

From the congregation's point of view, the experience of merger bears witness to two truths fundamental to a Christian sense of time. The first is that Christ, who resides in eternity, is nonetheless directly accessible in human time. The preacher emphasizes this view by repeatedly using the present tense in his religious ecstasy: "I sees de closin eyes" (369). After the service, blacks in the congregation acknowledge the minister's merger with Christ. One says, "He seed de power en de glory." Another agrees, "Yes, suh. He seed it. Face to face he seed it" (371). But who can fail to see that they too feel they have experienced merger? Their comments and Dilsey's tears are testament to that.

The experience also confirms a second truth for the blacks, the comfort brought by a larger view of Christian history. For Christians, eternity and the chronological time of human history converge after the Fall in the person of Christ and will do so again in His second coming. The guest minister at Dilsey's church sees Christ crucified and resurrected; and he also sees the scene of the Judgment Day. Thus he bears witness to the truth of the Christian view of history: the working out, in human history, of a Divine Plan conceived in eternity. Dilsey, he, and all the blacks also bear witness to the comfort such belief brings. Because this sense of time is a part of the durational selves of the blacks, those selves can transcend the myriad details of human history that characterize the succession of past, present, and future of chronological time. Such events seem trivial indeed when compared to the primary events that faith permits them to hold within themselves as measures of all other events; that is, the resurrection and the Second Coming. While living in the world of clock time, therefore, Dilsey gains the wisdom and comfort offered by a perspective definable as a Christian apprehension of duration. She lives *sub specie aeternitatis,* and her perspective is governed by that fact.

Although they have more than one meaning, Dilsey's remarks after the service point to this view and make the full significance of the black experience converge in her: "I've seed de first en de last," she tells Frony. "I seed de beginnin, en now I sees de endin" (371). Her words refer to the beginning and end of a family with whom she has spent her life, the Compsons, who are ravaged by chronological time because they cannot transcend it. Dilsey is different from them, and her difference appears in the second meaning of her words, the beginning of redemption through Christ's resurrection and its ending in His second coming. If physically she is ravaged by clock time, she cannot be spiritually ravaged. Her durational life contains both a past and future Christ. Faith prohibits the loss of that past, just as the hope that faith generates permits her to look confidently to that future.

One can now see the beauty of Faulkner's change from a personal narrator to a detached one in the last section of his novel. If all durational selves are beyond words, Dilsey's contains a sense of the eternal, which places it at an even greater distance from language than other such selves; so it is fitting that Faulkner have a narrator express the inadequacy of language for her, rather than to have her speak the inexpressible.

It is also fitting that the section in which she is most prominent should focus on Jason and Benjy as well. These parodied figures display the poles of naturalism's selves. Their presence here shows that Dilsey is a happy blend of moderate versions of these extremes of selfhood. In giving freedom to society's self, Faulkner shows that it can be as grotesque as a Jason—and morally contemptible, too, in a way that Crane's Jimmie cannot be, social product that he is. But in permitting the development of a durational self that a naturalist like Dos Passos saw forever suppressed, Faulkner permitted society's self to gain dignity as well, the dignity conferred on it by a durational self speaking through it. Dilsey's harmony of the two selves speaks on behalf of this view.

In a sense, however, there is another figure in this section, though he has been dead for eighteen years. Quentin is there by way of contrast to Dilsey. Like her, he longed for a merger with an infinite; but training and circumstance prohibited the fulfillment of his desires and threatened the very existence of his durational self. For some figures, the time is out of joint to achieve Dilsey's harmony. Even on such figures, however, Faulkner was able to confer dignity. By giving a developed voice to naturalism's yet undeveloped durational self, Faulkner gave it a freedom that a nascent durational self like Dos Passos's simply could not have. In doing so, he opened the way to tragedy in naturalism. Quentin Compson shows the direction in which it would move.

That harmony of self experienced by Dilsey is not shared by Quentin, who faces the prospect of losing his developed durational self because he can get no recognition for it from either his family or the world. Though on occasion his durational self converges with his shadow one, Quentin has good reason for believing that the convergence is temporary because of the times in which he lives, and that his moment in history dictates that he must lose his durational selfhood and live permanently in the world of the shadow self.

Nothing stated above is meant to suggest that Quentin is a tragic figure. What is asserted is that Quentin does have a durational self, an important point that critics have not seen. The usual critical complaints about Quentin, which often amount to moralizing, are mainly registered in terms that deny Quentin a durational self because they deny him, if not a knowledge of duration, then the experience of living within duration. The two principal ones concern his relations to time and to language. When Quentin tries to halt time by breaking his watch, for example, critics assume Quentin wishes to freeze time and to deny life's flow, both his own and Caddy's. They see him doing the same thing through his use of language. In his concern for virginity, they see him imposing on Caddy's life a verbal construct beyond which her life should not flow or change.[25]

Both views misinterpret Quentin's relations to time and to language and result in flawed interpretations of his monologue because they fail to see that Quentin has two selves. This failure misleads critics into thinking Quentin is trying to evade duration rather than to live within it and to express the self living there. The reverse is true.

Bergson provides the clue for understanding Faulkner's intent in Quentin's section:

> Now, if some bold novelist, tearing aside the cleverly woven curtain of our conventional ego, shows us under this appearance of logic a fundamental absurdity, under this juxtaposition of simple states an infinite permeation of a thousand different impressions which have already ceased to exist the instant they are named, we commend him for having known us better than we knew ourselves. This is not

the case, however, and the very fact that he spreads out our feeling in a homogeneous time, and expresses its elements by words, shows that he in his turn is only offering us its shadow: but he has arranged this shadow in such a way as to make us suspect the extraordinary and illogical nature of the object which projects it; he has made us reflect by giving outward expression to something of that contradiction, that interpenetration, which is the very essence of the elements expressed. Encouraged by him, we have put aside for an instant the veil which we interposed between our consciousness and ourselves. He has brought us back into our own presence.[26]

That "curtain" of the "conventional ego" or shadow self which must be removed is a curtain whose existence is a function of that chronological time which confronts one in waking, and which separates one from the durational self best apprehended as a quality in sleep. "Here we no longer measure duration, but we feel it; from quantity it returns to the state of quality; we no longer estimate past time mathematically."[27] Hence the significance of the first line of Quentin's monologue. He awakens from sleep, where the durational flow of the fundamental self is experienced most intensely, to the world of chronological time and the shadow self: "When the shadow of the sash appeared on the curtains it was between seven and eight oclock and then I was in time again, hearing the watch" (93).

Even after he awakes, however, Quentin has not abandoned duration, a point that must be kept in mind to understand his monologue. Bergson relies upon the image of strokes on a bell tower to explain two ways of apprehending time. To hear the strokes separately is to hear only a succession of sounds in space, to hear the passage of chronological time. But to hear them melting "into one another in such a way as to give the whole a peculiar quality, to make a kind of musical phrase out of it"[28] is akin to experiencing pure duration. One thus escapes "the self with well-defined states" and apprehends that "self in which *succeeding each other* means *melting into one another,*" though "we are generally content with the first, i.e. with the shadow of the self projected into homogeneous space."[29] Repeatedly Bergson refers to notes interpenetrating each other to express "the image of pure duration."[30] He writes of "the notes of a tune, melting, so to speak, into one another" and refers to a series of hammer blows that can be heard separate in a spatial world or as "pure sensations" forming "an indivisible melody."[31] To apprehend sounds in space indivisibly is the best equivalent he can find for experiencing pure duration as a quality.

Quentin's relations to sounds indicate that he can apprehend durational time and therefore has not lost contact with the durational self that unfolds in it. His fascination with the chimes striking the hour suggests his attempt to transcend the limitations of chronological time. "The quarter hour sounded," he says. "I stopped and listened to it until the chimes ceased" (99). It is not clear what he apprehends at this moment, and in the next reference to the chimes he seems to be still in the world of the shadow self, for he emphasizes the spacing of the notes: "I stood in the belly of my shadow and listened to the strokes *spaced* and tranquil along the sunlight, among the thin, still little leaves" (124, emphasis added). But later he specifically hears his watch, symbol of chronological time, and then turns to the chimes to apprehend them as symbols of pure duration: "Then I was hearing my watch and I began to listen for the chimes and I touched Shreve's letter through my coat, the bitten shadows of the elms flowing upon my hand. And then as I turned into the quad the chimes did begin and I went on while the notes came up like ripples on a pool and passed me and went on, saying Quarter to what? All right. Quarter to what" (212). Clock time becomes durational as the chimes' notes become like "ripples on a pool" and one forgets the utilitarian value of chronological time: "Quarter to what?"

Two other major references buttress the view that Quentin apprehends pure duration, one of them involving another relation to sound, specifically the way Quentin hears the sound of the bird's singing. "The bird whistled again, invisible, a sound meaningless [beyond reason] and profound [comprehended intuitively], inflexionless [no divisions in notes to spatialize the line]"; but then his sense of chronological time intrudes as the bird's song ceases "as though cut off with the blow of a knife" (168-169). Duration can be experienced only as quality; and hence the water imagery that succeeds this line, its flow also a symbol of duration,[32] is "felt, not seen not heard" (169). The same water imagery appears in his recalled encounter with Dalton Ames. After Ames leaves, Quentin looks at the water passing beneath the bridge on which he stands "and then the bird again . . . I heard the bird again and the water and then everything sort of rolled away. . . . I felt almost good" (201). The perfect apprehension of duration merges with the flow of his own psychic life, imaged in the water, to give him a moment of wholeness.

The other certain evidence that Quentin apprehends durational time appears in his mouthing sentiments of Benjy's: "*Hands can see,*" he says. "My nose could see gasoline" (215). Much of Quentin's narration, in short, is composed of memory images that recall the felt quality of his entire past—in this case, a childhood spent in part with Jason, who could not tolerate the smell of gasoline.

Quentin, however, is not a "pure" durational self because he is not an idiot like Benjy. His monologue reveals a developed social self through which the durational one repeatedly seeks expression. His memory images, existing within the pure memory of his durational self, converge with the sights and sounds he sees and hears on this last day of his life and thus form the bridge between his two selves, his shadow and durational ones. Quentin's own words indicate Faulkner's intention to render such a relationship between Quentin's selves. As Quentin boards a tram with his black eye, he observes, "I could see the twilight again, that quality of light as if time really had stopped for a while, with the sun hanging just under the horizon" (209-10). This time of day between full sunlight and full darkness is the perfect image to suggest the twilight state of Quentin's psyche, a state in which durational and shadow selves meet. Past becomes present, Quentin's reflections on twilight merge with "honeysuckle," which "was the saddest odour of all, I think" (210). Thus Faulkner portrays a durational self emerging through the resistant shadow world of the shadow self.

The resistance of that world to his durational self is the locus of Quentin's problem. To put the matter simply, Quentin's problem *is* his shadow self, which threatens the durational one with extinction. If the feelings that characterize the durational self develop in "a duration whose moments permeate one another," those feelings can easily be lost: "By separating these moments from each other, by spreading out time in space, we have caused this feeling to lose its life and its colour. Hence, we are now standing before our own shadow."[33]

If those words are Bergson's, the situation they portray is Quentin's. Although we need not go to Bergson to see that shadows are symbols of chronological time, sundials having always been used to express it, we do need his reasoning to understand Quentin's behavior, for it is Bergson who explains that the shadow is the social self because it exists in space. Quentin's attempts to trick his shadow and his breaking his watch thus reveal the terms of his problem: to preserve the durational self against the incursions of a chronological time that gives rise to a spatialized shadow self concealing his true identity.

Several references to Keats's "Ode to a Nightingale" support this view.[34] Keats's narrator hears a nightingale and unsuccessfully tries to merge with it in order to escape that "sole self" which is the equivalent of Quentin's shadow one. In the poem the bird is in the realm of the light of the moon, the speaker in the realm of shadows. Quentin similarly hears a bird on several occasions, only to be left in the realm of shadows. With the Italian girl he hears "a bird somewhere in the woods, beyond the broken and infrequent slanting of sunlight" (168). After his release by the judge, he "looked off into the trees where the afternoon slanted, thinking of afternoon and of the bird and the boys in swimming" (182-183). As he recalls his encounter with Dalton Ames (and as he literally fights with Gerald Bland) he hears "a bird singing somewhere beyond the sun" (199), and notes that Caddy's "face looked off into the trees where the sun slanted and where the bird" (203). The sun has replaced Keats's moon, so significantly the bird is "beyond the broken and infrequent slanting of sunlight" (168), a bird "beyond the sun," for the sun casts shadows and thus the bird must be in a realm beyond the source of the shadow. But his relationship to the bird is essentially that of Keats's speaker to his nightingale, and both remain in the shadow world. Hence Quentin recalls the story of a picture in a children's book of "a dark place into which a single weak ray of light came slanting upon two faces lifted out of the shadow" (215). They are his mother and father, and he and the other Compson children are "lost somewhere below even them without even a ray of light" (215). The image in this recollection thus sums up one aspect of Quentin's condition presented in these Keatsian references: "Here there is no light." He feels trapped in the realm of Keats's "sole self."

The trap has several implications for Quentin that cannot be understood unless one understands the nature of Quentin's durational self. Words, of course, freeze the flow of durational life and thus are inadequate to express it, but Faulkner nonetheless must manipulate his artistic medium, language, to express the self beyond words, just as he must permit an idiot verbal self-expression though the idiot cannot talk. He manipulates his medium well. Quentin's memory images depict a durational life profoundly melancholic (the sad odor of honeysuckle: 210) and also infer the reasons for the melancholia, a self whose commitments are orchestrated about several sharply conflicting polarities.

Quentin's devotion to an idealized Caddy associated with Eden (100, 130, 139) represents one pole of each polarity, so it is only necessary to list the other poles to which she is an opposite in order to understand the nature of Quentin's internalized system of values. In a durational self in which all past time merges into a present moment yielding in turn to a future one, the first of these poles is the threat of losing Caddy through her sexual dalliance; the second, her actual departure from his life; the third, his commitment to a Southern code of honor—here, that chivalric part of the code which values purity in women and demands the male's defense of the same—aroused by Caddy's sexual dalliance; and the last, his commitment to an absolute, his belief in the reality of sin on which that code rests.[35]

A recognition of an absolute in life is part of Quentin's durational self, though not of his shadow one, a point made emphatically clear through the familiar image of bells in a statement that shows that Quentin experiences durational time as "a quality and not as a quantity."[36] In the following, the time in which he apprehends Jesus and St. Francis is clearly "more felt than heard" by him: "It was a while before the last stroke ceased vibrating. It stayed in the air, more felt than heard, for a long time. Like all the bells that ever rang still ringing in the long dying light-rays and Jesus and Saint Francis talking about his sister" (97).

"More felt than heard." The phrase is an interesting one which appears somewhat earlier in variant form, and its earlier appearance is worth quoting because it speaks to Quentin's problem with his shadow self in a most telling way. Earlier Quentin remarks on clock time and then immediately transcends such time to show that a religious past exists in his self in a single continuum of time that defies the clock: "I dont suppose anybody ever deliberately listens to a watch or a clock. You dont have to. You can be oblivious to the sound for a long while, then in a second of ticking it can create in the mind unbroken the long diminishing parade of time you didn't hear. Like Father said down the long and lonely light-rays you might see Jesus walking, like. And the good Saint Francis that said Little Sister Death" (93–94).

"Time you didn't hear." Keats says, "Heard melodies are sweet, but those unheard are sweeter," and thereby points to the several implications of Quentin's feeling trapped in the realm of Keats's sole self. The first is that a self committed to "virginity" and the values it symbolizes, those associated with honor and an absolute, feels estranged from a world in which, as his father tells Quentin, virginity is but a word and Christ was but a man "not crucified" but "worn away by a minute clicking of little wheels" (94). The second is that the durational self can nonetheless be a source of comfort and value, a refuge, in such a world. It can still project private meanings on that world, though the world no longer acknowledges those meanings.

Even nonhuman things function to display the gulf between the self and the world and, at the same time, point to the value of possessing such a self in such a world. The trout Quentin sees is, of course, a Christian symbol, though the boys who seek to catch it are not aware of it as such. Significantly, Quentin sees it as a "shadow hanging like a fat arrow stemming into the current" (144), a view that displays his awareness that in the world of the shadow self the trout has lost its Christian meaning. Such a value does reside in his durational self, however, for he views the fish within a context of references to the resurrection and to hell that implicitly associate it with Christian values. Hence he metaphorically escapes the meaningless shadow world by contemplating a resurrection in which only his eyes will arise "to look on glory" (144). He fantasizes a state akin to the one Emerson feels when he describes himself as a "transparent eyeball" divorced from body and nature but in union with that god whose symbol is the eye (*Nature:* 1836).

Quentin's earlier encounter with the sparrow reveals the same pattern of awareness, a feeling of estrangement from the world and a feeling that the self offers refuge from it. He concentrates on the eye of the sparrow, and in so doing implicitly raises the larger question, Is God's eye truly on the sparrow associated with it in familiar adage? If it were, of course, Caddy's act would have some significance, but his father has taught him only too well that the social world contains no frame of reference by which to gain such significance. For Jason Compson God is but an indifferent "dark diceman" and the universe a mechanism dominated by chance, "by whatever issue the gods happen to be floating at the time" (221). And Quentin knows that this kind of world is not a Southern one alone, for he perceives that "God would be canaille too in Boston in Massachusetts. Or maybe just not a husband" (137–38). If Boston acknowledges any God, it is not one responsible for the immaculate conception, as his reference to "husband" indicates. But after Quentin sees the sparrow's eye, he escapes that world by taking refuge in durational time, apprehending bells "more felt than heard" and finding in duration's self that sense of Jesus and Saint Francis so conspicuously absent from the world of space and clock time.

But Quentin's story of incest is an even more illuminating example of the vital importance to Quentin of his durational self, as well as an example of the gap between it and the world. For Quentin, the tale of incest is a metaphor for the conflicting commitments of his durational self. It resolves those conflicts by showing allegiance to Caddy through assuming partial responsibility for her sin. It also shows allegiance to principle by his punishing them both through casting them into hell. An eternity in hell, in turn, expresses the self's commitment to rival values and to its desire to transcend the world of the shadow self, dominated by the laws of cause and effect, by living from the durational self. This metaphoric situation thus represents a convergence in words between Quentin's durational self and the spatial reality of Caddy's transgression.

Unfortunately, his telling the tale issues in a knowledge that raises a fatal implication for being trapped in the world of the "sole self." His father's response to the tale not only confirms for Quentin the gap between the world and his durational self but also points to the threat posed by that world to his cherished self's very existence. His father responds by calling Quentin blind to "that part of general truth the sequence of natural events and their causes which shadows every mans brow even benjys" (220). By reducing metaphor to the language of causation the father illustrates the gap between Quentin's self and the world. But Quentin's echoing of the word "temporary" shows that he acknowledges the truth of the comment, the truth that the self that is a source of comfort even as it suffers will disappear in time. Its melancholia and suffering will evaporate into the thin air of the spatial world, and thus it will be no refuge at all.

Threatened it already is.[37] The massiveness of the shadow world's assault on Quentin's durational self is shown by the way in which Quentin senses the spatial world invading his inner being: "Eating the business of eating inside of you *space too space and time* confused Stomach saying noon brain saying eat oclock" (129: emphasis added). This view that the spatial world will defeat the durational self is foreshadowed by the aftermath of Quentin's fight with Gerald Bland. To Quentin, Gerald's words about women are fighting ones, strong enough to endow Quentin's durational self with the strength to overpower his social one during the course of a fight in which he relives his earlier fight with Dalton Ames. The durational self thus fights the world, but it is Quentin who gets the black eye.

Finally, the defeat of that self is shown not only by the world's invading Quentin's psyche and bruising him in battle, but by its diminished power to reverse the process of invasion by projecting its own meanings onto the world. That is the real point of Quention's recollection of falling asleep at home while smelling the fragrance of honeysuckle:

> The whole thing came to symbolize night and unrest I
> seemed to be lying neither asleep nor awake looking down a
> long corridor of grey halflight where all stable things had
> become shadowy paradoxical all I had done shadows all I
> had felt suffered taking visible form antic and perverse
> mocking without relevance inherent themselves with the
> denial of the significance they should have affirmed thinking
> I was I was not who was not was not who. (211)

When even the objects by which the durational self expresses its
values assume sufficient autonomy in the shadow world to deny
the significance Quentin gave them, the self that once gave significance to the world without is clearly a hostage to that world and
about to be destroyed by it.

The self in danger of extinction must either permit itself to be
absorbed by the world (in a sense, permit itself to become the
world), or it must commit suicide both as an act of defiance
against the world and as an act of affirmation for the self and its
values. Quentin confronts a situation in which he must ask himself, In whose eye shall I live? He cannot, like Dilsey, live in the eye
of God, for his social self has been denied that possibility by his
father. The alternative is therefore clear. He must live in the
world's eye, as Deacon does (123), or in the electric eye of Mottson, where Jason lives.

That Quentin will reject that situation in the only way possible
has been prepared for by those many comments that show him
taking refuge in the durational self as an escape from the world
and that at the same time point to his suicide. If he escapes the
shadow world for the world of a self that can contemplate a
resurrection in which only his eyes will rise to "look on glory," he
also forecasts an act of suicide committed not to preserve that self
in an afterlife but (paradoxically) to forestall the extinction in this
life of a self that expresses its values through such terms. Quentin's act of suicide is thus free and affirmative—all the more free
and affirmative because it proceeds from the durational self, not
the shadow one. As Bergson put the matter, "The free action
drops from it like an over-ripe fruit."[38]

Although Quentin's suicide is a philosophical one, this action does not make him a tragic figure. He is only *potentially* tragic because the world in which he lives proscribes the possibility for tragic action. If his suicide illustrates one core truth from which Faulkner's tragic vision emanates, that the world assaults and even destroys the durational self, it also illustrates that in modern times the acts of durational selves cannot be tragic because the world to some degree must mirror that self by honoring its conflicting values and thus bear witness that the action to which the conflict leads can legitimately be viewed as tragic.

This last factor is clearly absent in *The Sound and the Fury*, a world in which, according to Quentin's father, "tragedy is second hand." Put Quentin in another world, however, and his potential for tragic action might very well be realized. For that matter, even a shadow self might assume the proportions of tragic hero responsible for the unfolding tragic action constituting the plot of tragedy. That world, of course, is the world of *Absalom, Absalom!* There the selves of naturalism produce "tragedy wrought to its uttermost" in the nauralistic tradition. The quotation is from Yeats's poem "Lapis Lazuli." It beautifully describes Faulkner's enrichment of the classic phase of American literary naturalism by his writing *Absalom, Absalom!*

For naturalism's selves to become tragic, one needed development and both needed freedom. Faulkner endowed Bergson's shadow self with freedom and permitted the potentially free durational self to gain its freedom through developing it. In portraying that self in the Quentin Compson of *The Sound and the Fury*, Faulkner also located the potential source of tragic action in conflicts in the durational self. What was missing was a world honoring its conflicting values and therefore capable of comprehending "tragedy" as more than the mere word that "virginity" is in the world of 1910. In *Absalom, Absalom!*, Faulkner provided that missing ingredient.

As a joint creator of that world, Quentin Compson can project his own conflict between love of person (Caddy) and loyalty to the Southern code onto Henry's particular version of that conflict as it focuses on Charles. If his personal conflict could not issue in tragic action because "tragedy is second hand" in 1910, he could experience tragic action through an imaginative merging with Henry in 1865 because that world honored the conflicting values and could perceive tragedy in the action resolving that conflict. This statement, however, can be misleading if one thinks the representative of that world is Thomas Sutpen. Certainly the designer of the abstract symbol of the social structure, Sutpen's Design, would not experience the tragic dilemma as Henry does, for Sutpen's durational life was innocent of connecting honor with race. Any commitment to honor that Charles poses for him is simply an appearance behind which is the reality of his desire to fulfill the Design by which this plantation society is patterned.[39] Were the person of Sutpen the representative of this world, therefore, one could not say that the world honors the conflicting values that impel Henry to tragic action. But it is the other people who live within the social structure symbolized by Sutpen's Design who share those values. The Rosas and Henrys of this society cherish them, they far outnumber the exceptional Thomas Sutpen, and they provide the connections between Henry's values and the world's.

Sutpen's affective life seems a vacuum in contrast to the lives of those around him, and so he deserves to be called "a walking shadow," one term Rosa uses when describing him to Quentin. Nevertheless, Quentin has good reason to endow this shadow self with tragic stature. If Quentin were to experience participation in a true tragic action in his role as Henry, then Henry's father had to have a stature that Quentin's did not. In 1910 Quentin's father urges him, in effect, to accept his shadow self, so Quentin logically identifies his own father with the world of the shadow self and the limitations of that self. Clearly conflict with such a father could not have the resonance of tragic collision. That kind of resonance would be possible only if the father who is shadow self also had stature. Since Quentin does endow that "walking shadow," Thomas Sutpen, with stature, he becomes the tragic hero of *Absalom, Absalom!*—the source of the tragic action destroying both his sons.

In the Quentin-Shreve section of the novel, the process of elevating Sutpen to tragic stature depends on investing Sutpen's life with a tragic irony of a kind to be expected from a young man

(Quentin) who values the durational self so highly. Sutpen becomes a shadow self at the behest of his durational self.[40] Insulted at the door, he internally debates ways of vindicating himself, through revenge by killing the plantation owner, or through meeting the terms that the young boy perceives as the demands set by this world for gaining recognition. Although the action he takes is not spurred by conflicting values in the durational self, it is spurred by that self's sense of honor and desire for recognition, and the decision Sutpen makes drops from that self "like an overripe fruit," to use Bergson's phrase: "All of a sudden he discovered, not what he wanted to do but what he just had to do, had to do it whether he wanted to or not, because if he did not do it he knew he could never live with himself for the rest of his life, never live with what all the men and women that had died to make him had left inside of him for him to pass on" (220).* What was left inside him was the durational self, that "something shouting it" (237) that set Sutpen on his future course.

Other critics have described many ways by which Sutpen achieves tragic stature.[41] Here we need only note that his tragedy and the entire tragic action issue from his durational self, and part of Sutpen's tragic stature resides in the consequences of his seeking to vindicate that self through his Design, this point of vindicating the boy turned away from the door emerging more than once in re-creations of his talks with Quentin's grandfather. Unwittingly he enters the shadow world of the shadow self, develops the hubris that is really the innocence of the undeveloped durational self of the child he was (children usually being egotistical and blind to the needs of others), continually tries to vindicate that child at any cost to others, and pays the price of the tragic shadow self by becoming self-defeating. He is defeated by the very world from which he sought recognition for his durational self because in his effort to vindicate that self, he halted its growth and could never develp the rapport that self has with others.

Tragic heroes, even those ruthless as Sutpen, must still command some sympathy, and Quentin permits him some. What Sutpen becomes is in fact a projection of part of Rosa's durational

---

*William Faulkner, *Absalom, Absalom!* (New York: Random House, 1936). The page numbers in the text also apply to the Vintage Edition.

self and, if one will grant a durational self to the nameless planta-tion owner whose slave turns Sutpen away from the front door, he is a projection of part of that self too. He becomes their shadow projected into space; innocent of their internalized values, it is true, but still a projection of the durational selves of the plantation owners and the Rosas and Henrys of this world. Sutpen's dura-tional self, recall, is innocent of a sense of race and caste as theirs is not. By making Sutpen a man who loses his essence by attempt-ing to meet the terms of a social structure proceeding from such selves, all in the interest of vindicating the little boy he remains within, Quentin (and Faulkner through him) permits Sutpen to lay greater claims on the reader's sympathy than a Rosa Coldfield, one member of that society, can acknowledge. Without such selves, society would have a different structure and the Design pursued by Sutpen, if pursued at all, need not have required the rejection of a first wife and child, nor the subsequent events leading up to Rosa's insult.

Quentin is not only a figure who gains psychological release, a sense of tragedy, by creating this story and merging with it. He is also a vehicle used by Faulkner for creating a story of the past that can be seen as tragic even by readers in a modern naturalistic world whose sense of the tragic is lost, or is distorted by slipshod usages of the term in newspapers or on television. Within the world of the story created, sound connections between the values of the character and his world can be established to permit the magnification of a tragic action. The story taking place in a past when tragedy was possible can then be related to the modern world denying its existence through the use of a modernist device. Breaking down the barrier between the fictional world and the reader's by showing the story in the process of being created secures sound value connections between the past world being re-created and the present world in which it is created, for the world of Quentin and Shreve is the world of the reader. If even Shreve can merge with that world and experience the legitimacy of these connections aesthetically, then so can the reader.

The modernist device serves another purpose, working as it does toward an enlarged view of the capacities of the self—or, rather, of the selves—the two selves of Quentin. His shadow self is naturalism's spatialized self; his durational self is naturalism's undeveloped second self, that of Dos Passos and Dreiser. Faulkner has not only developed this second self, he has not simply given each self freedom, he has also invested them with an ability for self-transcendence of a kind available to figures who experience tragic joy.

Yeats's poem "Lapis Lazuli" can illuminate this last point. [42] In that poem a sculptor has worked with defects in the lapis lazuli of the title to make them appear part of the work of art, a sculpture depicting three Chinamen climbing a mountain, and whose eyes, so the speaker imagines, will sparkle with tragic joy once they reach their "halfway house." In the poem actors become the tragic heroes whom they play; actresses, the tragic heroines. Actors *become* Hamlet and Lear; actresses *become* Ophelia and Cordelia. Their imaginative acts of transcendence permit them to escape the selves that they are offstage, to transcend the banality of their existence in their private worlds, and to experience as artists the joy of expanding the self to the largest dimensions possible, the dimensions of tragic self.

Perhaps Faulkner resurrected the dead Quentin of *The Sound and the Fury* because he had discovered this way out of the predicament leading to Quentin's suicide. For in *Absalom, Absalom!* Quentin can experience the self-transcendence available to the figures who experience tragic joy in Yeats's poem. In helping to create the story and in merging with it, he does what Yeats's sculptor and actors do. In his role as playwright, Quentin is like the sculptor because he transforms the defects or limitations of the pathetic shadow self by making it that larger-than-life "walking shadow," Thomas Sutpen. Like the actor he invests his durational self with tragic dignity by merging with Henry to become part of the tragic action and experience the tragic joy denied him when he committed suicide.

Of course, if we read the novels in terms of their internal chronology, then we must conclude that self-transcendence was not enough for Quentin. Though *Absalom, Absalom!* appeared after *The Sound and the Fury* and so provided Quentin the opportunity for self-transcendence, his experiences in the later novel need to have taken place before those of the earlier novel, in which he commits suicide. Read in this way, the novels show that for some sensitive souls, the imaginative displacement of self simply cannot compensate for the pain of existence in the meaningless modern world, the naturalistic world of *The Sound and the Fury,* nor preserve the durational self living there.

Whichever of the meanings Faulkner intended for Quentin's total experience as it appears in both novels, it is clear what function Quentin's presence in *Absalom, Absalom!* serves. His presence permits Faulkner to make *Absalom, Absalom!* a tragedy firmly rooted in naturalism, for the naturalistic world of *The Sound and the Fury* appears in it in the person of Quentin. If the selves of naturalism can experience self-transcendence in *Absalom, Absalom!,* however, the process also involves a transcendence of the naturalistic world. A figure who is a central character in a naturalistic novel transcends self and the world in which that self lives to move to another world, which is tragic. The naturalistic world where there can be no tragic love becomes, in Fitzgerald's words, "that country well left behind" in favor of the world of tragic love.[43]

This is not to say that novels that portray naturalistic worlds are novels well left behind, however. Each work coming out of a shared milieu develops a literary tradition by giving that milieu a special literary dimension. Juxtaposing these unique works displays a development in that tradition, just as it shows some special potential within the milieu reflected in each work within the tradition. The development in the tradition studied here is from determinism to self-determination, a movement to be found among the works of individual writers—Dreiser would not be the only example—as well as among the individual works of differing naturalistic writers. Within the tradition, Steinbeck brought self-fulfillment to individuals by moving a group from determinism to self-determination. By so doing he moved the naturalistic tradition from the grim hopelessness of "The Blue Hotel" or of *McTeague* to hope triumphant. But the tradition itself raised another challenge: to endow the naturalist's self with tragic dimensions and involve it in a tragic action. Faulkner met this challenge by showing that self transcending itself and its society in the brilliant triumph of self-immolation that constitutes the tragic joy of tragedy. In publishing their greatest novels, Steinbeck and Faulkner did not end the tradition of naturalism in American fiction, but they did bring its classic phase to a close.

NOTES

1. AMERICAN LITERARY NATURALISM

1. For representative views of the difference between American literary realism and American literary naturalism, see the following: Edwin H. Cady, *The Light of Common Day: Realism in American Fiction* (Bloomington: Indiana Univ. Press, 1971), pp. 43–52; Everett Carter, *Howells and the Age of Realism* (Hamden, Conn., Archon Books, 1966), chap. 5, esp. pp. 238–39 for Howells's own recognition of a change. See also Ronald E. Martin, *American Literature and the Universe of Force* (Durham: Duke Univ. Press, 1981), esp. chap. 3, for a discussion of the force philosophy which subsequently affected the course of American fiction.

2. See Lars Ahnebrink, *The Beginnings of Naturalism in American Fiction* (Upsala: Upsala Univ. Press, 1950), p. 185; George J. Becker, "Introduction: Modern Realism as a Literary Movement," in George J. Becker, ed., *Documents of Modern Literary Realism* (Princeton: Princeton Univ. Press, 1963), p. 35; Oscar Cargill, *Intellectual America: Ideas on the March* (New York: Macmillan, 1941), pp. 13, 85, 97-98, 107; Richard Chase, *The American Novel and Its Tradition* (Garden City, N.Y.: Doubleday, 1957), p. 186n., pp. 185-204; Malcolm Cowley, "A Natural History of American Naturalism," in Becker, ed., *Documents*, pp. 430, 431, 447; Harry Hartwick, *The Foreground of American Fiction* (New York: American Book Co., 1934), pp. 17-20, 45; Stuart P. Sherman, in Becker, ed., *Documents*, pp. 456-59. Ahnebrink and Cowley part from others in finding Norris a determinist but really optimistic (Ahnebrink, p. 232), or partly so (Cowley, p. 430).

3. For a composite list, with some overlap of works and writers and modest degrees of differences about the depth of the pessimism, see the following: Cargill, *Intellectual America*, pp. 159-60; Cowley, "American Naturalism," p. 447; Leslie Fiedler, "Naturalism and Ritual Slaughter," *New Leader* 21 (18 December 1948), 10; Hartwick, *American Fiction*, 43, 160; Michael Millgate, *American Social Fiction: James to Cozzens* (New York: Barnes & Noble, 1964), p. 131; Randall Stewart, *American Literature and Christian Doctrine* (Baton Rouge: Louisiana State Univ. Press, 1958), pp. 107, 113, 120.

4. For such a denial of Crane's naturalism, see Marston LaFrance, *A Reading of Stephen Crane* (Oxford: Clarendon Press, 1971), pp. 38-43, 96-97, 199, 221-22. For Cady's denial of the movement, see *Light of Common Day*, pp. 51, 45. Denials of the naturalism of other writers or works will appear in notes or bibliographical essays for future chapters.

5. Charles Child Walcutt, *American Literary Naturalism: A Divided Stream* (Minneapolis: Univ. of Minn. Press, 1956), p. 20.

6. Ibid., p. 27. See also pp. 23–27 for fuller development of this view.

7. On failure, see Ibid., p. 28; on Crane, pp. 66–67.

8. For an especially clear rendering of Walcutt's view of these *parallel* conflicts, see his treatment of Norris's *The Octopus,* Ibid., pp. 142–150. For his view of a doctrinal conflict alone, see his treatment of *Vandover and the Brute,* in which Vandover lacks freedom but is judged morally: Ibid., pp. 119–122.

9. In his bibliographical essay on Stephen Crane, Pizer assesses his own relation to Walcutt. See Robert A. Rees and Earl N. Harbert, eds., *15 American Authors Before 1900: Bibliographic Essays on Research and Criticism* (Madison: Univ. of Wisconsin Press, 1971), pp. 114–15. See also his denial of coherence to the movement in Donald Pizer, *Realism and Naturalism in Nineteenth-Century American Literature* (Carbondale: Southern Illinois Univ. Press, 1966), p. 36.

10. Quoted phrase is in Pizer, *Realism and Naturalism,* p. 31. For role of determinism, see my bibliographical essay for this chapter.

11. The point is made especially clear by the reason Walcutt finds Crane a supreme naturalist: "Nowhere does a character operate as a genuinely free ethical agent in defiance of the author's intentions" (*Naturalism,* p. 67).

12. Cf. Pizer on moral ambiguity, *Realism and Naturalism,* pp. 12–14, 30.

13. In *Naturalism,* Walcutt finds both Crane and true naturalism monistic. On naturalism, see p. 12. On Crane as "pure naturalist," see pp. 66, 67. Edwin Cady agrees that naturalism is monistic but denies Crane's monism-naturalism: *Stephen Crane* (New York: Twayne Publishers, 1962), p. 131; (revised edition 1980), pp. 131–32. Pizer's description of Crane makes Crane a dualist: *Realism and Naturalism,* p. 28. Yet he clearly thinks Crane is a naturalist: p. 32.

14. James T. Farrell, "Some Observations on Naturalism, So Called, in Fiction," in *Reflections at Fifty and Other Essays* (New York: Vanguard Press, 1954), p. 150.

15. Ibid., p. 148, n. 2.

16. Ibid., p. 150.

17. For this distinction between methodological and ontological monism, see Arthur C. Danto, "Naturalism," *Encyclopedia of Philosophy,* ed. Paul Edwards. 8 Vols. (New York: Macmillan, 1967) 5:448.

18. Quoted from Roland Hall, "Monism and Pluralism," *Encyclopedia,* 5:363. On naturalistic posture, see Danto, n. 17.

19. Sterling P. Lamprecht, *The Metaphysics of Naturalism* (New York: Appleton-Century-Crofts, 1967), p. 160.

20. Ibid., p. 161.

21. Ibid., p. 196.

22. Ibid., p. 172.

23. Ibid., pp. 162, 199.

24. Ibid., p. 162.

25. Ibid.

26. Farrell would accept Lamprecht's ontological monism and the view that man is

free, but Farrell's view of character is geared not to stress that man *is* free but that the relationship between character and environment creates a complicated vision of freedom. On his ontological monism, see Edgar M. Branch, "Freedom and Determinism in James T. Farrell's Fiction," in Sydney J. Krause, ed., *Essays on Determinism in American Literature* (Kent, Ohio: Kent State Univ. Press, 1964), pp. 89, 90, 93. For an expanded discussion of *Studs Lonigan* which includes the complex view of freedom, see Edgar M. Branch, *James T. Farrell* (New York: Twayne, 1971), esp. chap. 3. He quotes Farrell as follows: "Environment affected character, and character itself is a social product which is a result of society. In turn, character affects and changes environment": p. 52.

27. Farrell, "Observations," p. 148 n.

28. Ibid., p. 148 text and p. 148 n.

29. Cf. Frank Bergon's view of current criticism of Crane: *Stephen Crane's Artistry* (New York: Columbia Univ. Press, 1975), pp. ix-x.

30. Farrell, "Observations," p. 148.

31. William F Edwards, "Foreword," in Lamprecht, *Metaphysics*, p. x.

32. See my bibliographical essay on Crane.

33. Farrell, "Observations," p. 150.

34. Ibid., p. 152.

35. Richard Taylor, "Determinism," in *Encyclopedia of Philosophy*, 2:359.

36. On this point cf. Taylor, p. 365. I find Taylor's account of Hobbes's relation to determinism useful because it is so comprehensive, and my discussion parallels and echoes his. I identify the original source of Taylor's quotations from Hobbes.

37. Thomas Hobbes, "Of Liberty and Necessity," in *The English Works of Thomas Hobbes*, ed. Sir William Molesworth. 11 vols. (London, 1840), 4:274. Hereafter cited as *Works of Hobbes*.

38. For Hobbes on voluntary action, deliberation, "last appetite" (or "last will"), see *Works of Hobbes*, 4:272-73. See p. 274 for "voluntary actions" as "necessitated."

39. Ibid., 273.

40. Ibid., 273-74.

41. The quoted words are Taylor's, *Encyclopedia*, 2:365. The view is a standard one. See Sidney Morgenbesser and James Walsh, eds., *Free Will* (Englewood Cliffs, N. J.: Prentice-Hall, 1962), p. 6.

42. Quoted words are Taylor's, *Encyclopedia*, 2:365. See *Works of Hobbes*, 4:275, for original words. Taylor concisely highlights the problems in Hobbes's view and Hobbes's defense against them.

43. William James, "The Dilemma of Determinism," in *Essays in Pragmatism* (New York: Hafner, 1969), p. 40.

44. See Ahnebrink, *Beginnings of Naturalism*, pp. 7 ff. For more recent and extensive background, see Martin, *Universe of Force*, esp. chap. 2 ("Herbert Spencer's Universe of Force") and chap. 3 ("The Americanization of the Universe of Force").

45. Quoted words are Taylor's, *Encyclopedia*, 2:367. For an ironic contrast between scientific and literary views of causation, see Martin, *Universe of Force*, pp. 28, 94-95.

I agree with Malcolm Cowley's emphasis on "conditions, forces, physical laws, or nature herself" (Becker, ed., *Documents*, p. 435) as important to the naturalistic novel, but he does not see how they manifest themselves within a Hobbesian vision.

46. Cady, *Stephen Crane* (New York: Twayne, 1962), p. 109. Cady quotes from Walcutt's *Naturalism*, p. 67.

47. On dual selves, see Henri Bergson, *Time and Free Will: An Essay on the Immediate Data of Consciousness*, trans. by F. L. Pogson (London: George Allen & Unwin, 1910), pp. 128 ff. On views of science, see Henri Bergson, *The Creative Mind: An Introduction to Metaphysics*, trans. by Mabelle L. Andison (New York: The Wisdom Library, 1946), pp. 43, 44, 46. On man as part of nature, see H. Wilson Carr, *The Philosophy of Change* (London: Macmillan, 1914), p. 160. On the English school of philosophers, see Bergson, *Time and Free Will*, pp. 99 ff. For a general overview of Bergson's thought which I found helpful, see T. A. Goudge, "Henri Bergson," *Encyclopedia* 1: esp. pp. 290, 292, 287, 288.

48. See Bergson, *Time and Free Will*, pp. 140-48.

49. On psychological determinism, see Bergson, *Time and Free Will*, pp. 148-63. On escape from determinism through duration or pure time, see pp. 158-221, esp. pp. 175 ff. On pure time or duration, see also pp. 100, 110, 229, 231.

50. On freedom of the self living in pure time, see Bergson, *Time and Free Will*, pp. 167, 172, 173. For dual selves, see pp. 129-139, 240; and for one reference to the spatialized (social) self as a shadow, see p. 231. For free acts as rare, see pp. 167, 231.

51. Marguerite Tjader and John J. McAleer, eds., *Notes on Life* by Theodore Dreiser (University, Ala.: Univ. of Alabama Press, 1974), p. 87.

52. My phrasing is indebted to Donald Pizer's contrasting view of man and nature in *The Red Badge*. He writes: "Crane dramatizes Fleming's realization that . . . nature and man are really two, not one" (*Realism and Naturalism*, p. 28); and he links Fleming's view and Crane's.

2. STEPHEN CRANE

1. Frank Bergon also comments on the correspondent's "disinterested vision" (p. 61), but his view of the story's ending denies the correspondent a formulated education and so denies the story much intellectual meaning (p. 93): *Stephen Crane's Artistry* (New York: Columbia Univ. Press, 1975).

2. Richard Taylor, "Determinism," *The Encyclopedia of Philosophy*, Paul Edwards, ed. (New York: Macmillan Publishing Co., Inc. and The Free Press, 1967), 2:359.

3. The care Crane took in writing the story supports this view. See J. C. Levenson, in *Tales of Adventure*, The University of Virginia Edition of the Works of Stephen Crane, ed. Fredson Bowers, 5:xcviii.

4. *Works of Thomas Hobbes* 4:273.

5. On the various classes of primary colors and the results of their blending, see Faber Birren, *Principles of Color: A Review of Past Traditions and Modern Theories of Color Harmony* (New York: Van Nostrand Reinhold, 1969), p. 22.

6. *Works of Hobbes*, 4:273.

7. R. W. Stallman and Lillian Gilkes, eds. *Stephen Crane: Letters* (New York: New York Univ. Press, 1960), no. 17, p. 14. See also no. 18 and n. 18.

8. Ibid., no. 178, p. 133.

9. Bergon would agree about the effect (an unclear moral focus), if not the cause (the Hobbesian vision): *Stephen Crane's Artistry*: pp. ix-x, 71.

10. For a discussion of "respectability" exposing society's hypocrisy, see Joseph X.

Brennan, "Ironic and Symbolic Structure in Crane's *Maggie*," *Nineteenth-Century Fiction* 16 (March 1962): 305. See also Bergon, *Stephen Crane's Artistry*, for comments on "respectability," "moral posturing," and "social status": pp. 72-73.

11. For a Darwinian interpretation of *Maggie*, see David Fitelson, "Stephen Crane's *Maggie* and Darwinism," *American Quarterly* 16 (Summer 1964): 182-94.

12. Marston LaFrance uses these passages to argue that Jimmie is a responsible agent. *A Reading of Stephen Crane* (Oxford: Clarendon Press, 1971), pp.62-63.

13. For discussion of a tension in Crane's "best fiction" between "two ironically divergent points of view," the character's and the narrator's, see James B. Colvert, "Structure and Theme in Stephen Crane's Fiction," *Modern Fiction Studies* 5 (Autumn 1959): 199-208. Quoted material on p. 200.

14. See Fitelson's association of irony with the novel's Darwinian determinism: "*Maggie* and Darwinism," pp. 186-88. For a discussion of a possible "bifurcation" in the novel, see LaFrance, *Reading of Crane*, pp. 54-56.

15. Eric Solomon's *Stephen Crane, From Parody to Realism* (Cambridge: Harvard Univ. Press, 1966), pp. 23-44.

16. For James Trammel Cox's idiosyncratic development of this point, see his "The Imagery of 'The Red Badge of Courage,' " *Modern Fiction Studies* 5 (1959), 210 ff.

17. Outside a deterministic framework, the point is also made by LaFrance, *Reading of Crane*, pp. 116-17; Donald Gibson, *Fiction of Crane* (Carbondale, Ill.: Southern Illinois Univ. Press, 1968), p. 83. For Gibson's view that the novel fails to reconcile freedom and determinism, see p. 89.

18. The point is also made by LaFrance, *Reading of Crane*, within an argument showing Henry maturing: pp. 117, 119, 122.

19. William P. Safranek shows that later descriptions of changes in Henry echo the language of Henry's initial perceptions of the change in the loud soldier, a fact that creates a parallel between the two characters and makes Wilson's change a foreshadowing of Henry's: "Crane's *The Red Badge of Courage*," *Explicator* 26 (November 1967): item 21.

20. I am in partial sympathy with Stanley B. Greenfield's sense of a change in Henry and Greenfield's sense of the future's uncertainty, but I think Crane's emphasis on conditions undermines Greenfield's view of the efficacy of the will: "The Unmistakable Stephen Crane," *PMLA* 73 (December 1958): 571-72.

21. Warren French rejects the novel's naturalism because he thinks Henry is able to engage in "self-conscious analysis" and thus gain the freedom of the "lover" permitting Henry to "advance on his own initiative," but I believe this view is undermined for the same reason that Greenfield's (above) is: it fails to take conditions into account; in this case, conditions dictating the content of the analysis and the "lover's" view of the world: "John Steinbeck: A Usable Concept of Naturalism," in *American Literary Naturalism: A Reassessment* (Heidelberg: Carl Winter, Universitätsverlag., 1975), ed. Yoshinobu Hakutani and Lewis Fried, pp. 125-27. With minor changes in phrasing, the same view appears in Warren French, *John Steinbeck* (Boston: Twayne, 2nd ed. rev., 1975), pp. 40, 42, 43.

3. FRANK NORRIS

1. In *The American Novel and Its Tradition* (Garden City, N.Y.: Doubleday, 1957), Richard Chase calls McTeague a " 'Darwinian' Adam" (p. 191). Warren French initially

treats Polk Street as "a kind of run-down Eden": *Frank Norris* (New York: Twayne, 1962), p. 64.

2. For a summary of his discussion of the efficacy of these themes in Norris's later work, see Ronald Martin, *American Literature and the Universe of Force* (Durham: Duke Univ. Press, 1981), p. 183.

3. See, for example, Ernest Marchand, *Frank Norris: A Study* (New York: Octagon Books, 1964), p. 69. (This is a reprint of an edition published by Stanford Univ. Press, 1942).

4. It goes without saying that these symbols have attracted numerous commentaries. For the most recent and extended discussion of them in relation to McTeague's aesthetic sense as it interacts with the world around him, see Don Graham, *The Fiction of Frank Norris: The Aesthetic Context* (Columbia: Univ. of Missouri Press, 1978), chap. 3: "Art and Humanity in *McTeague*," esp. pp. 50-53, 59 ff.

5. I have been partly influenced here by Donald R. McPheron, who gave a report on the novel's wall symbolism in my graduate seminar in American literary naturalism (Vanderbilt, Spring 1975). I also find French insightful in noting that "both the vignettes of the romantic old people and of the snarling beasts exemplify the way in which civilization builds barriers that keep 'Nature' from exercising its benign influence": *Frank Norris*, p. 66.

6. I have never seen evidence that Norris read Zola's "Le Roman expérimental," so he probably arrived at the formulae established within that work in the way Franklin Walker suggests. (See my bibliographical essay.) For influences from Zola (and others) relevant to the writing of *McTeague*, see the following: Graham, *Fiction of Norris*, p. 56n.; Marchand, *Frank Norris*, pp. 90-96; Martin, *Universe of Force*, pp. 151-55; Donald Pizer, *Novels of Norris*, (Bloomington: Indiana Univ. Press, 1966), pp. 52-63.

7. Emile Zola, "The Experimental Novel," in *The Experimental Novel and Other Essays*, tr. by Belle Sherman (New York: Haskell House, 1964), p. 8.

8. Ibid., p. 8.

9. William Dillingham has written that Norris shows that "the same forces which destroy his main characters also can create happiness"; "The Old Folks of *McTeague*," *Nineteenth-Century Fiction* 16 (September 1961): 171.

10. William James, "The Dilemma of Determinism," in *Essays in Pragmatism* (New York: Hafner Publishing Co., 1969), p. 56.

4. THEODORE DREISER

1. William James, "The Dilemma of Determinism," in *Essays in Pragmatism* (New York: Hafner Publishing Co., 1969), pp. 42, 43.

2. Taylor, "Determinism," *Encyclopedia of Philosophy*, 2:359.

3. Marguerite Tjader and John J. McAleer, eds., *Notes on Life* by Theodore Dreiser (University: Univ. of Alabama Press, 1974), pp. 42, 43.

4. Richard Lehan emphasizes that Dreiser uses chance as a catalyst to expose a determined realm which Lehan associates with the "quintessential quality of a character": *Theodore Dreiser: His World and His Novels* (Carbondale: Southern Illinois Univ. Press, 1969), p. 111.

5. For strong expressions of such views, see Charles Shapiro, *Theodore Dreiser: Our Bitter Patriot* (Carbondale: Southern Illinois Univ. Press, 1962), p. 43; Donald Pizer, *The Novels of Theodore Dreiser: A Critical Study* (Minneapolis: Univ. of Minnesota Press, 1976), pp. 343, 345.

6. John J. McAleer, *Theodore Dreiser: An Introduction and Interpretation* (New York: Holt, Rinehart and Winston, 1968), pp. 108, 110-11, 117-19.

7. W. A. Swanberg, *Dreiser* (New York: Scribner, 1965), p. 181.

8. Tjader and McAleer, eds., *Notes,* pp. 14, 325.

9. Ibid., p. 186.

10. McAleer makes such a distinction: *Dreiser,* p. 106. My next two paragraphs also embrace some points he makes on p. 106, but our emphases are different here and our arguments, though not incompatible, soon part ways. He tries to expose social hypocrisy through this distinction, and he retains the distinction to study a pattern of light and solar imagery associated with special characters and binding the trilogy together. His is not a deterministic argument, as suggested by his statement: "The only Dreiser characters without free will are conventionalists, and they have abdicated their will to society or synod" (p. 72). My interest, on the other hand, is to collapse the distinction between the groups of characters in order to show Dreiser pursuing the implications of determinism.

11. Maxwell Geismar, *Rebels and Ancestors: The American Novel, 1890-1915* (Boston: Houghton Mifflin, 1953), p. 314.

12. Tjader and McAleer, eds., *Notes,* p. 289. In the next line Dreiser asks, "But of what import is that?" *The Titan* and *The Stoic* explore that import.

13. Ibid., p. 258.

14. Ibid., p. 188.

15. Pizer also sees a hierarchy among women: *Novels of Dreiser,* pp. 173-74. For a discussion of the influence of Jacques Loeb and tropism on Dreiser, see Ellen Moers, *Two Dreisers* (New York: Viking, 1969), pp. 240-55.

16. Theodore Dreiser, "A Counsel to Perfection" in *Hey Rub-A-Dub-Dub: A Book of the Mystery and Wonder and Terror of Life* (New York: Boni and Liveright, 1920), p. 115.

17. Tjader and McAleer, eds., *Notes,* p. 81.

18. See Oscar Cargill, *Intellectual America: Ideas on the March* (New York: Macmillan, 1941), p. 121; Michael Millgate, *American Social Fiction: James to Cozzens* (New York: Barnes & Noble, 1964), pp. 77-79; Pizer, *Novels of Dreiser,* pp. 169-70,198, 200.

19. See Robert Penn Warren's general but incisive and eloquent discussion of the subject: *Homage to Theodore Dreiser* (New York: Random House, 1971), pp. 80-86.

20. Dreiser, "The Essential Tragedy of Life," in *Rub-A-Dub-Dub,* p. 245.

21. Tjader and McAleer, eds., *Notes,* p. 87.

22. Swanberg, *Dreiser,* pp. 445, 444.

23. Compare and contrast Robert Elias's view of the equation inevitable as compensation: *Theodore Dreiser: Apostle of Nature* (Ithaca: Cornell Univ. Press, 1970), pp. 172-74.

24. Tjader and McAleer, eds., *Notes,* p. 251.

25. Dreiser, "The Equation Inevitable," in *Rub-A-Dub-Dub*, p. 179.
26. Ibid., p. 180.
27. James, *Pragmatism*, p. 52.
28. Ibid., p. 49.
29. Ibid., pp. 51-52.
30. Tjader and McAleer, eds., *Notes*, pp. 198, 195, 195.
31. James, *Pragmatism*, pp. 55-57.
32. Tjader and McAleer, eds., *Notes*, pp. 286-87.
33. Ibid., p. 287.
34. Paul Edwards, "Life, the Meaning and Value of," *Encyclopedia*, 4:471-73. Edwards uses the phrase " 'terrestrial' sense" in opposition to the phrase " 'cosmic' sense" on p. 472.
35. A similar observation is made by Lehan, *Dreiser*, p. 112; and Tjader and McAleer, eds., *Notes* shows no evidence of his abandoning determinism.
36. Elias, *Apostle of Nature*, pp. 289-90.
37. Ibid., p. 298.
38. Ibid., p. 302.
39. Tjader and McAleer, eds., *Notes*, p. 93.
40. On this particular point see "Hinduism" in *The New Encyclopedia Britannica* (1974 ed. Macropopaedia, vol. 8), p. 889. See the same entry for my general views in the previous paragraph.
41. See R. N. Mookerjee, "Dreiser's Use of Hindu Thought in *The Stoic*," *American Literature* 43 (May 1971), 273-78, for errors in Dreiser's view of Hinduism. See esp. p. 275.
42. James, *Pragmatism*, p. 51.

5. JOHN DOS PASSOS

1. The amount of literature on the subject of alienation is vast. The breakdown of types of alienation and related discussion by Gajo Petrovic in his overview of the subject provides a comprehensive, organized background, some of which I have found appropriate to the needs of literary analysis: "Alienation," *Encyclopedia of Philosophy* 1:76-80. For a relation between alienation and economic determinism, see p. 80.
2. On his being mistaken as a Marxist, see Melvin Landsberg, *Dos Passos' Path to "U.S.A.," A Political Biography 1912-1936* (Boulder: The Colorado Associated Univ. Press, 1972), pp. 150, 225. For the possible influence of Veblen on Dos Passos during the writing of *Manahattan Transfer*, and for the influences which are certain, see pp. 103-6, 65.
3. John Dos Passos, "The Backwash of Our First Crusade," in *The Theme is Freedom* (New York: Dodd, Mead, 1956), p. 2.
4. Jean-Paul Sartre, "John Dos Passos and *1919*," in *Dos Passos: A Collection of Critical Essays*, ed. Andrew Hook (Englewood, N.J.: Prentice-Hall, 1974), p. 68, 69.
5. On this point, see Petrovic, *Encyclopedia*, 1:79.
6. See Henri Bergson, *Time and Free Will* (London: George Allen & Unwin, 1910), pp. 231-32.

7. Blanche Housman Gelfant, *American City Novel* (Norman: Univ. of Oklahoma Press, 1954), p. 161.

8. John Dos Passos, "A Question of Elbow Room," in *Occasions and Protests* (Chicago: Henry Regnery Co., 1964), p. 52.

9. *Works of Hobbes*, 4:273.

10. Others have noted a resemblance between the work of the two writers. See George J. Becker, *John Dos Passos* (New York: Frederick Ungar Publishing Co., 1974), p. 39; John D. Brantley, *The Fiction of John Dos Passos* (The Hague: Mouton, 1968), p. 53.

11. For an account of Whitman's well-known influence on Dos Passos, see Linda W. Wagner, *Dos Passos: Artist as American* (Austin: Univ. of Texas Press, 1979), pp. 102-3, 161-63, 165-69.

12. Gelfant's study of imagery sees loneliness and impersonality as functions of perceiving people and things on the same level: *American City Novel*, p. 147.

13. The man is identified as Jimmy's father by John H. Wrenn, *John Dos Passos* (New York: Twayne, 1961), p. 127.

14. Wagner, *Dos Passos*, p. 48.

15. Charles Child Walcutt thinks the method eliminates will: *American Literary Naturalism: A Divided Stream* (Minneapolis: Univ. of Minn. Press, 1956), p. 281. Joseph Warren Beach sees the method as reducing action to "a matter of stimulus and response": *American Fiction: 1920-1940* (New York: Macmillan, 1941), p. 38.

16. Claude-Edmonde Magny, "Time in Dos Passos," in *Dos Passos*, Hook, ed., p. 130.

17. Ibid., p. 130.

18. Dos Passos, "A Question of Elbow Room," in *Occasions and Protests*, p. 52.

19. The point is developed at length by David Vanderwerken, "*Manhattan Transfer*: Dos Passos' Babel Story," *American Literature* 49 (May 1977): 253-67.

20. See Malcolm Cowley's view: "John Dos Passos: The Poet and the World," in *Dos Passos*, Hook, ed., pp. 83-4, 86.

21. Alfred Kazin, *On Native Grounds: An Interpretation of Modern American Prose Literature* (New York: Harcourt Brace, 1942), p. 345.

22. Dos Passos, *Occasions and Protests*, p. 72.

6. JOHN STEINBECK

1. In *Thematic Design in the Novels of John Steinbeck* (The Hague: Mouton, 1969), Lester Jay Marks argues that the group possesses will from the very beginning (a point he stresses several times: pp. 68, 73-74, 75-76), and that Steinbeck uses the interchapters as "a second structural element . . . [supporting] the idea of willful movement in the novel" (p. 69). My own judgment is that the interchapters stress determinism, not will, and that Marks's opposite view necessarily fails to see the complexities of Steinbeck's literary implementation of his biological concept of group man.

2. John Steinbeck, *The Log from the Sea of Cortez: The narrative portion of the book "Sea of Cortez" with a profile 'About Ed Ricketts'* (London: Heinemann, 1958), p. 165. Quotation and idea identified by Astro as added and endorsed by Steinbeck:

Richard Astro, *John Steinbeck and Edward F Ricketts* (Minneapolis: Univ. of Minnesota Press, 1973), pp. 45-46. See my bibliographical essay for comments on the collaboration between Steinbeck and Ricketts in *Sea of Cortez*.

3. Steinbeck, *Log*, pp. 240-41. Passage and concept identified by Astro as added and endorsed by Steinbeck: *Steinbeck and Ricketts*, p. 47.

4. Steinbeck, "Some Thoughts on Juvenile Delinquency," *Saturday Review* 37 (28 May 1955): 22.

5. Steinbeck, *Log*, p. 217. Astro believes that both Ricketts and Steinbeck shared this belief: *Steinbeck and Ricketts*, p. 31.

6. Steinbeck, *Log*, pp. 216-17. Comment of n. 5 applies.

7. Steinbeck, *Log*, pp. 264-65. I do not know whether this was originally Ricketts' sentiment or Steinbeck's, but I find nothing in Steinbeck's thought to suggest that he disagrees with it.

7. WILLIAM FAULKNER

1. H. Wildon Carr, *Philosophy of Change* (London: Macmillan, 1914), p. 103.

2. T. A. Goudge, "Henri Bergson," in *Encyclopedia of Philosophy* (New York: Macmillan, 1967) 1:288.

3. Henri Bergson. *Time and Free Will* (London: George Allen & Unwin, 1910), p. 106.

4. Ibid., p. 100.

5. Carr, *Philosophy of Change*, p. 29.

6. Bergson, *Time and Free Will*, p. 101.

7. Ibid.

8. Ibid., p. 133.

9. Ibid., p. 127.

10. Henri Bergson, *Matter and Memory*, tr. by Nancy Margaret Paul and W. Scott Palmer (London: George Allen & Unwin, 1919), p. 96.

11. Ibid., p. 92.

12. See n. 50 to chap. 1.

13. Henri Bergson, *Creative Evolution*, tr. by Arthur Mitchell (New York: Henry Holt, 1911), p. 176.

14. Bergson, *Time and Free Will*, p. 172.

15. Ibid., p. 176.

16. Jacques Maritain, *Bergsonian Philosophy and Thomism*, tr. by Mabelle L. Andison in collaboration with J. Gordon Andison (New York: Philosophical Library, 1955), p. 261 n.

17. Ibid., pp. 260-61.

18. Ibid., p. 263.

19. On this point see James B. Meriwether, "The Textual History of *The Sound and the Fury*," in *The Merrill Studies in "The Sound and the Fury*," comp. James B. Meriwether (Columbus, Ohio: Charles E Merrill, 1970), pp. 25-31.

20. For specific examples of the literary form called a complaint, see C. Hugh Holman, *A Handbook to Literature* (Indianapolis: Bobbs-Merrill, 4th ed., 1980), p. 95.

21. Donald M.Kartiganer, *The Fragile Thread: The Meaning of Form in Faulkner's Novels* (Amherst: Univ. of Massachusetts Press, 1979), p. 17. Kartiganer sees some comedy here (p. 17) but is concerned to deny the commonly held view that Jason represents the analytic mind, a denial made possible because he misses the parody. See also Melvin Backman's comments about the "brilliant satire" of this "comic villain": *Faulkner: The Major Years* (Bloomington: Indiana Univ. Press, 1966), pp. 29-30.

22. On Bergson's view of language as a violation of the self, see Bergson, *Time and Free Will*, pp. 137-39, 160f. See also Parthea Reid Broughton, *William Faulkner: The Abstract and the Actual* (Baton Rouge: Louisiana State Univ. Press, 1974), pp. 53-54, 109, 127, and all of chap. 6, "Conceptualizing." Her remarks on the word "nigger" (p. 128) have their own clear relevance to Jason's use of linguistic abstractions, though she does little with Jason in this regard. Susan Dale Resnick Parr does more: "And by Bergson, Obviously." "Faulkner's *The Sound and the Fury, As I Lay Dying,* and *Absalom, Absalom!* from a Bergsonian Perspective." Ph.D. diss. (Univ. of Wisconsin, 1972), pp. 98-102.

23. See Cleanth Brooks, "Primitivism in *The Sound and the Fury,*" in *English Institute Essays: 1952,* ed. by Alan S. Downer (New York: Columbia Univ. Press, 1954), pp. 5-7.

24. Bergson, *Time and Free Will,* p. 100.

25. For examples of views that have become commonplace, see Olga Vickery on Quentin and time: *Faulkner* (Baton Rouge: Louisiana State Univ. Press, rev. ed., 1964), p. 39; on Quentin and language, see Vickery, p. 37. On this second point see Peter Swiggart's much stronger statement: *The Art of Faulkner's Novels* (Austin: Univ. of Texas Press, 1962), pp. 93-94. Margaret Church, on the other hand, grants Quentin a "sense of duration," but "one that Quentin protests against; he would live outside of time": *Time and Reality: Studies in Contemporary Fiction* (Chapel Hill: Univ. of North Carolina Press, 1949), pp. 234-35. Parr, "And by Bergson, Obviously," thinks Quentin knows "the nature of duration" but develops an argument that he cannot "merge with real time" (p. 64) because he is permanently prey to "involuntary memories" (p. 65). Her view that Quentin "objectifies or thingifies" (p. 68) is parallel to the standard views I have noted.

26. Bergson, *Time and Free Will,* pp. 133-34.

27. Ibid., p. 126.

28. Ibid., p. 127.

29. Ibid., p. 128.

30. Ibid., p. 105.

31. Ibid., pp. 100, 125.

32. See Bergson's parallel between duration and the melting "crystals of a snowflake": *Time and Free Will,* pp.138-39.

33. Bergson, *Time and Free Will,* p. 133.

34. Joan S. Korenman uses "Ode on a GrecianUrn" to discuss a Keatsian stasis as the perfect fulfillment Quentin desires: "Faulkner's Grecian Urn," *The Southern Literary Journal* 7 (Fall 1974): 9-13.

35. My explanation of the terms of Quentin's problem shows the enduring influence of Hyatt H. Waggoner's study, *William Faulkner: From Jefferson to the*

World (Lexington: Univ. of Kentucky Press, Kentucky Paperbacks, 1966), pp. 47-52.

36. Bergson, *Time and Free Will*, p. 128.

37. For discussions of an identity crisis in Quentin, see Michael Gressett, "Psychological Aspects of Evil in *The Sound and the Fury*," in Meriwether, ed., *Merrill Studies*, pp. 118-19; Sally R. Page, "Faulkner's Sense of the Sacred," in George H. Wolfe, ed., *Faulkner: Fifty Years after "The Marble Faun"* (University: Univ. of Alabama Press, 1976), pp. 102, 108-9, 113.

38. Bergson, *Time and Free Will*, p. 176.

39. The point about Sutpen's view of race is made by Cleanth Brooks in *William Faulkner: The Yoknapatawpha Country* (New Haven: Yale Univ. Press, 1963), p. 299.

40. To argue that Faulkner's characters are always free, even in childhood, Shirley Parker Callen cites Sutpen as one of three Faulkner characters who freely act from the fundamental or "inner" self even as children: "Bergsonian Dynamism in the Writings of William Faulkner." Ph.D. diss. (Tulane Univ., 1962), pp. 132-33.

41. See esp. Walter Sullivan's partly Hegelian view in "The Tragic Design of *Absalom, Absalom!*," *South Atlantic Quarterly* 50 (October 1951): 552-65. A Hegelian approach seems the most plausible for a Bergsonian reading and harmonizes well with Wadlington's view of "binary consciousness" in *The Sound and the Fury*. (See bibliographical essay.) For an essentially Aristotelian approach, see Lynn Gartrell Levins, *Faulkner's Heroic Design: The Yoknapatawpha Novels* (Athens: Univ. of Georgia Press, 1976), pp. 38-54. For other discussions of classical tragedy in the novel, see Levins's n. 7, pp. 184-85.

42. The parallel between the poem and the novel, as well as the kind of transcendence achieved here, was suggested by my wife, Prof. Barbara McCamus Conder.

43. The words quoted are from F. Scott Fitzgerald, *Tender Is the Night* (New York: Scribner, 1933), p. 34.

BIBLIOGRAPHICAL ESSAYS

1. AMERICAN LITERARY NATURALISM

Because of the responses it provoked, Charles Child Walcutt's *American Literary Naturalism: A Divided Stream* (Minneapolis: Univ. of Minn. Press, 1956) has sustained interest in its subject for many years. Walcutt's insistence that "the theme of determinism . . . is of course basic" (p. 20) is in fact correct. His attempt to retain this focus, however, had a reverse effect because of the book's major shortcomings: it fails to show persuasively how determinism manifests itself in naturalistic works, and it fails to show that freedom can logically coexist with determinism within a naturalistic work.

One unfortunate result of these two failures is that various critics withdrew one author after another from the naturalist movement until there seemed to be no movement left at all. Thus it now seems no surprise that Edwin Cady did in fact deny the existence of literary naturalism in America: *The Light of Common Day: Realism in American Fiction* (Bloomington: Indiana Univ. Press, 1971), pp. 51, 45.

Walcutt's work had another unfortunate result, this one stemming from his failure to show that freedom can logically coexist with determinism within a naturalistic work. In thinking a work flawed if it contained these two doctrines (as well as the parallel attitudes accompanying them: optimism and pessimism), he ironically opened the way for diminishing the importance of determinism as a serious doctrine within the works—the very determinism he called "basic" to the works and the movement.

Donald Pizer's work illustrates this ironic consequence. He finds that Walcutt "paradoxically" has been instrumental in leading many critics to accept American literary naturalism "as a complex literary phenomenon rather than as merely a weak-minded illustration of a particular philosophical doctrine": "Stephen Crane," in *15 American Authors Before 1900: Bibliographic Essays on Research and Criticism*, ed. by Robert A. Rees and Earl N. Harbert (Madison: Univ. of Wisconsin Press, 1971), p. 114. The paradox refers to Walcutt's view that determinism is central to naturalism, and Pizer's description of a movement definable by it points to his own view of determinism as a doctrine and to his view of its role in the naturalistic novel. For example, he writes of *Maggie*: "Crane, then, is a naturalistic writer in the sense that he believes that environment molds lives. But he is much more

than this"—in this case, Crane is also a social critic assaulting social hypocrisy: *Realism and Naturalism in Nineteenth-Century American Literature* (Carbondale: Southern Illinois Univ. Press, 1966), p. 130.

This point of view fails to comprehend the possibilities inherent in a
deterministic vision. That failure handicaps even the most enthusiastic
critics of naturalistic writers, for it not only limits their sense of the essential
richness of individual works but also blinds them to a sound theoretical
view giving the movement unity in its classic phase, a phase in which
determinism plays a central role. Thus, for example, Pizer's *Twentieth-
Century American Literary Naturalism: An Interpretation* (Carbondale: Southern Illinois Univ. Press, 1982) is essentially discontinuous with the relevant
chapters in his earlier study, *Realism and Naturalism.* And, as an insightful
review indicates, the limitations of this later work can be traced to Pizer's
distrust of theory, his decision not to formulate " 'a single, static definition'
of naturalism" (*Modern Language Studies* 13, no. 2 [Spring 1983]: 117. Re-
viewer Alice Hall Petry quotes Pizer.) Petry also sees that a theory need not
be " 'single' " or " 'static' " and can profit from those " 'constant reference[s] to philosophical and cultural ideas' which Pizer has so studiously
avoided" (p. 117. Petry again quotes Pizer.)

But of course such references do not themselves guarantee seeing a
continuity within the diversity of the movement's classic phase. Employing
the concept of "force" derived from physics for an understanding of some
earlier naturalistic American writers, Henry Adams included, Ronald E.
Martin spends a good third of his study establishing such a framework:
American Literature and the Universe of Force (Durham: Duke Univ. Press,
1981). He concludes that by the 1920s and 1930s "literary naturalism of the
sort practiced by London, Norris, and Dreiser [the novelists who are his
focus] also seemed to be played out" (p. 256). His concept thus leaves us with
what Adams would call a "break of continuity": *The Education of Henry
Adams* (Boston: Houghton Mifflin, 1918), p. 381. It also leaves us without
Stephen Crane. But Harold Kaplan also has a force philosophy, one that
treats human groups as a force, and he does include Crane: *Henry Adams and
the Naturalist Tradition in American Fiction* (Chicago: Univ. of Chicago Press,
1981), pp. 99-101, 121-28.

2. STEPHEN CRANE

"The Open Boat"

My analysis should in part be read against the background of Marston
LaFrance's view of the story as a paradigm of a clear moral vision existing

in all of Crane's world: *A Reading of Stephen Crane* (Oxford: Clarendon Press, 1971), p. 196; pp. 195-205 for a full analysis emphasizing the word "moral." Much of my opposition to his view depends on my point that the world of the boat is emphatically different from the world of the shore. This point suggests one major difference between my approach and another parallel to it in its emphasis on the value of community. Although Robert Shulman acknowledges the complexities of shore life, he thinks the worlds are not radically different and that the story points to "the possibilities implicit but usually concealed in ordinary life": see his "Community, Perception, and the Development of Stephen Crane: From *The Red Badge* to 'The Open Boat,' " *American Literature* 50 (November 1978): 455. Because his article is also a (valuable) response to critics who see the story as "undermining . . . man's mind, character, and language in an epistemologically absurd universe" (450-51), he does not capture the depths of the correspondent's education.

My view that the story exposes society as a fiction, a creation of man's in a godless world, makes Milne Holton's remarks on Crane's larger world view relevant: *Cylinder of Vision: The Fiction and Journalistic Writing of Stephen Crane* (Baton Rouge: Louisiana State Univ. Press, 1972), esp. pp. 13-14.

"The Blue Hotel"

James Trammell Cox's reading of "The Blue Hotel" as a "total conceit" (p. 148) issuing in determinism will remain a classic specimen of this approach to the story: "Stephen Crane as Symbolic Naturalist: An Analysis of 'The Blue Hotel,' " *Modern Fiction Studies* 3 (Summer 1957): 147-58. The very comprehensiveness of his approach to what is a *short* story makes it inevitable that we use some of the same features of the story and employ a couple of similar critical points, but we interpret these features and use these points in very different ways to arrive at our shared conclusion that the story is indeed deterministic. The sheer number and complexity of the contrasts and parallels Cox draws in transforming the story's disparate elements into a spinning "firewheel" (158) set our treatments apart.

In spite of its comprehensiveness, however, his approach fails to persuade for at least two reasons. First, he does not develop the blurring of the human and animal kingdoms in the person of the Easterner, leaving the point made in a general statement (152). But the major problem is that in one essential regard Cox fails to see any blurring at all. His sense of determinism depends heavily on the wind, but he interprets the wind as a deterministic force of the nonhuman world, though invading the human world symbolized by the card game. Hence the deterministic wind is really a "fate or a vast, indifferent . . . force" (155) external to man. Such a separation between worlds, of course, easily leads to the moralist reading of a Marston LaFrance, who finds that "man's moral world and external nature's pointless energy are as sharply distinct in this story as elsewhere in Crane's work": *Reading of Crane*, p. 221. It also may be behind Donald Gibson's view that critics who find determinism in the story "have little more than the weather to point to as proof of their claim": *The Fiction of Stephen Crane* (Carbondale, Ill.: Southern Illinois Univ. Press, 1968), p. 110.

Of course, the appearance of ethical choice has also been seen as a factor denying the story's determinism, even by Max Westbrook, who states that "the relation of Crane's characters to society . . . is not properly described as either 'black' determinism or 'white' free will, but rather as a 'grey struggle' ": "Stephen Crane: The Pattern of Affirmation," *Nineteenth-Century Fiction* 14 (December 1959): 220. But he denies that Crane "took up" social determinism and thinks the fact that Johnnie cheats and that the Easterner fails to corroborate the fact "militate against concluding that ethical failure is inevitable or that ethical failure is blamed exclusively on circumstance": "Stephen Crane's Social Ethic," *American Quarterly* 14 (Winter 1962): 590. My definition of determinism and its application to the story are designed to counter such views.

Maggie

The seminal work here is Walcutt's *American Literary Naturalism*, especially his comment "that these people are not free agents, and that their freedom is limited as much by their conventional beliefs as by their poverty" (p. 69). Because Marston LaFrance's *Reading of Crane* is the most intensive of many moralist readings, my analysis of *Maggie* should be read against his: pp. 38–43, 51–66. Some of these readings are generated by a failure to see that irony and determinism are perfectly compatible (cf. Gibson, p. 28, or LaFrance, p. 53); but I think the chief element leading to moralist interpretations is the appearance of choice made by characters within the work, an element that Walcutt does not really account for. Edwin Cady has changed his sense of the novel's focus from Maggie to her environment (cf. his *Stephen Crane*, 1962, p. 110, to his *Stephen Crane*, 1980, p. 110), but he still denies Crane's naturalism on the basis of the existence of "personal moral responsibility and guilt" (1980 edition: p. 111; cf. to comments on "ethical choices" in 1963 edition: p. 110). And the realistic Max Westbrook retains a moralist view of *Maggie* just as he does of "The Blue Hotel."

Westbrook uses the famous letter to John Northern Hilliard to argue his case for *Maggie*. (The letter is to be found in Robert Stallman and Lillian Gilkes, eds., *Stephen Crane: Letters* [New York: New York Univ. Press, 1960, no. 137, pp. 108–110].) Westbrook says the letter "argues that ethics are real" and adds, quoting the letter, that "what has value, meaning, is the

attempt to be 'as nearly honest' as a 'weak mental machinery will allow.' "
He then finds Jimmie responsible for failing to see that "what is wrong for
Pete cannot be right for him. . . . He is not doing the best he is capable of
doing under the given circumstances": "Crane's Social Ethic," 590-91. It
seems to me, however, that when implemented into the form of fiction, this
letter produces the same Hobbesian vision which Crane's two comments on
Maggie produce. Man's "weak mental machinery" is at the mercy of conditions. Irony can emphasize how much at the mercy of conditions that
machinery is even while implying that a character is rationalizing. Include
the weak mental machinery as one of the conditions and one sees without
doubt that conditions undermine moral judgment.

I find Frank Bergon much closer to the mark than moralist critics when
he argues that "Crane's belief in man's 'weak mental machinery' . . . would
not let him give interpretive responsibility to a single point of view for very
long": *Stephen Crane's Artistry* (New York: Columbia Univ. Press, 1975), p.
65. He thus can see that *Maggie* catches the reader in "a moral contradiction"
(p. 74) demanding that the forgiveness offered to Maggie be offered to
others also and, unlike Gibson (p. 27), he does not find this a flaw because
"his art calls into question" assumptions that we impose on it (p. x). But he
wrongly asserts that "there is no strong representation of a coherent vision"
(p. ix) in Crane; that Crane treats detail "seriously and significantly . . .
often at the expense of a larger design or even of the dominant subject" (p.
xi), and that "Crane refuses to be explicit about causality" in *Maggie* (p. 69).
The Hobbesian vision has its coherence—and its determinism—neither of
which is a principal concern of Bergon's.

The Red Badge of Courage

Since 1979, the major critical issue concerning *The Red Badge of Courage* is
which of two editions gives the authoritative text—the one edited by
Fredson Bowers in the University of Virginia Edition of the Works of
Stephen Crane (Charlottesville: Univ. Press of Virginia, 1975), which follows the original Appleton edition at least in omitting the major material
omitted by the Appleton edition; or the one edited by Henry Binder, which
is based on Binder's reconstructed version of a longer manuscript: *The Red
Badge of Courage: An Episode of the American Civil War* (New York: Norton,
1982). This study uses the Bowers edition rather than the Binder edition for
many reasons, all of which can be summed up thus: my view of the novel in
fact applies to both editions, but it shows that the Bowers edition is actually
artistically superior to the Binder edition. This essay is not the place to argue
this point extensively, but a few examples concerning one representative
deletion, a discarded chapter 12, will illustrate the greater conciseness of the
Bowers edition.

The premise on which my view of the novel rests is that Henry's actions and thoughts are dictated by conditions. One major pattern that emerges, as the analysis in chapter 2 of my text shows, is a pattern of guilt (cause) and rationalization (effect). The point of the pattern is to show that as conditions change—as a rationalization fails, for example—so too does Henry's vision of self, society, or nature as he strives to relieve himself of guilt. That point has been amply made by chapter 11; the discarded chapter 12 is simply an unnecessary extension of this pattern. Edwin Cady's aesthetic (*not* interpretive) sense of the discarded chapter seems more valid than Binder's, although I think the chapter is superfluous whereas Cady argues it would have added to "discursive patches" blemishing the novel: *Stephen Crane* (New York: Twayne, 1962), p. 129; *Stephen Crane*, Revised Edition (Boston: Twayne, 1980), p. 130.

It is also unnecessary to the coherence of the conclusion of the Bowers edition, although Binder's central claim is that this together with other deletions in that edition not only make the final chapter incoherent but in fact conceal the meaning of the entire novel. My own analysis will have to stand as my testimony to the coherence of the Bowers conclusion, but one point should be stressed here. Though the specific pattern of cause and effect involving guilt and rationalization is complete by chapter 11, the larger pattern of cause and effect continues throughout the novel. Thus it comes as no surprise that when conditions change—when Henry is in the "new condition" of a release from battle at the novel's end (Bowers, p. 133; Binder, p. 106)—his view of nature should change so he no longer views it as his enemy. Nor do we need Binder's passage about the new relation to nature ("that he was tiny but not inconsequent to the sun": Binder, p. 108), since that is but an extension of the view of the relation to nature apparent in the Bowers ending. Furthermore, the irony of both versions does not deflate Henry so much as it points out the ironic situation of man that Henry portrays. Henry is not unchanged; he has *been* changed (again) by conditions.

Finally, in my view there are no "problem passages" of the sort Binder singles out. To cite one simple example, the phrase, the "small shoutings in his brain about these *matters*" (Bowers, p. 134: emphasis added) is not illogical in the Bowers edition, as Binder claims. If the reader understands "matters" to mean Henry's flight and subsequent rationalizations, of which the discarded chapter 12 is but one overextended example, the plural noun becomes logical and economical. A somewhat more complicated example raises an interesting point about the limitations of Binder's own edition. Commenting on the sentence: "Yet gradually he [Henry] mustered force to put the sin at a distance" (Binder, p. 108; Bowers, p. 135), Binder complains that "the reader never learns about the nature of Henry's 'force' or what kind of 'distance' is involved" in the Bowers edition (Binder, p. 131). But compare my interpretation of this sentence, and note that my view—that the source of the force distancing Henry from his sin is his tranquil philosophy—is necessary even to understanding the sentence in Binder's edition. Though Binder thinks it is explained by the subsequent lines referring to Henry's decision to utilize his sin to create "a sobering balance" moderating his "egotism," this decision actually is an *effect* of Henry's distancing himself from his sin, not the cause of his distancing himself. Apparently Binder's ending is not as explicit as he claims.

For further details and views of the controversy, see the following: Henry Binder, "*The Red Badge of Courage* Nobody Knows," *Studies in the Novel* 10 (Spring 1978): 9–47; reprinted in his edition listed above, pp. 111–58, from which I have quoted here; Donald Pizer, " '*The Red Badge of Courage* Nobody Knows': A Brief Rejoinder," *Studies in the Novel* 11 (Spring 1979): 77–81; Henry Binder, "Donald Pizer, Ripley Hitchcock, and *The Red Badge of Courage,*" *Studies in the Novel* 11 (Summer 1979): 216–23. For a view of the effects the "maimed text" has had on criticism, see Steven Mailloux, "*The Red Badge of Courage* and Interpretive Conventions: Critical Response to a Maimed Text," *Studies in the Novel* 10 (Spring 1978): 48–63. For a reporter's view of the controversy, see *The New York Times*, 2 April 1982, p. 1, col. 2.

3. FRANK NORRIS

In the past twenty years, criticism of *McTeague* has drifted away from the subject of determinism. Warren French set the tone of this criticism by importing Norris's private moral views into the novel: *Frank Norris* (New York: Twayne, 1962). For him, the "naturalistic devices" are "a means to tractarian [moral] ends" (p. 9). Thus he saw Norris manipulating plot (he offers the ending as a good example) and using deterministic elements for the purpose of making characters get their just deserts "without a word of direct preaching" (p. 68).

But this kind of approach has led other critics such as George M. Spangler to find special defects: "The Structure of *McTeague,*" *English Studies* 59 (February 1978): 48-56. Spangler assumes the existence of an obvious moral vision in the work: "The statement that a moralistic view of man's instinctual nature overtly dominates the first part of the novel hardly requires defense" (p. 50). From this premise proceeds his argument that the two parts of the novel possess no "rational coherence" (p. 53) and hence the novel lacks "structural coherence" (p. 56). The major contradiction that he finds within the work is that the overt moral view of the novel's first part—a view that sex is destructive—is not consistent with the moral view of greed in the novel's second part: the "economic theme is virtually discontinuous

with the sexual concerns of part one" (p. 52). This discontinuity is emphasized by the fact that the milieu of the city important to the first part
disappears as a center of attention in the second part, where it is replaced by
Trina's avarice (p. 52). If Norris's aim was to criticize the morality of the
milieu, why should the milieu disappear?

Spangler cannot see the logical relationship that is there between both
parts of the novel because he cannot adapt Trina's erotic relationship to her
coins to the novel's two overt moral aspects. His circuitous attempt to find a
unifying element still leaves the novel's structure impaired. The account of
the relationship between sex and greed offered by Joseph H. Gardner has a
valid and less complicated logic. (See "Dickens, Romance, and *McTeague*: A
Study in Mutual Interpretation," *Essays in Literature* 1 [Spring 1974]: 69–82).
But it still leaves the structural problems Spangler finds within the novel,
problems that can only be resolved by a thoroughly deterministic reading.

Such a reading unites the parts of the novel by finding a unified relation
between social and sexual determinism. It is open to the question that is
implicit in Franklin Walker's comment that Norris "had assimilated [conti-
nental naturalism] empirically, . . . by analyzing *L'Assommoir* and *Madame
Bovary* rather than by studying *Le Roman expérimental*": *Frank Norris: A
Biography* (Garden City, N.Y.: Doubleday, 1932), p. 232. If this is so, and if in
private Norris really accepted those "ideals of free will and of moral order"
to which Donald Pizer refers (p. 22) in *The Novels of Frank Norris* (Bloomington: Indiana Univ. Press, 1966), then perhaps one should find implicit
moralizing in a deterministic work written by a moralist.

But this approach creates the kind of problems discussed above and is,
however unintentionally, unfair to the novelist. One need not be a Christian
to create a work of art expressing Christian vision with admirable intricacy
and consistency. Much the same thing can be said of Norris and the
determinism of *McTeague*. To deny the novel's thoroughgoing determinism
is to deny its superb artistry.

4. THEODORE DREISER

Warner Berthoff, Alfred Kazin, and Larzer Ziff do not accept the naturalism of Dreiser's novels as a philosophy. Either it is seen as a state of
mind and temperament congenial to the expression of his personal view
of life, or as superfluous to the essential truth presented about American
character. (Warner Berthoff, *The Ferment of Realism: American Literature,
1884-1919* [New York: Free Press, 1965], p. 239; Alfred Kazin, *On Native
Grounds: An Interpretation of Modern American Prose Literature* [New York:
Harcourt, Brace & World, 1942], p. 87; Larzer Ziff, *The American 1890s:
Life and Times of a Lost Generation* [New York: Viking, 1966], p. 336.)

In such general critical estimates as these, one expects to find generalizations often at odds with fact; but this view that Dreiser is far from a coherent philosopher is also standard fare for more specialized academic treatments of him. Ronald Martin is clearly speaking for more than himself in *Universe of Force* when he writes: "By now no one should need further cautioning that Dreiser is not coherent" (p. 237). In context, his remark refers to *Sister Carrie*, but this view has an at least indirect application to his center of interest, "the trilogy of desire," which he finds unsatisfying because it is *static*, a word that Martin does not use but that best describes his dissatisfaction with a work whose amoral viewpoint makes it "difficult to locate what would matter to . . . [readers] in such a context" (p. 246). And there is a larger problem, both aesthetic and philosophical. Finally, in his trilogy, Dreiser "lacked the art and the insight to successfully bring together amoral realism, the business-world hero, and the universe of force" (p. 247).

If, however, one sees Dreiser as a serious philosophical novelist in *these* novels at least, the art surfaces through the unfolding philosophical vision that unites them. By and large, the stumbling block has been *The Stoic*. I reserve to my text and notes a challenging of the conventional wisdom about a work that was never brought to full development. But a questioning of the inner integrity of *The Stoic* is not the only hindrance to seeing Dreiser as a philosophical novelist in the trilogy. For Sidney Richman the problem is not only that the novel is "too sketchy" but also that it is "too dependent upon the lines of development already charted by *The Financier* and *The Titan* to serve so clearly as *The Bulwark* as a model of Dreiser's philosophy": "Theodore Dreiser's *The Bulwark*: A Final Resolution," *American Literature* 34 (May 1962), 244. In fact, it is precisely because of this dependency that the trilogy shows most clearly the harmonious unfolding of Dreiser's thought.

5. JOHN DOS PASSOS

The naturalism of *Manhattan Transfer* has been denied on three basic grounds. Melvin Landsberg, in *Dos Passos' Path to "U.S.A.": A Political Biography, 1912-1936* (Boulder: Colorado Associated Univ. Press, 1972), argues that some of its characters do make choices defying social pressure (p. 123); E.D. Lowry, in "*Manhattan Transfer*: Dos Passos's Wasteland," *Dos Passos: A Collection of Critical Essays*, ed. Andrew Hook (Englewood Cliffs, N.J.: Prentice-Hall, 1974), that it is "attuned . . . to the problem of evil" and therefore has a moral vision (p. 60); and Robert C. Rosen, in *John Dos Passos: Politics and the Writer* (Lincoln: Univ. of Nebraska Press, 1981), that it does not emphasize that causality which is central to the naturalistic novel (pp. 46–47). My analysis is designed to meet such objections, and it bears the influence of some seminal work on Dos Passos.

The seminal American work is by Blanche Gelfant, both in her article, "The Search for Identity in the Novels of John Dos Passos," *PMLA* 76 (1961): 133-49, and in the relevant chapter of her study, *The American City Novel* (Norman: Univ. of Oklahoma Press, 1954). The comprehensive article covering all of Dos Passos's novels shows how all pervasive the theme of identity is, and how unfailingly the characters fail to find an identity. (She divides characters into four classes: pp. 143-44). Of the many insights in her *American City Novel*, her treatment of imagery is especially fertile. Taken together, Gelfant's article and book give us a comprehensive and detailed study of Dos Passos's work.

The French critics whom I have found most intriguing are comprehensive in their generalizations, though not detailed in their analyses. The generalizations of Jean-Paul Sartre and Claude-Edmonde Magny are nonetheless magnificent in their sweep and accuracy, and I have tried to give them some substance of determinism within the texture of the work itself which, I hope, is not at odds with the authors' own intentions. The relevant material by each is as follows: Magny, "Time in Dos Passos;" Sartre, "John Dos Passos and *1919*," both in the collection *Dos Passos* edited by Andrew Hook.

Perhaps because of his special conception of the novelist as a "second-class historian of the age he lives in" (and we live in), a historian building "a reality more nearly out of his own factual experience than a plain historian or biographer can" ("Statement of Belief," *Bookman* 68 [September 1928] 26), Dos Passos's work seems strikingly relevant and bears correspondences to a host of socio-philosophical commentaries. I found the novel enlightened by Herbert Marcuse's *One Dimensional Man: Studies in the Ideology of Advanced Industrial Society* (Boston: Beacon Press, 1968)—(just as I in fact found Marcuse's work clearer from my own understanding of Dos Passos). In particular, I found Marcuse's comments on the need to liberate the imagination especially relevant to the marked emphasis on fantasies in the novel. Anna Cohen seems to me the perfect embodiment of Marcuse's enslaved imagination (pp. 8ff, 250ff).

6. JOHN STEINBECK

I use the term "species self" instead of the terminology used by Steinbeck, whose concept of the "phalanx" or "group" self is set forth at length in Richard Astro's first four chapters of a comparative study of the thought of the men in his title: *John Steinbeck and Edward F. Ricketts: The Shaping of a Novelist* (Minneapolis: Univ. of Minnesota Press, 1973). See esp. chap. 4,

"The Argument of Phalanx" (pp. 61-74). I chose the term "species self" because its connotations are more definite in linking man not simply to the human world but to the nonhuman world as well, and this dual linkage is indispensable for understanding *The Grapes of Wrath*.

In contrasting Ricketts's view that "man's highest function is to uncover his emotional relationship with the world as a whole" (p. 43) to Steinbeck's view that man and the cosmos are "goal oriented" (p. 51), Astro insists that Ricketts is a monist (pp. 43, 72, 73) while Steinbeck is a dualist (pp. 57, 73). Nothing he says of Steinbeck, however, is inconsistent with my view of naturalism as monistic in my first chapter.

Astro's emphasis is on the contrast between the thought of these two men because his work was in large part stimulated by his desire to expose as a fallacy the commonly held notion that Steinbeck wrote the narrative portion of *The Sea of Cortez* and his friend Ricketts composed the second part, the catalogue of biological life. In fact Steinbeck wrote the narrative portion on the basis of a journal kept by Ricketts and, although he included some of his own views, he also rendered beliefs of Ricketts with which he was not in agreement. See Astro, *Steinbeck and Ricketts*, pp. 13, 18-19. But Astro's study does not lead him into any such error as to deny Ricketts's presence in *The Grapes of Wrath* (cf. Astro on Casy, p. 134), and nothing he states compels one to dismiss as insignificant Steinbeck's use of Ricketts's ideas there. Unlike Astro, I am not concerned to identify Ricketts's influence in a novel *written by* Steinbeck; but where I can, I do point out in my notes passages from *The Sea of Cortez* that were written by Steinbeck and represent his own thought.

I am concerned by the form of Astro's response to critics whom Astro feels distort the meaning of Steinbeck's frequent analogies between the human and animal worlds. Accepting a symbolic relation between the turtle and the Joads, he feels compelled to state that "never does Steinbeck suggest that the Joads are turtles in the biological sense of the term" (p. 54). This statement, whose truth is beyond challenge, brings out a larger problem provoking it, the problem bedeviling understandings of literary naturalism all along: that to see man as a part of nature is to see him as only an animal; or that to see him as part of nature is always to deny his freedom in some absolute sense. The latter (not the former) restrictive definition of naturalism is probably behind the comment Warren French makes in his reading of the novel. "In *The Grapes of Wrath* [Steinbeck] turned what had started to be a Naturalistic novel into a drama of consciousness": *John Steinbeck* (Boston: Twayne, 2nd ed. rev., 1975), p. 44. My treatment is designed to harmonize the poles of thought implied by French's comment.

Those very poles explain why I find so valuable criticism stressing

Steinbeck's romanticism (or mysticism) and pragmatism (or empiricism). Although the central polarity is between freedom and determinism, these other polarities enrich it. Such supplementary oppositions have been expressed in two classic essays: Frederick I. Carpenter, "The Philosophical Joads," *College English* 2 (1941): 315-25; Woodburn O. Ross, "John Steinbeck: Naturalism's Priest," *College English* 10 (1949): 432-37.

Although his interpretation appeared after mine was essentially completed, mine can usefully be read against that of Donald Pizer: "The Grapes of Wrath," *Twentieth-Century American Literary Naturalism: An Interpretation* (Carbondale: Southern Illinois Univ. Press, 1982), pp. 65-81. Despite some details on which we agree, he concentrates on the " 'conversion' of Tom, Ma, and Casy from I to We consciousness within a traditional moral framework, not a deterministic one. See especially p. 70, where he argues that "the real evils in the Joads' life are . . . not the abstractions of the mechanical or the institutional but the human failings of fear, anger, and selfishness."

7. WILLIAM FAULKNER

Donald M. Kartiganer has written that "the philosophy of Bergson is a clear presence in Faulkner's fiction, whether there by design or a common understanding": *The Fragile Thread: The Meaning of Form in Faulkner's Novels* (Amherst: Univ. of Massachusetts Press, 1979), p. 166. Much the same thing can be said of the criticism of Faulkner. It is a testament to the sensitive readings of the past that a good many of them are implicitly Bergsonian, especially in their treatment of time, even though neither the name "Bergson" nor the word "duration" appears. I cannot give the long list of examples which I would like, so I offer but two chosen not only for their merit but for their age and form—one an article, the other a book: Karl E. Zink, "Flux and the Frozen Moment: The Imagery of Stasis in Faulkner's Prose," *PMLA* 71 (1956): 285-301; Olga W. Vickery, *The Novels of William Faulkner: A Critical Interpretation* (Baton Rouge: Louisiana State Univ. Press, 1959), esp. pp. 255-65.

Explicit Bergsonian criticisms, of which Kartiganer's is one, are increasingly more common. Again, I cannot be complete: Richard P. Adams, "The Apprenticeship of William Faulkner," in *William Faulkner: Four Decades of Criticism*, ed. by Linda Welshimer Wagner (East Lansing: Michigan State Univ. Press, 1973), pp. 39–41; Panthea Reid Broughton, *William Faulkner: The Abstract and the Actual* (Baton Rouge: Louisiana State Univ. Press, 1974), which seems to me largely Bergsonian despite its many references to other philosophers. Two dissertations also employ a

Bergsonian frame of reference: Shirley Parker Callen, "Bergsonian Dynamism in the Writings of William Faulkner," Tulane Univ., 1962; Susan
Dale Resneck Parr, " 'And by Bergson, Obviously': Faulkner's *The Sound
and the Fury, As I Lay Dying*, and *Absalom, Absalom!* from a Bergsonian
Perspective," Univ. of Wisconsin-Madison, 1972. The first part of Parr's
title refers to Faulkner's own acknowledgment of his debt to Bergson:
James B. Meriwether and Michael Millgate, eds., *Lion in the Garden:
Interviews with William Faulkner 1926–1962* (New York: Random House,
1968), p. 72.

If work that is implicitly Bergsonian is added to work that is explicitly
so, then there is an abundance of such criticism. For that reason, the
reader may find a capsule summary of my differences from other ap-
proaches useful. My emphases are on Faulkner's connections to naturalism and on the existence of dual selves in his novel, in particular the
existence of a self which lives in duration. Since these selves grow out of
naturalism, the two emphases merge to provide the effective differences
between my approach and others. I find in *The Sound and the Fury* what
Donald M. Kartiganer claims it lacks: a "resolution of action into meaning" and a "reconciliation of fragments into a controlling system" (p. 21).
For him, "the four fragments . . . remain separate and incoherent" (p. 19).
His is a version of a view fostered by Faulkner (see Kartiganer's pp. 4–5)
that the novel is a failure "of telling" (p. 6), but that the failure in a sense
constitutes its success because it captures the "process quality" (p. xv) of
life as viewed by Bergson and by moderns generally.

My own view is that even a Bergsonian metaphysic provides a sense of
order in the work based on types of selves presented, just as it provides a
source of meaning in seeing the durational self as a refuge from the world.
The novel is therefore quite coherent structurally and thematically. Even
Dilsey's Christian vision becomes an effective part of the whole in this
nonChristian novel because the novel's unifying center is not Dilsey's
Christianity but a durational self which in her case happens to be characterized by Christian belief and values.

This emphasis on a durational self shows what so many critics have
missed, the true source of transcendence of life's difficulties for Faulkner.
Transcendence takes place when one character can move from his social
to his durational self, even though someone like Dilsey may think she
transcends by moving from an earthly realm to an authentic perception of
a divine one. My view of a durational self and transcendence is meant to
act as a corrective to views like those expressed by Margaret Church,
Time and Reality: Studies in Contemporary Fiction (Chapel Hill: Univ. of
North Carolina Press, 1949), pp. 233–35. See esp. p. 235, where she

remarks that Dilsey has the ability to transcend "a sense of duration." For a related misunderstanding of transcendence, see Douglas Messerli, "The Problem of Time in *The Sound and the Fury*: A Critical Reassessment and Reinterpretation," *The Southern Literary Journal* 6 (1974): 19–41.

This same emphasis on a durational self is designed as a response to critics who moralize about Quentin's refusal to accept change. Broughton, for example, writes: "To Quentin, progression bears no relation to the Bergsonian concept of fluidity; with Quentin it is strictly mechanical" (p. 113). In fact Quentin is trying to preserve a self living in duration and through which durational time flows. He is caught in the situation of confronting the likelihood of losing his refuge from the world: duration and duration's self.

This point about Quentin explains why I am not persuaded by Warwick Wadlington's view of him. He finds Quentin's suicide "a bid for tragic recognition": "*The Sound and the Fury*: A Logic of Tragedy," *American Literature* 53 (November 1981): 422. Although I believe that Quentin affirms the values of his durational self through his suicide, I do not believe that the suicide is induced because others fail to see "that his pain is significant" (422); rather it is induced by his fear of losing the self which with that pain is still his source of refuge from the world. In this regard I am closer to critics who see Quentin fearing the loss of a sense of loss. See, as examples, John W. Hunt, *William Faulkner: Art in Theological Tension* (Syracuse: Syracuse Univ. Press, 1965), p. 67; Walter J. Slatoff, *Quest for Failure: A Study of William Faulkner* (Ithaca: Cornell Univ. Press, 1960), p. 69. Because of the way I characterize Quentin's durational values, I am also closer to critics who see Quentin as a traditionalist: George Marion O'Donnell, "Faulkner's Mythology," in *William Faulkner: Two Decades of Criticism*, ed. by Frederick J. Hoffman and Olga W. Vickery (East Lansing: Michigan State College Press, 1951), p. 43; Walter Brylowski, *Faulkner's Olympian Laugh: Myth in the Novels* (Detroit: Wayne State Univ. Press, 1968), pp. 72–73; and Mark Spilka, "Quentin Compson's Universal Grief," *Contemporary Literature* 11 (Autumn 1970): 451–69. See esp. 454, 460.

I also disagree with the conclusions that Wadlington draws from his view that the novel has "the logic of tragedy." He sees it as a modern form of Hegelian tragedy based now on an all-pervasive "binary consciousness" (p. 421)—and as modern tragedy he finds it replete with "attempt at reversal" (p. 421) and "catharsis" (p. 422), though both are displaced from their traditional sources. Since Faulkner resurrected Quentin to permit him to participate in a tragic action in *Absalom, Absalom!*, however, I do not think that this "binary consciousness" is the source of a modern tragic sense. I think it functions instead to show that tragedy really *is* second hand, as Quentin's father would have it. I do value, however, Wadlington's theoretical approach to modern tragedy. Because of it, his use of the term "tragedy" never seems superficial.

Most relevant to my discussion of *Absalom* are studies that see the story as a reflection of Quentin. Too often they view Quentin as a psychological case, a view Spilka argues against: "Universal Grief," p. 454. For such critics, see Spilka's n. 6, p. 454. I would add to his list John T. Irwin, *Doubling and Incest/Repetition and Revenge: A Speculative Reading of Faulkner* (Baltimore: Johns Hopkins Univ. Press, 1975), especially pp. 74–99. Most pertinent is Estelle Schoenberg's treatment of the work as personal to Quentin: *Old Tales and Talking: Quentin Compson in William Faulkner's "Absalom, Absalom!" and Related Works* (Jackson: Univ. Press of Mississippi, 1977), esp. chaps. 1–2, 5–8. I do not agree with her that, because Quentin is responsible for the shape of the story's final re-creation, Faulkner "thereby demotes Sutpen and promotes Quentin to star billing in the cast of *Absalom, Absalom!*" (p. 83). That approach can lead psychoanalytically oriented readers to a reductive view that ignores the fact that, even if the story has its source in Quentin's psyche, a story *is* created and possesses an aesthetic legitimacy of its own.

INDEX

alienation. *See* Dos Passos, *Manhattan Transfer*
Astro, Richard, 218-19

Bailey, Benjamin, 167
Bergon, Frank, 213
Bergson, Henri, 124, 161-92 passim; *Time and Free Will,* 14, 161; and two kinds of time, 14-15; and two selves, 15-16; and Faulkner, 20-21. *See also* determinism
Berofsky, Bernard, 9n
Berthoff, Warner, 216
Binder, Henry, 213, 214-15
Bowers, Fredson, 213, 214-15
Brooks, Cleanth, 176
Broughton, Panthea Reid, 220, 222

Cady, Edwin, 13, 212, 214
Callen, Shirley Parker, 208n. 40
Carpenter, Frederick I., 220
Church, Margaret, 221-22
Comte, Auguste, 13
Cox, James Trammell, 211
Crane, Stephen: and naturalism as pessimistic determinism, 1; his pessimistic or monistic determinism, 1, 4, 8; denied a coherent philosophical vision, 9, 10; and freedom, 13; and Hobbesian vision, 16; as soft determinist, 16; reference to, 19, 20, 159, 160
—"The Blue Hotel," 18-19, 30-42, 68, 118, 195, 211-12; determinism as issue in, 31-34, 37; moral axis blurred in, 34-36; conception of character in, 36, 37-38, 40-41; moral reading illogical for, 37;

Hobbesian paradox in, 37, 42; man's relation to nature in, 38-40; conception of freedom in, 40; kinds of determinism in, 41-42
—*Maggie,* 18, 42-52, 53, 212-13; Hobbesian view of liberty of self in, 42-45; inscription on copies of, 43; determinism in, 44, 45, 46-47, 49-50, 50-51; concept of freedom in, 45, 52; concept of morality in, 46-47, 47-49; view of self and irony in, 50; Hobbesian paradox and form of, 51-52
—"The Open Boat," 18, 21, 22-30, 45, 159, 210-11; conception of nature in: 22-23, 27; naturalism of, 22-24; origins of ethical and moral systems, 23, 24; society as a fiction, 24-25, 27-28; two types of society, 24, 25-26, 28; conception of responsibility in, 26-27; determinism forecast in, 28-30
—*The Red Badge of Courage,* 18, 19, 52-68, 118, 213-15; contrasted to *Maggie,* 53; man's relation to nature in, 53; flashback in, 53-55; role of emotions in, 53, 56, 57, 59-61; and determinism, 54, 55, 56, 61, 62; views of morality and freedom, 55; role of illusion in, 55-56, 62-63, 67-68; Hobbesian vision, 67

Darwinism, 47
determinism: as pessimistic, 1; and views of relation to literary naturalism, 1, 2, 4, 17, 18, 19; and philosophic naturalism, 6-7, 8; defined, 9, 32; Hobbesian vision

leads to, 11-12; and soft determinists, 12, 16; and emphasis on
conditions, 13-14; and Bergson's
view of two selves as escape from,
15-16; and Crane's work, 16, 18-19;
and Dreiser, 16-17, 19; and Norris,
16, 18; central to American literary
naturalism, 17; and causation in
portraying self and choice, 17; and
Steinbeck, 20. *See also* freedom of
the will; entries under individual
works
Dewey, John, 5, 7
Dos Passos, John, and naturalism as
pessimistic determinism, 1; Sartre
on *1919*, 121-22; reference to, 21,
117, 142, 160, 161, 162, 179
—*Manhattan Transfer*, 17, 18, 19-20,
118-41, 146, 158, 217-18; alienation
in, 118, 119, 120, 121, 123, 123-24,
140; determinism in, 118, 119,
121-22, 123-24, 125, 126; nature in,
118, 141; role of chance in, 122-23;
choice and freedom in, 122, 123,
125; naturalism of, 123, 140-41;
view of self in, 123-24, 125, 126,
137, 141; Hobbes's definition of
liberty of self applies to, 126; view
of self and imagery of, 126-34;
compared to Whitman, 129, 141;
view of self and structure of,
134-35; view of self and use of
newspapers in, 135-37; view of self
and historical perspective of,
137-39; compared to Eliot's
"Preludes," 141
Dreiser, Theodore: and naturalism as
pessimistic determinism, 1; as die-
hard determinist, 3; as free-will
determinist, 16-17; explores
implications of determinism, 19;
reference to, 20, 21, 85, 142, 159,
195
—*The Financier*, 87, 88-95;
determinism and: view of nature in,
89-90; creative power in, 89-90, 92;
two sets of characters in, 90, 91;
man's relation to nature in, 91, 112;
naturalistic axis of, 92; ethics and
morality in, 92, 93; role of illusion

in, 92-93, 94-95; central question
of, 92, 94
—*Notes on Life*, 16-17, 86, 90, 94, 97,
103, 105, 106, 108
—*The Stoic*, 87, 108-17; the fated self
and the problem of meaning in,
108-12; and the creative power,
112-13; and a true self, 113; and
man's relationship to nature, 114;
and Brahmanism, 114-16, 117
—*The Titan*, 87, 95-108;
Cowperwood as artist in, 98-101:
and central question of, 97; and
major theme of, 98; and naturalistic
vision of, 99; and the problem of
compensation in, 101-08
—"Trilogy of Desire," 19, 160, 217;
significance of, 86-88; determinism
in, 86-87; and "the dilemma of
determinism," 88, 106-08; and
individual goals, 93; and Dreiser's
naturalistic vision, 93-94; and the
pleasure principle, 94, 95; and the
problem of compensation, 101-02;
and ethical action, 103; and free
will, 103, 112; and the equation
inevitable, 103-06; and morality,
104-05; and the creative power,
108-09
dualism, 4, 6, 219
duration. *See* Bergson, Henri;
Faulkner, William, *The Sound and
the Fury*

Edwards, Paul, 109
Elias, Robert, 103, 112
Eliot, T.S., 141
Emerson, Ralph Waldo, 117, 154,
157-58, 159; references to works by:
Nature, 99, 158, 187; *Self-Reliance*,
113; "The Problem," 116; *The Poet*,
163

Farrell, James T.: and naturalism as
pessimistic determinism, 1; "Some
Observations on Naturalism, So
Called" (quoted), 5, 7, 8, 9;
compared to Sterling Power
Lamprecht, 6; *Studs Lonigan*, 17
Faulkner, William: and naturalism as

pessimistic determinism, 1; and naturalism, 20-21; conception of self in novels of, 21; reference to, 141
—*Absalom, Absalom!*, 21, 223; introduces tragedy into naturalism, 190; Quentin's two selves and tragedy of, 190-95
—*The Sound and the Fury*, 21, 160-95, 221-23; and naturalism, 160-62; Benjy as parody of durational self in, 162-63, 165, 167-68; Jason as parody of shadow self in, 169; Jason's narration as parody of literary complaint in, 171-73; parody as criticism of shadow self in, 173-75; Dilsey and dual self in, 175-76; Dilsey and time in, 175-76, 177; Christian history in, 178; and tragedy, 179; Quentin and two selves in, 180, 183-84; Bergson as guide to Faulkner's intention in, 180-81; Quentin and duration in, 180, 181-83; Quentin and shadow self in, 184-85; Quentin and durational self in, 185-89
freedom of the will: seen as contradiction in naturalistic fiction, 2, 3; compatible with determinism in fiction, 4; and competing critical views of naturalism: 4, 6, 8, 9; as crucial question in Crane's work, 8, 9; as crucial question in American literary naturalism, 8, 12-13; and double vision, 10; and contingency, 13; and Bergson's two selves, 15-16. *See also* determinism; entries under individual works
French, Warren, 201n, 215, 219

Gardner, Joseph H., 216
Geismar, Maxwell, 92
Gelfant, Blanche, 125, 218
Gibson, Donald, 212
Godiva, 127
Greenfield, Stanley B., 201n

Hemingway, Ernest, 1
Hobbes, Thomas: definition of liberty of self quoted, 11, 12, 38, 42, 126.

See also determinism; naturalism (American literary); naturalism (philosophical); entries under individual works
Holton, Milne, 211

Irony. *See* Crane, Stephen, *Maggie*

James, William, 85; "The Dilemma of Determinism," 12, 86, 106-07, 117
Jefferson, Thomas, 137

Kant, Immanuel, 13
Kaplan, Harold, 210
Kartiganer, Donald M., 220, 221
Kazin, Alfred, 140, 216
Keats, John, 95, 139, 167, 184-85, 186

LaFrance, Marston, 210-11, 212
Lamprecht, Sterling Power, 18; *The Metaphysics of Naturalism*, 6, 7
Landsberg, Melvin, 217
Lowry, E.D., 217

McAleer, John J., 87
McPheron, Donald R., 202n
Magny, Claude-Edmonde, 136, 218
Marcuse, Herbert, 218
Maritain, Jacques, 167
Marks, Lester Jay, 205n
Martin, Ronald E., 210, 217
melodrama, 52, 83-84
Melville, Herman: *Moby-Dick,* 39
monism. *See* naturalism (American literary)
Mont Blanc, 39
moral judgment: relation of to naturalism, 3, 4, 23, 45. *See also* entries under individual works

naturalism (American literary): and pessimistic determinism seen in, 1-4; and optimism seen in, 2, 3; and monism, 4, 5-6; logical contradictions absent from works of, 4, 9; philosophical coherence of, 4, 16-17, 18-21; defined by Farrell, 5; attitudes toward role of will in, 7-8; Crane's vision touchstone of status of will in, 8-9, 16; causality and determinism in, 9-10, 12-14; Hobbesian vision in, 13, 14, 16-17, 18-19, 20; Bergsonian selves in, 14-16, 20-21; determinism central to classic phase of, 17; as term, applicable to two kinds of literary works, 18; bibliographical essay on, 209-10. *See also* self; entries under individual works

naturalism (philosophical): and monism, 5-6; defined by Lamprecht, 6; human freedom and monism seen as compatible in, 6-7; versus modern literary naturalism, 8; and Hobbes's views of will and liberty, 10-12

nature: man as part of, 4, 5, 6-7; and term "naturalistic," 4-5, 18; and Bergson, 14; and "The Open Boat," 18; as benign in Dos Passos and Steinbeck, 19-20; as destructive in Crane, Norris, and Dreiser, 20; and *The Sound and the Fury*, 21. *See also* entries under individual works

Norris, Frank: and naturalism as pessimistic determinism, 1; views in *The Octopus*, 16, 17-18; reference to, 20, 87, 159

—*McTeague*, 16, 19, 69-85, 118, 159, 160, 195, 215-16; freedom of will questioned in, 69-70, 71; story of individuals treated as archetypes, 70; hard determinism in, 70, 71; sexual determinism in, 70, 71-72, 78-80; social determinism in, 70, 72-75; sexual and social determinism merged in, 78-80, 81-83; structure of, 83-85

Parr, Susan Dale Resneck, 207nn. 22, 25

Petry, Alice Hall, 210

Pizer, Donald, 2, 34, 209-10, 216, 220

Pynchon, Thomas, 17

realism, American literary, 1

Richman, Sidney, 217

Rosen, Robert C., 217

Ross, Woodburn O., 220

Sartre, Jean-Paul, 121-22, 218

Schoenberg, Estelle, 223

self: and determinism in American literary naturalism, 14, 16, 18, 19, 20; Bergson's view of, 14-16; durational, 15, 21; shadow (social), 15-16, 21; appearance in American literary naturalism of a dual, 19-21. *See also* entries under individual works

Shelley, Percy Bysshe, 39

Shulman, Robert, 211

society: and determinism, 29-30. *See also* entries under individual works

Solomon, Eric, 52

Spangler, George M., 215-16

Spencer, Herbert, 13

Spilka, Mark, 222, 223

Steinbeck, John: and naturalism as pessimistic determinism, 1; and a dual self, 20; reference to, 19, 141, 160-61, 195

—*The Grapes of Wrath*: 18, 142-59, 218-20; varieties of determinism in, 143-47; function of interchapters in, 145, 146-47, 148, 149; freedom harmonizes with determinism in, 146-47, 149; dual selves in, 148, 150; species self and, 150, 158; freedom and species self in, 150, 154; social criticism and species self in, 151-53, 156-57; man's relation to nature in, 154-56

—*Sea of Cortez*, 147-48, 155, 156, 219

Stevens, Wallace, "The Snow Man," 27

Sullivan, Walter, 208n. 41

Swanberg, W.A., 88, 103

Thoreau, Henry David, 154-55; *Walden*, 157

time. *See* Bergson, Henri; Faulkner, William, *The Sound and the Fury*

tragedy, 162, 179, 189-95

Vickery, Olga, 220

Wadlington, Warwick, 222-23

Walcutt, Charles Child, 2, 3, 4, 13, 209, 212

Walker, Franklin, 216
Westbrook, Max, 212-13
Whitman, Walt, 129, 141, 160; *Song of
  Myself,* 155
will. *See* freedom of the will

Yeats, William Butler: "Lapis Lazuli,"
  190, 194

Ziff, Larzer, 216
Zink, Karl E., 220
Zola, Émile, *L'Assommoir,* 84; "The
  Experimental Novel," 84, 85